ENGLISH
FOR EVERYONE

COURSE BOOK

LEVEL 4 ADVANCED

Editors Lili Bryant, Ben Ffrancon Davies
Art Editors Daniela Boraschi, Clare Joyce,
Clare Shedden, Michelle Staples
Editorial Assistants Jessica Cawthra, Sarah Edwards
Illustrators Edwood Burn, Denise Joos, Clare Joyce,
Michael Parkin, Jemma Westing
Audio Producer Liz Hammond
Managing Editor Daniel Mills
Managing Art Editor Anna Hall
Project Manager Christine Stroyan
Jacket Designer Natalie Godwin
Jacket Editor Claire Gell
Jacket Design Development Manager
Sophia MTT
Producer, Pre-Production Luca Frassinetti
Producer Mary Slater
Publisher Andrew Macintyre
Art Director Karen Self
Publishing Director Jonathan Metcalf

DK India
Jacket Designer Surabhi Wadhwa
Managing Jackets Editor Saloni Singh
Senior DTP Designer Harish Aggarwal

First published in Great Britain in 2016 by
Dorling Kindersley Limited
80 Strand, London, WC2R 0RL

A CIP catalogue record for this book
is available from the British Library.
ISBN: 978-0-2412-4232-2

Printed and bound in China

All images © Dorling Kindersley Limited
For further information see: www.dkimages.com

A WORLD OF IDEAS:
SEE ALL THERE IS TO KNOW

www.dk.com

Contents

How the course works — 8

01 Making conversation — 12
New language Present tenses
Vocabulary Meeting new people
New skill Using question tags

02 Action and state verbs — 16
New language State verbs in continuous forms
Vocabulary Action and state verbs
New skill Describing states

03 Using collocations — 18
New language Collocations
Vocabulary Beliefs and opinions
New skill Talking about your life

04 Complex descriptions — 22
New language General and specific adjectives
Vocabulary Personalities
New skill Ordering adjectives

05 Making general statements — 26
New language Introductory "it"
Vocabulary Talents and abilities
New skill Expressing general truths

06 Vocabulary Travel and tourism — 30

07 Phrasal verbs — 32
New language Phrasal verbs overview
Vocabulary Travel
New skill Using complex phrasal verbs

08 Narrative tenses — 36
New language The past perfect continuous
Vocabulary Travel adjectives and idioms
New skill Talking about a variety of past actions

09 Giving advice and opinions — 40
New language Modals for advice and opinion
Vocabulary Recommendations
New skill Giving advice and opinions

10 Making predictions — 44
New language Degrees of likelihood
Vocabulary Idioms about time
New skill Talking about possibilities

11 Vocabulary Family and relationships — 48

12 Using discourse markers — 50
New language Linking information
Vocabulary Family history
New skill Talking about relationships

13 Past habits and states — 54
New language "Used to" and "would"
Vocabulary Family values
New skill Contrasting the past with the present

14 Comparing and contrasting — 58
New language "As... as" comparisons
Vocabulary Adjective-noun collocations
New skill Comparing and contrasting

15 Two comparatives together — 62
New language Two comparatives together
Vocabulary Age and population
New skill Expressing cause, effect, and change

16 Vocabulary Studying — 66

17 Taking notes — 68
New language Organizing information
Vocabulary Academic life
New skill Taking notes

18 Speaking approximately — 72
New language Generalization
Vocabulary Approximate quantity phrases
New skill Talking about numbers

19 Changing emphasis — 76
New language The passive voice
Vocabulary Online learning
New skill Changing sentence emphasis

20 Things that might happen — 80
New language "What if," "suppose," "in case"
Vocabulary Exams and assessment
New skill Talking about hypothetical situations

21 Vocabulary Working — 84

22 Job applications — 86
New language Prepositions and gerunds
Vocabulary Job applications
New skill Writing a résumé and cover letter

23 Asking polite questions — 90
New language Direct and indirect questions
Vocabulary Job interviews
New skill Asking questions politely

24 Complex verb patterns — 94
New language Verb + infintive / gerund
Vocabulary World of work
New skill Using complex verb patterns

25 Double object verbs — 98
New language Double object verbs
Vocabulary New businesses
New skill Talking about starting a business

26 Vocabulary Meeting and presenting — 102

27 Reflexive pronouns — 104
New language Reflexive pronouns
Vocabulary Workplace language
New skill Talking about work issues

28 Meeting and planning — 108
New language Combining verbs
Vocabulary Office tasks
New skill Taking part in meetings

29 Qualifying descriptions — 112
New language Non-gradable adjectives
Vocabulary Qualifying words
New skill Adding detail to descriptions

30 Expressing purpose — 118
New language "In order to," "so that"
Vocabulary Language of apology
New skill Expressing purpose

31 **Vocabulary** Environmental concerns · 122

32 **Conditional tenses** · 124
New language The third conditional
Vocabulary Environmental threats
New skill Talking about an unreal past

33 **Past regrets** · 130
New language "Should have" and "ought to have"
Vocabulary Time markers
New skill Expressing regret about the past

34 **Actions and consequences** · 134
New language Dependent prepositions
Vocabulary Actions and consequences
New skill Changing sentence stress

35 **Few or little?** · 138
New language "Few," "little," "fewer," "less"
Vocabulary Nature and environment
New skill Describing quantities

36 **Vocabulary** Tradition and superstition · 144

37 **Past possibility** · 146
New language "Might / may / could" in the past
Vocabulary Urban myths
New skill Talking about past possibility

38 **Speculation and deduction** · 150
New language More uses for modal verbs
Vocabulary Phrasal verbs with "out"
New skill Speculating and making deductions

39 **Mixed conditionals** · 154
New language Mixed conditionals
Vocabulary Personality traits
New skill Talking about hypothetical situations

40 **Adding "-ever" to question words** · 158
New language Words with "-ever"
Vocabulary Chance and weather phrases
New skill Joining a clause to a sentence

41 **Vocabulary** Media and celebrity · 162

42 **Reporting with passives** · 164
New language Passive voice for reporting
Vocabulary Reporting language
New skill Distancing yourself from facts

43 **Making indirect statements** · 168
New language Indirect statements
Vocabulary Hedging language
New skill Expressing uncertainty

44 **Adding emphasis** · 172
New language Inversion after adverbials
Vocabulary Media and celebrity
New skill Adding emphasis to statements

45 **Shifting focus** · 176
New language Focusing with clauses
Vocabulary Phrases for emphasis
New skill Shifting focus

46 **Vocabulary** Crime and the law · 180

47 **Relative clauses** · 182
New language Relative clauses
Vocabulary Crime and criminals
New skill Specifying and elaborating

48 **More relative clauses** · 186
New language Where, when, whereby, whose
Vocabulary Courtroom phrases
New skill Using relative words

49 **Modal verbs in the future** · 190
New language "Will be able to," "will have to"
Vocabulary Legal terms
New skill Expressing future ability and obligation

50 **Modal verbs overview** · 194
New language Using modal verbs
Vocabulary Modal verbs
New skill Asking, offering, and predicting

| 51 | **Vocabulary** Customs and cultures | 198 |

| 52 | **Talking about groups** | 200 |

New language Using adjectives as nouns
Vocabulary Countries and nationalities
New skill Generalizing politely

| 53 | **Old and new situations** | 204 |

New language "Be used to" and "get used to"
Vocabulary Moving and living abroad
New skill Talking about old and new situations

| 54 | **Articles** | 208 |

New language Articles
Vocabulary Commonly misspelled words
New skill Saying words with silent letters

| 55 | **Abstract ideas** | 212 |

New language Concrete and abstract nouns
Vocabulary Education systems
New skill Talking about abstract ideas

| 56 | **Vocabulary** Technology and the future | 216 |

| 57 | **Future hopes** | 218 |

New language "Wish" with "would" or "could"
Vocabulary Hopes for the future
New skill Talking about future hopes and wishes

| 58 | **The future continuous** | 220 |

New language The future continuous with "will"
Vocabulary Polite requests
New skill Planning your career

| 59 | **The future perfect** | 226 |

New language The future perfect
Vocabulary Life plans
New skill Making plans and predictions

| 60 | **The future in the past** | 230 |

New language "Would" and "was going to"
Vocabulary Changing plans
New skill Saying what you thought

| 61 | **Vocabulary** Art and culture | 234 |

| 62 | **Leaving words out** | 236 |

New language Ellipsis
Vocabulary Entertainment
New skill Leaving out unneccessary words

| 63 | **Substituting words** | 240 |

New language Substitution
Vocabulary Books and reading
New skill Replacing phrases

| 64 | **Shortening infinitives** | 244 |

New language Reduced infinitives
Vocabulary Music and performance
New skill Avoiding repetition

| 65 | **Expressing reactions** | 248 |

New language Informal discourse markers
Vocabulary Advanced prefixes
New skill Structuring conversation

| 66 | **Getting things done** | 252 |

New language "Have / get something done"
Vocabulary Services and repairs
New skill Describing things people do for you

| 67 | **Complex agreement** | 256 |

New language Complex agreement
Vocabulary Collective nouns
New skill Using the correct agreement

| 68 | **"So" and "such"** | 260 |

New language "So" and "such" for emphasis
Vocabulary Medical science
New skill Emphasizing descriptions

| 69 | **Using articles to generalize** | 264 |

New language Generic "the"
Vocabulary Exploration and invention
New skill Using advanced articles

| **Answers** | 268 |
| **Index** | 28 |

How the course works

English for Everyone is designed for people who want to teach themselves the English language. Like all language courses, it covers the core skills: grammar, vocabulary, pronunciation, listening, speaking, reading, and writing. Unlike in other courses, the skills are taught and practiced as visually as possible, using images and graphics to help you understand and remember. The best way to learn is to work through the book in order, making full use of the audio available on the website and app. Turn to the practice book at the end of each unit to reinforce your learning with additional exercises.

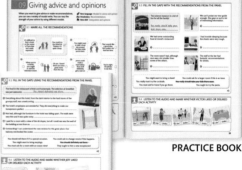

PRACTICE BOOK

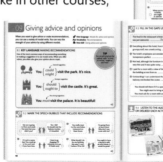

COURSE BOOK

Unit number The book is divided into units. The unit number helps you keep track of your progress.

Learning points Every unit begins with a summary of the key learning points.

Modules Each unit is broken down into modules, which should be done in order. You can take a break from learning after completing any module.

Language learning Modules with colored backgrounds teach new vocabulary and grammar. Study these carefully before moving on to the exercises.

32 Conditional tenses

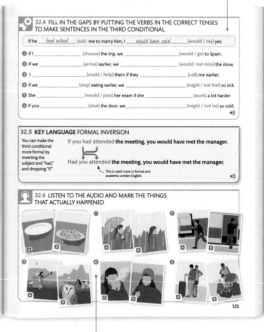

Audio support Most modules have supporting audio recordings of native English speakers to help you improve your speaking and listening skills.

Exercises Modules with white backgrounds contain exercises that help you practice your new skills to reinforce learning.

FREE AUDIO website and app www.dkefe.com

Language modules

New language points are taught in carefully graded stages, starting with a simple explanation of when they are used, then offering further examples of common usage, and a detailed breakdown of how key constructions are formed.

Module number Every module is identified with a unique number, so you can track your progress and easily locate any related audio.

Module heading The teaching topic appears here, along with a brief introduction.

15.1 KEY LANGUAGE TWO COMPARATIVES TOGETHER

You can make comparisons that show cause and effect by using two comparatives in one sentence.

The harder I train, the stronger I get.

Implies that training causes you to get stronger.

Sample language New language points are introduced in context. Colored highlights make new constructions easy to spot, and annotations explain them.

15.2 FURTHER EXAMPLES TWO COMPARATIVES TOGETHER

The worse the children behave, the angrier the teacher gets.

The louder the cat meows, the louder the dog barks.

Graphic guide Clear, simple visuals help to explain the meaning of new language forms and when to use them, and also act as an aid to learning and recall.

Supporting audio This symbol indicates that the model sentences featured in the module are available as audio recordings.

15.3 HOW TO FORM TWO COMPARATIVES TOGETHER

"THE"	COMPARATIVE EXPRESSION	SUBJECT	VERB	"THE"	COMPARATIVE EXPRESSION	SUBJECT	VERB
The	harder	I	train,	the	stronger	I	get.

Formation guide Visual guides break down English grammar into its simplest parts, showing you how to recreate even complex formations.

Vocabulary Throughout the book, vocabulary modules list the most useful English words and phrases, with visual cues to help you remember them.

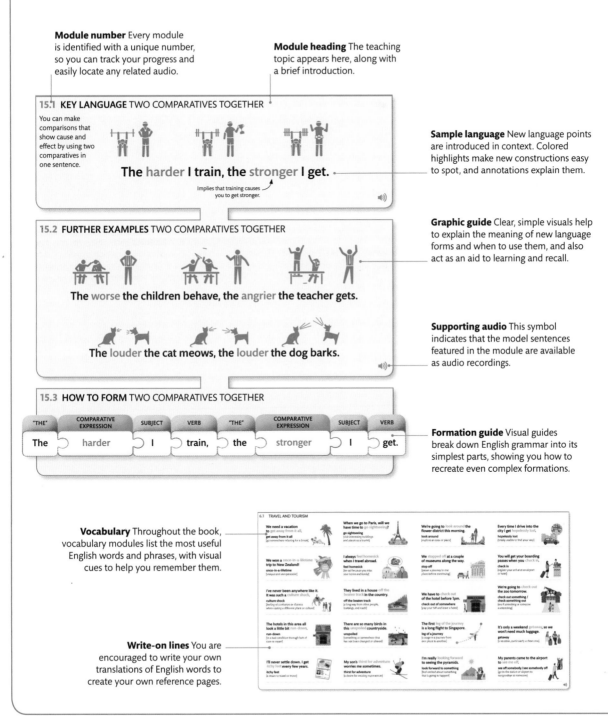

Write-on lines You are encouraged to write your own translations of English words to create your own reference pages.

Practice modules

Each exercise is carefully graded to drill and test the language taught in the corresponding course book units. Working through the exercises alongside the course book will help you remember what you have learned and become more fluent. Every exercise is introduced with a symbol to indicate which skill is being practiced.

 GRAMMAR
Apply new language rules in different contexts.

 READING
Examine target language in real-life English contexts.

 LISTENING
Test your understanding of spoken English.

 VOCABULARY
Cement your understanding of key vocabulary.

 WRITING
Practice producing written passages of English text.

 SPEAKING
Compare your spoken English to model audio recordings.

Module number Every module is identified with a unique number, so you can easily locate answers and related audio.

Exercise instruction Every exercise is introduced with a brief instruction, telling you what you need to do.

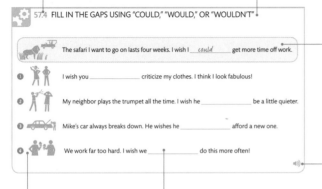

57.4 FILL IN THE GAPS USING "COULD," "WOULD," OR "WOULDN'T"

The safari I want to go on lasts four weeks. I wish I _could_ get more time off work.

1. I wish you _____ criticize my clothes. I think I look fabulous!

2. My neighbor plays the trumpet all the time. I wish he _____ be a little quieter.

3. Mike's car always breaks down. He wishes he _____ afford a new one.

4. We work far too hard. I wish we _____ do this more often!

Sample answer The first question of each exercise is answered for you, to help make the task easy to understand.

Supporting audio This symbol shows that the answers to the exercise are available as audio tracks. Listen to them after completing the exercise.

Supporting graphics Visual cues are given to help you understand the exercises.

Space for writing You are encouraged to write your answers in the book for future reference.

Listening exercise This symbol indicates that you should listen to an audio track in order to answer the questions in the exercise.

63.10 RESPOND TO THE AUDIO, SPEAKING OUT LOUD USING SUBSTITUTION

Do you go to bookstores often?
[suppose] _Yes, I suppose so._

Who wrote your favorite novel?
[did] _____

Do you think all books will be digital soon?
[hope] _____

Would you like to write a book?
[think] _____

Speaking exercise This symbol indicates that you should say your answers out loud, then compare them to model recordings included in your audio files.

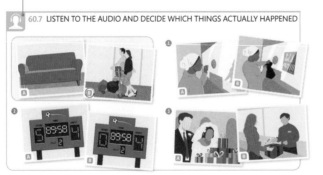

60.7 LISTEN TO THE AUDIO AND DECIDE WHICH THINGS ACTUALLY HAPPENED

Audio

English for Everyone features extensive supporting audio materials. You are encouraged to use them as much as you can, to improve your understanding of spoken English, and to make your own accent and pronunciation more natural. Each file can be played, paused, and repeated as often as you like, until you are confident you understand what has been said.

LISTENING EXERCISES
This symbol indicates that you should listen to an audio track in order to answer the questions in the exercise.

SUPPORTING AUDIO
This symbol indicates that extra audio material is available for you to listen to after completing the module.

FREE AUDIO
website and app
www.dkefe.com

Track your progress

The course is designed to make it easy to monitor your progress, with regular summary and review modules. Answers are provided for every exercise, so you can see how well you have understood each teaching point.

Checklists Every unit ends with a checklist, where you can check off the new skills you have learned.

05 ✔ CHECKLIST
☊ Introductory "it" ☐   **Aa** Talents and abilities ☐   ♣ Talking about your abilities ☐

Review modules At the end of a group of units, you will find a more detailed review module, summarizing the language you have learned.

Check boxes Use these boxes to mark the skills you feel comfortable with. Go back and review anything you feel you need to practice further.

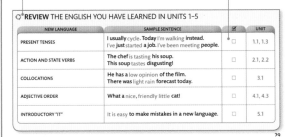

☊ **REVIEW** THE ENGLISH YOU HAVE LEARNED IN UNITS 1–5

NEW LANGUAGE	SAMPLE SENTENCE	☑	UNIT
PRESENT TENSES	I usually cycle. Today I'm walking instead. I've just started a job. I've been meeting people.	☐	1.1, 1.3
ACTION AND STATE VERBS	The chef is tasting his soup. This soup tastes disgusting!	☐	2.1, 2.2
COLLOCATIONS	He has a low opinion of the film. There was light rain forecast today.	☐	3.1
ADJECTIVE ORDER	What a nice, friendly little cat!	☐	4.1, 4.3
INTRODUCTORY "IT"	It is easy to make mistakes in a new language.	☐	5.1

29

01

1.2
Hi José,
Today **is** my first day in my new job, so **I am leaving** the house early.
I'm a bit nervous, but **I'm also** very excited! Anyway, **I'm already running** late, and **I need** to leave to catch the bus. **Don't forget** to pick up some milk on your way home from work tonight!
See you later!

1.4 ◄))
① **I have been reading** for hours. My eyes **have started hurting.**
② Has the mail **arrived** yet? **I have been expecting** a letter all week.
③ My leg **has been hurting** all day, but I **haven't seen** a doctor yet.
④ Have you **seen** my keys? **I have been looking** for them for ages.
⑤ Have you **heard** about Carl? He **has decided** to move.
⑥ **I have finished! I have been writing** this essay for ages.
⑦ Have you ever **visited** France? We **have been looking** at brochures.
⑧ **I have been trying** to reach Tao all day, but he **has not answered** yet.

1.6 ◄))
① They aren't very welcoming, **are they?**
② He should try harder to be friendly, **shouldn't he?**
③ She hasn't made many friends here, **has she?**
④ He doesn't like going to new places, **does he?**
⑤ They're so happy to be here, **aren't they?**
⑥ They would be here if they could, **wouldn't they?**

1.8 ●
① Answer required
② Answer not required
③ Answer not required
④ Answer required
⑤ Answer not required
⑥ Answer not required

Answers Find the answers to every exercise printed at the back of the book.

Audio This symbol indicates that the answers can also be listened to.

Exercise numbers Match these numbers to the unique identifier at the top-left corner of each exercise.

01 Making conversation

Verbs have various forms in the present tense, including continuous and perfect. You need to understand these differences when making question tags.

⚙ **New language** Present tenses
Aa Vocabulary Meeting new people
🧩 **New skill** Using question tags

1.1 KEY LANGUAGE PRESENT SIMPLE AND PRESENT CONTINUOUS

PRESENT SIMPLE	PRESENT CONTINUOUS
The present simple refers to something that happens in general or as part of a daily routine.	The present continuous refers to something that is happening right now and will continue for a limited amount of time.

I usually cycle to work, but today I'm walking instead.

 ## 1.2 REWRITE THE NOTE, CORRECTING THE HIGHLIGHTED ERRORS

Hi José,

Today is being my first day in my new job, so I leave the house early. I'm being a bit nervous, but I'm also being very excited! Anyway, I already run late, and I'm needing to leave to catch the bus. Don't be forgetting to pick up some milk on your way home from work tonight!

See you later!

Hi José,

Today is my first day...!

12

1.3 KEY LANGUAGE PRESENT PERFECT AND PRESENT PERFECT CONTINUOUS

PRESENT PERFECT

Use the present perfect to talk about the recent past or general experiences in a lifetime up until now.

PRESENT PERFECT CONTINUOUS

Use the present perfect continuous to talk about an action that started in the past, but is continuing until now or has present results.

I've **just** started **a new job.** I've **been meeting** **new people all week.**

◀))

1.4 FILL IN THE GAPS BY PUTTING THE VERBS IN THE PRESENT PERFECT OR THE PRESENT PERFECT CONTINUOUS

I _have been waiting_ (wait) for a bus all morning, but I still _haven't seen_ (not see) one!

1. I _____ (read) for hours. My eyes _____ (start) hurting.

2. Has the mail _____ (arrive) yet? I _____ (expect) a letter all week.

3. My leg _____ (hurt) all day, but I _____ (not see) a doctor yet.

4. Have you _____ (see) my keys? I _____ (look) for them for ages.

5. Have you _____ (hear) about Carl? He _____ (decide) to move.

6. I _____ (finish)! I _____ (write) this essay for ages.

7. Have you ever _____ (visit) France? We _____ (look) at brochures.

8. I _____ (try) to reach Tao all day, but he _____ (not answer) yet.

◀))

1.5 KEY LANGUAGE QUESTION TAGS

If the main clause of the sentence is positive, the question tag is negative, and vice versa. In most cases, the question tag uses the verb "do."

Question tags are small questions added to the end of a statement in informal conversation.

You like **meeting new people,** don't you?

You don't like **meeting new people,** do you?

If the main verb is "be," "be" is also used in the question tag.

The negative question form of "I am" is "aren't I."

I am **working tomorrow,** aren't I?

George isn't **working today,** is he?

If the main clause of the sentence contains an auxiliary verb or a modal verb, the question tag uses this verb.

You have **met the new boss,** haven't you?

We shouldn't **interrupt him,** should we?

1.6 MATCH THE STATEMENTS TO THE CORRECT QUESTION TAGS

Nina's always late for work,   isn't she?

1. They aren't very welcoming,   are they?

2. He should try harder to be friendly,   does he?

3. She hasn't made many friends here,   has she?

4. He doesn't like going to new places,   wouldn't they?

5. They're so happy to be here,   aren't they?

6. They would be here if they could,   shouldn't he?

1.7 KEY LANGUAGE INTONATION WITH QUESTION TAGS

If the intonation goes up at the end of the question tag, it is a question requiring an answer.

You'd like to move offices, wouldn't you?

[I am asking whether or not you would like to move offices.]

If the intonation goes down at the end of a question tag, the speaker is just inviting the listener to agree.

You've already met Evelyn, haven't you?

[I already know you've met Evelyn.]

1.8 LISTEN TO THE SENTENCES AND MARK WHETHER OR NOT AN ANSWER IS REQUIRED

You came here last year, didn't you?
Answer required ☑ **Answer not required** ☐

1 You moved to the other side of town, didn't you?
Answer required ☐ **Answer not required** ☐

2 They haven't treated you very well, have they?
Answer required ☐ **Answer not required** ☐

3 You're staying with your dad tonight, aren't you?
Answer required ☐ **Answer not required** ☐

4 You bought something for dinner, didn't you?
Answer required ☐ **Answer not required** ☐

5 You don't have any money for a taxi, do you?
Answer required ☐ **Answer not required** ☐

6 Maria doesn't seem to like Sue, does she?
Answer required ☐ **Answer not required** ☐

1.9 ADD QUESTION TAGS TO THE SENTENCES AND SAY THEM WITH BOTH TYPES OF INTONATION

Clara doesn't still work for the same company, _____*does she*_____?

1 People don't have their own office space here, _____?

2 You have been introduced to Mr. Thomas, _____?

3 You'd like to come to dinner with us all tonight, _____?

4 Oscar and Kate aren't here yet, _____?

02 Action and state verbs

Verbs that describe actions or events are known as "action" or "dynamic" verbs, whereas those that describe states are known as "state" or "stative" verbs.

✿ New language State verbs in continuous forms
Aa Vocabulary Action and state verbs
✚ New skill Describing states

2.1 KEY LANGUAGE ACTION AND STATE VERBS

Action verbs can be used in simple and continuous forms.
State verbs are not usually used in continuous forms.

ACTION	STATE
I read every day. ✓	 **I own two cars.** ✓
I am reading right now. ✓	**I am owning two cars.** ✗

2.2 KEY LANGUAGE USING STATE VERBS IN CONTINUOUS FORMS

Some verbs can be both action and state verbs. When these verbs are describing an action, they can be used in continuous forms.

ACTION	STATE
I am thinking about taking up fencing. [Right now, I'm considering taking up fencing.]	**I think fencing is a great sport.** [In my opinion, fencing is a great sport.]
The chef is tasting his soup. [The chef is testing the soup's flavor.]	**This soup tastes disgusting!** [The soup has a disgusting flavor.]

Other state verbs can be used in continuous forms. They keep their stative meaning, but emphasize a change, development, or temporary situation.

CONTINUOUS FORM	SIMPLE FORM
Are you feeling better today? **You seemed sick yesterday.**	 **How do you feel about Modern art?**

2.3 MARK THE SENTENCES THAT ARE CORRECT

He's wanting to buy a house. ☐
He wants to buy a house. ☑

1. She has long, wavy hair. ☐
   She's having long, wavy hair. ☐

2. Sorry, I'm not believing you. ☐
   Sorry, I don't believe you. ☐

3. That jacket fits you very well. ☐
   That jacket is fitting you very well. ☐

4. I rarely think about the past. ☐
   I'm rarely thinking about the past. ☐

5. Jess is having a great time at the party. ☐
   Jess has a great time at the party. ☐

6. That milk is smelling dreadful. ☐
   That milk smells dreadful. ☐

7. I'm thinking about going home soon. ☐
   I think about going home soon. ☐

8. I'm slowly realizing the problem here. ☐
   I slowly realize the problem here. ☐

9. You seem unhappy. Can I help? ☐
   You're seeming unhappy. Can I help? ☐

◀))

2.4 FILL IN THE GAPS USING THE WORDS IN THE PANEL

Hi Sara,

I'm writing about Gavin. I _____think_____ there's something wrong. I'm not _____ that it's anything serious, but he doesn't _____ to be his usual happy self. Maybe he's not _____ in well in his new job. I was going to _____ that the three of us go out for a drink, or perhaps you would _____ a meal. Let me know what you think.

Tina

| seem | suggest | ~~think~~ | suggesting | prefer | fitting |

02 ✓ CHECKLIST

✿° State verbs in continuous forms ☐   **Aa** Action and state verbs ☐   🧩 Describing states ☐

03 Using collocations

Collocations are often formed of two words, but can contain more. Using them will make you a more fluent English speaker.

🔧 **New language** Collocations
Aa Vocabulary Beliefs and opinions
🧩 **New skill** Talking about your life

3.1 KEY LANGUAGE COLLOCATIONS

Collocations are pairs or groups of words that naturally go together and sound "right" to experienced users of a language.

He has a low opinion of the film. ✅
He has a light opinion of the film. ❌

"Light" can have a similar meaning to "low" ("not much"), but does not sound natural next to "opinion."

There was light rain forecast today. ✅
There was low rain forecast today. ❌

"Low" can have a similar meaning to "light," but does not collocate with "rain."

🔊

Aa 3.2 FILL IN THE GAPS USING THE WORDS IN THE PANEL TO CREATE MORE COLLOCATIONS

It is [extremely *unlikely*] that there will be a happy ending.

1. She doesn't have any [family] left, only an uncle.

2. Sometimes the only solution is to [your best] and hope.

3. All their lives they appeared to be [married] .

4. Unfortunately, the financial crisis [ruined his] .

5. He first [into business] when he was only 17.

6. Looking at old photographs can [stir up] .

7. I can [distinctly] meeting him 20 years ago.

8. Looking at them, the difference in age is [visible] .

Panel
close
career
went
do
happily
~~unlikely~~
memories
clearly
remember

🔊

3.3 READ THE ARTICLE AND ANSWER THE QUESTIONS

Lara Estelle has recently died.
True ☐ **False** ☑

1 Lara was a famous fashion designer.
True ☐ **False** ☐

2 The author's mother does not like Lara Estelle's music.
True ☐ **False** ☐

3 The author's father was a soccer fan.
True ☐ **False** ☐

4 Lara became famous in the 1980s.
True ☐ **False** ☐

5 Steven was Lara's second husband.
True ☐ **False** ☐

6 Lara and Steven are no longer married.
True ☐ **False** ☐

7 The author's father has forgiven Lara now.
True ☐ **False** ☐

LIFE, LOVE, AND LARA

Lara Estelle celebrates her 70th birthday today

It's difficult to imagine now, but in her younger days Lara "The Shades" Estelle was always in the news. How did she create such a sensation? Opinions are divided. Some people say that she was a brilliant musician with an iconic fashion sense. Others believe she was the cause of one of the country's most dramatic sporting upsets.

My parents' views on Lara Estelle are poles apart and, therefore, typical of many of their generation. My mother still loves Lara's music and used to have the same platinum white hair and dark sunglasses as her idol. My father, however, remembers 1980 and his favorite soccer team losing in the final game of the season. He still firmly believes that Lara caused Dun City to lose. But how could a singer cause such drama?

The quality of her music is a matter of opinion, but in 1979 Lara was a top-selling artist. She met her first husband Steven Jones, Dun City's star player, backstage at one of her concerts. Within weeks they were engaged. Lara told Steven that, to prove his love for her, their wedding must be on the same day as the league final that season. He agreed, and there is still a popular belief among City fans that their team lost because Jones did not play. The couple divorced a year later and City never won any trophies again. To this day, my father dislikes Lara's music.

Steven and Lara were married in a glamorous ceremony in 1979.

Aa   3.4 MATCH THE DEFINITIONS TO THE COLLOCATIONS

a subject on which people hold different views

1 completely opposed

2 an opinion held by a lot of people

3 people hold differing points of view

4 to hold a strong opinion that something is true

opinions are divided

a popular belief

a matter of opinion

firmly believe

poles apart

3.5 READ MARIAM'S BLOG AND ANSWER THE QUESTIONS USING FULL SENTENCES

Mariam Davies
• WILDLIFE PHOTOGRAPHER •

 ## ABOUT ME

I was born in a small town in northern France and went to college in Scotland to study architecture. While at college, I joined the photography club. We used to go on field trips to amazing places and I met my husband, the landscape photographer Julian Davies, while photographing dolphins from a boat. During my last year in college, a wildlife magazine published a number of my photos of birds. This was a major turning point for me and, after we graduated, Julian and I became freelance photographers. We were based in Europe while our twin boys were growing up, but since they both graduated last year, we have started exploring and photographing further afield. We spent some time in Africa this year, and want to take photographs in Japan and Korea next year.

What is Mariam's profession?
Mariam is a wildlife photographer.

❶ Where is Mariam from?

_____

❷ What subject did she study in college?

_____

❸ How did she meet her husband?

_____

❹ What important turning point in her life does she mention?

_____

❺ Do Mariam and Julian have children?

_____

❻ Where are they planning to travel next year?

_____

 ### 3.6 LISTEN TO THE AUDIO AND MATCH THE EVENTS TO WHEN THEY HAPPENED

| 23 years ago | This morning | One month ago | 25 years ago | 3 years ago |

3.7 CROSS OUT THE INCORRECT WORDS IN EACH SENTENCE

Lisa ~~was receiving~~ / received an email from her friend ~~every morning~~ / this morning.

1. Lisa **was going** / **went** to Thailand 25 years **since** / **ago**.

2. Bill **had taught** / **was teaching** when Lisa arrived in Thailand.

3. Lisa and Bill **were getting married** / **got married** 23 years ago, **on** / **in** March

4. Lisa **had been traveling** / **has traveled** for 25 years before she returned.

5. Barbara **has graduated** / **graduated** from college **previous** / **last** month.

🔊

3.8 USE "WHEN" AND "WHILE" TO DESCRIBE THE EVENTS ON THE TIMELINE, SPEAKING OUT LOUD

TIP
Use "when" for completed actions and "while" for continuous actions.

| MOVED TO CHINA | GOT MARRIED | HAD A BABY | WROTE MY THESIS | STARTED A SMALL BUSINESS |

STUDYING FULL-TIME   LIVING IN CHINA   STUDYING PART-TIME

I moved to China _____ *while I was studying full-time.* _____ 🗣

1. I got married _____ 🗣

2. I was _____ I had a baby. 🗣

3. I wrote my thesis _____ 🗣

4. I was _____ I started a small business. 🗣

🔊

04 Complex descriptions

When you describe something using more than one adjective, the adjectives usually have to go in a specific order. There are several categories of adjectives.

4.1 KEY LANGUAGE ADJECTIVE ORDER

Opinion adjectives come before factual ones in a sentence. General opinion adjectives always come before specific opinion adjectives.

OPINION ADJECTIVES   FACT ADJECTIVE

What a nice, friendly little cat!

"Nice" is a general opinion adjective. It can describe lots of different things.

"Friendly" is a specific opinion adjective. It usually only describes people or animals.

🔊

4.2 FURTHER EXAMPLES ADJECTIVE ORDER

 It's a fantastic, exciting new movie.

 He's a wonderful, kind old man.

 What a horrible, ugly plastic table.

 That's a lovely, stylish cotton shirt.

🔊

4.3 HOW TO FORM ADJECTIVE ORDER

Like opinion adjectives, fact adjectives must go in a particular order.

OPINION ADJECTIVES   FACT ADJECTIVES

	GENERAL	SPECIFIC	SIZE	SHAPE	AGE	COLOR	MATERIAL	
What a	nice,	friendly	little					cat!
He's a	wonderful,	kind			old			man.
That's a	lovely,	stylish					cotton	shirt.

4.4 WRITE THE ADJECTIVES FROM THE PANEL IN THE CORRECT GROUPS

GENERAL	SPECIFIC	SIZE	SHAPE	AGE	COLOR	MATERIAL
awful						

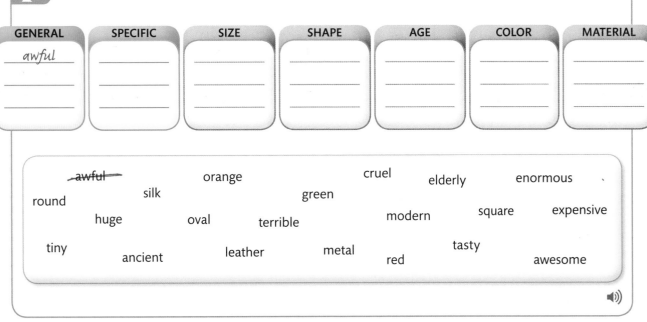

awful   orange   cruel   elderly   enormous

round   silk   green

huge   oval   terrible   modern   square   expensive

tiny   ancient   leather   metal   tasty   awesome

red

4.5 WRITE THE ADJECTIVES IN THE CORRECT ORDER

uncomfortable   wooden   horrible

It's a ___*horrible*___ , ___*uncomfortable*___ ___*wooden*___ chair. I don't want to buy it.

rude   terrible

1 I don't like him at all. He's a _____ , _____ man. Let's not invite him to the party.

nice   young   intelligent

2 My mother thinks he's a _____ , _____ _____ boy.

brown   friendly   sweet

3 Dad, look at this _____ , _____ _____ puppy! Can we take him for a walk?

comfortable   wonderful

4 Should we buy this _____ , _____ sofa for the living room? We really need a new one.

23

4.6 READ THE PERFORMANCE REVIEWS AND ANSWER THE QUESTIONS

Performance Review: Jorge Perez

Jorge is very hard-working and his confidence has grown considerably since he joined the company last summer. He often looks beyond the immediate issues and is proactive in dealing with any potential problems before they arise. He has shown himself to be fair-minded, and he often helps others in his team. In fact, he has proved that he has a natural flair for communication and leadership. We are delighted that Jorge has recently started a leadership skills course, and we will look to promote him when it is completed.

Performance Review: Maria Moran

Given that Maria works in the HR department, we were hoping that her communication skills would have developed more. Calling one of her colleagues "bone-idle" during an appraisal is typical of her blunt approach. Fortunately, the colleague in question is broad-minded and accepted an apology. Despite taking part in several training opportunities, Maria continues to take a narrow-minded approach to her work. Her refusal to acknowledge other people's opinions can make her seem big-headed and arrogant.

Jorge has worked for the same company for several years.
True ☐ **False** ☐ **Not given** ☑

1. The author is pleased that Jorge is taking a leadership course.
True ☐ **False** ☐ **Not given** ☐

2. Jorge is going to be promoted next month.
True ☐ **False** ☐ **Not given** ☐

3. Maria works in the Sales department.
True ☐ **False** ☐ **Not given** ☐

4. Maria has taken part in a number of training courses.
True ☐ **False** ☐ **Not given** ☐

5. Maria is fairly broad-minded in terms of her approach to work.
True ☐ **False** ☐ **Not given** ☐

4.7 LISTEN TO THE AUDIO AND MARK THE CORRECT SUMMARY

A manager is talking to her employee, Paul, about his performance at work during the past year.

1. On the whole, Paul hasn't really settled in very well in his new role. He is hard-working, but needs to work on his team-building and communication skills. ☐

2. On the whole, Paul has settled in really well in his new role. He is a hard-working and popular member of the team, but he needs to work on his communication skills. ☐

3. On the whole, Paul has settled in really well in his new role. He is hard-working, but needs to try to become more popular and improve his communication skills. ☐

4.8 FILL IN THE GAPS USING THE NEGATIVE PREFIXES IN THE PANEL

They were really rude and __un__ friendly.

1. His last employer said he was ____ trustworthy.

2. She doesn't realize how ____ sensitive she is.

3. He's 25 now, but he's rather ____ mature at work.

4. I'm afraid she's quite an ____ efficient worker.

5. He gossips and is ____ kind to his co-workers.

6. Her office desk and her work are ____ organized.

7. He makes mistakes because he's ____ patient.

8. She's ____ loyal to the company.

im	dis	un	in

Aa 4.9 FIND 10 ADJECTIVES IN THE GRID AND WRITE THEM UNDER THE CORRECT HEADING

```
G E X C E L L E N T O N S
N E B N L L N R T Q E P V
N D E F J P O P U L A R D
R I N R E R T I U T C O I
Q U V U E P C A M D C A I
E D I S L O Y A L A E C D
H Z L T S L O Z C O U T Z
E A V R T S V V J S N I D
L C M A T U R E G J K V I
P H I T P A I L I E I E S
F W C I M P A T I E N T D
U B C N A F G E I J D L M
L N Q G A R R O G A N T D
```

POSITIVE ADJECTIVES

1. helpful
2. _____
3. _____
4. _____
5. _____

NEGATIVE ADJECTIVES

6. disloyal
7. _____
8. _____
9. _____
10. _____

05 Making general statements

It is very useful to know how to start sentences with the word "it" in English. You can use "it is" at the beginning of a sentence to make a general statement about something.

⚙ **New language** Introductory "it"
Aa Vocabulary Talents and abilities
🧩 **New skill** Expressing general truths

5.1 KEY LANGUAGE INTRODUCTORY "IT"

Certain set phrases beginning "it is" can be used at the start of a sentence. "It" is the subject of the sentence, and can be used to express a general truth or belief.

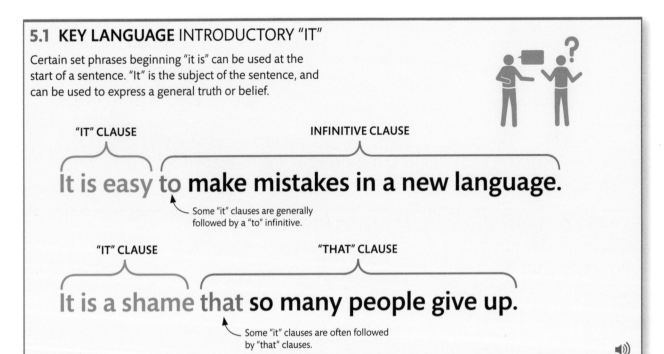

"IT" CLAUSE   INFINITIVE CLAUSE

It is easy to make mistakes in a new language.

Some "it" clauses are generally followed by a "to" infinitive.

"IT" CLAUSE   "THAT" CLAUSE

It is a shame that so many people give up.

Some "it" clauses are often followed by "that" clauses.

5.2 FURTHER EXAMPLES INTRODUCTORY "IT"

 It is important to **be relaxed about making mistakes.**

 It is essential to **give yourself time to study regularly.**

 It's true that **being able to speak a second language is useful.**

 It's unlikely that **you will be comfortable speaking aloud at first.**

 It is difficult to **remember new words if you don't write them down.**

5.3 FILL IN THE GAPS USING THE WORDS IN THE PANEL

It's _____*important to*_____ have the skills to communicate globally.

1 With busy work and social lives, it's _____ most people have little time to study.

2 Languages are so useful. It is _____ so few people learn a second language.

3 Learning doesn't have to be expensive. It is not _____ spend a lot of money.

4 Try internet study groups. It is _____ meet other language learners online.

5 Don't worry if you need time. It's _____ you'll be able to speak fluently quickly.

easy to   a shame that   unlikely that   essential to   ~~important to~~   true that

5.4 KEY LANGUAGE LEADING WITH AN INFINITIVE PHRASE

When you want to emphasize the contents of the infinitive clause, you can put it at the front of the sentence.

The construction with "it" at the start is much more common.

It is easy to begin learning.

To begin learning is easy! Keeping it going is harder.

Placing the infinitive clause at the start works particularly well with short sentences.

5.5 CROSS OUT THE INCORRECT WORDS IN EACH SENTENCE

It is worth working hard. To / ~~That~~ / ~~It~~ give up now would be a shame.

1 Remember, it's important to / that / it be relaxed about making mistakes.

2 With so many options, it's no longer difficult to / that / it find language courses online.

3 To / That / It take the exam now would be a waste of time. She hasn't studied at all.

4 To / That / It is unlikely that he will finish the class before the end of the year.

5 Don't give up! It's true to / that / it the more you study, the better you will become.

5.6 READ THE FORUM POSTS AND ANSWER THE QUESTIONS

Who is learning a language which involves clicking?
Alice ☐ Dave ☐ Mei ☐ Sam ☑

1. Who finds their language lessons a little boring?
Alice ☐ Dave ☐ Mei ☐ Sam ☐

2. Who can speak a number of different languages very well?
Alice ☐ Dave ☐ Mei ☐ Sam ☐

3. Who was encouraged to learn a language by someone else?
Alice ☐ Dave ☐ Mei ☐ Sam ☐

4. Who thinks they have a natural ability for learning languages?
Alice ☐ Dave ☐ Mei ☐ Sam ☐

5. Who is conducting research about learning languages?
Alice ☐ Dave ☐ Mei ☐ Sam ☐

Lingo-net

ABOUT | NEWS | FORUM | CONTACT

ARE YOU A LANGUAGE LEARNER?

Alice: I'm working on a TV program and am looking for people to share language learning experiences. Do you have a hidden talent or even a complete inability to learn languages? Get in touch!

Dave: I'm trying to learn Native American Pawnee. I don't have any natural ability and most words have at least 10 syllables! The lessons drag on a bit but I'll keep on doing them until I'm fluent.

Mei: I think I have an aptitude for language-learning. I'm fluent in four languages. I'd love to learn Sentinelese but it's impossible because no-one knows what it sounds like!

Sam: I've only ever spoken English, but one of my professors has a remarkable capacity for languages and speaks Xhosa (a South African language with click sounds). He asked if I'd like to learn it, and I took him up on the offer. It's very difficult, but he's shown me some online videos to help.

5.7 FILL IN THE GAPS TO CREATE COLLOCATIONS USING THE PHRASES IN 5.6

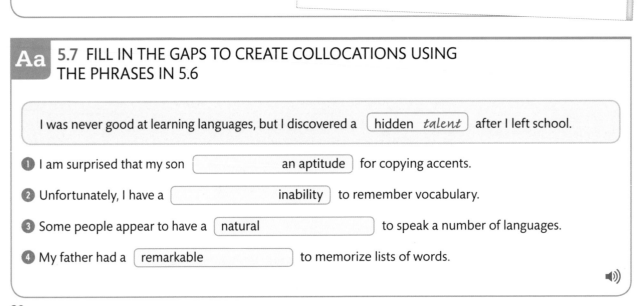

I was never good at learning languages, but I discovered a [hidden *talent*] after I left school.

1. I am surprised that my son [an aptitude] for copying accents.

2. Unfortunately, I have a [inability] to remember vocabulary.

3. Some people appear to have a [natural   ] to speak a number of languages.

4. My father had a [remarkable   ] to memorize lists of words.

5.8 RESPOND TO THE AUDIO, SPEAKING OUT LOUD

Do you like learning new languages?

It isn't easy to _learn a new language, but I find it a lot of fun._

1 Why do you think learning languages is important?

It is important to _____

2 What advice would you give to new learners?

It's best to _____

3 What is the hardest thing about learning languages?

It is difficult to _____

---

05 ✓ CHECKLIST

⚙ Introductory "it" ☐   **Aa** Talents and abilities ☐   🧩 Expressing general truths ☐

♻ REVIEW THE ENGLISH YOU HAVE LEARNED IN UNITS 1–5

NEW LANGUAGE	SAMPLE SENTENCE	☑	UNIT
PRESENT TENSES	I usually cycle. Today I'm walking instead. I've just started a job. I've been meeting people.	☐	1.1, 1.3
ACTION AND STATE VERBS	The chef is tasting his soup. This soup tastes disgusting!	☐	2.1, 2.2
COLLOCATIONS	He has a low opinion of the film. There was light rain forecast today.	☐	3.1
ADJECTIVE ORDER	What a nice, friendly little cat!	☐	4.1, 4.3
INTRODUCTORY "IT"	It is easy to make mistakes in a new language.	☐	5.1

06 Vocabulary

6.1 TRAVEL AND TOURISM

We need a vacation to get away from it all.

get away from it all
[go somewhere relaxing for a break]

When we go to Paris, will we have time to go sightseeing?

go sightseeing
[visit interesting buildings and places as a tourist]

We won a once-in-a-lifetime **trip to New Zealand!**

once-in-a-lifetime
[unique and unrepeatable]

I always feel homesick **when I travel abroad.**

feel homesick
[be sad because you miss your home and family]

I've never been anywhere like it. It was such a culture shock.

culture shock
[feeling of confusion or distress when visiting a different place or culture]

They lived in a house off the beaten track **in the country.**

off the beaten track
[a long way from other people, buildings, and roads]

The hotels in this area all look a little bit run-down.

run-down
[in a bad condition through lack of care or repair]

There are so many birds in this unspoiled **countryside.**

unspoiled
[something or somewhere that has not been changed or altered]

I'll never settle down. I get itchy feet **every few years.**

itchy feet
[a desire to travel or move]

My son's thirst for adventure **worries me sometimes.**

thirst for adventure
[a desire for exciting experiences]

We're going to look around the flower district this morning.

look around
[explore an area or place]

We stopped off at a couple of museums along the way.

stop off
[pause a journey in one place before continuing]

We have to check out of the hotel before 1pm.

check out of somewhere
[pay your bill and leave a hotel]

The first leg of the journey is a long flight to Singapore.

leg of a journey
[a stage in a journey from one place to another]

I'm really looking forward to seeing the pyramids.

look forward to something
[feel excited about something that is going to happen]

Every time I drive into the city I get hopelessly lost.

hopelessly lost
[totally unable to find your way]

You will get your boarding passes when you check in.

check in
[register your arrival at an airport or hotel]

We're going to check out the zoo tomorrow.

check out something / check something out
[see if something or someone is interesting]

It's only a weekend getaway, so we won't need much luggage.

getaway
[a vacation, particularly a short one]

My parents came to the airport to see me off.

see off somebody / see somebody off
[go to the station or airport to say goodbye to someone]

07 Phrasal verbs

Phrasal verbs occur in many different forms. They have two or more parts, which are sometimes separable. They are very common, especially in spoken English.

 New language Phrasal verbs overview
Aa Vocabulary Travel
New skill Using complex phrasal verbs

7.1 KEY LANGUAGE PHRASAL VERBS

Phrasal verbs contain a verb and one or more particles. One verb can use different particles to form many different phrasal verbs.

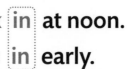 

We must check in at noon.

She always checks in early.

The verb agrees with the subject. ⟋ ⟍ The particle never changes.

7.2 REWRITE THE SENTENCES CORRECTING THE ERRORS IN THE PHRASAL VERBS

He **work outs** at least twice a week.
He works out at least twice a week.

① Be careful, it's absolutely **pour downing** with rain.

_____

② He's behind on his work, so he needs to **catch-up**.

_____

③ They are **take downing** the offensive posters today.

_____

④ She'll have a backup. She always **backs ups** her files.

_____

⑤ They **split ups** every time they have an argument.

_____

7.3 KEY LANGUAGE SEPARABLE PHRASAL VERBS

If a phrasal verb has a direct object, the direct object can sometimes go between the verb and the particle.

He filled in the customs form.

He filled the customs form in.

If the direct object is a pronoun, it must go between the verb and the particle.

He filled it in.   **He filled in it.**

7.4 REWRITE THE SENTENCES SEPARATING THE PHRASAL VERBS

> The school is putting on a show.
> *The school is putting a show on.*

1 I'll pick up your shopping for you.

_____

2 They're putting up posters outside again.

_____

3 Have you checked out the restaurant menu?

_____

4 He hasn't set up the computer yet.

_____

7.5 REWRITE THE SENTENCES USING PRONOUNS

> She is looking up the location.
> *She is looking it up.*

1 He should ask Mary out if he wants to.

_____

2 Remember to take out the recycling later.

_____

3 You should send the phone back if it's broken.

_____

4 Could you turn off the lights when you leave?

_____

7.6 KEY LANGUAGE THREE-WORD PHRASAL VERBS

Some phrasal verbs are made up of more than two words. In such cases, the spoken stress falls on the second word.

VERB + PARTICLE + PREPOSITION

She always comes up with exciting travel plans.

The stress is on "up" here.

7.7 SAY THE SENTENCES OUT LOUD, FILLING IN THE GAPS USING THE PHRASAL VERBS IN THE PANEL

> My sister's always ___*coming up with*___ ways to save money.

1 My big brother is a CEO. I have a lot to _____ .

2 Slow down! I can't _____ you any more, I'm tired.

3 His parents aren't very strict. He _____ everything!

keep up with

get away with

live up to

~~come up with~~

33

7.8 READ THE ARTICLE AND NUMBER THE PICTURES IN THE ORDER THEY HAPPENED

A ☐

B ☑1

C ☐

D ☐

E ☐

F ☐

YOUR LIFE STORY

My year off turned into a career

When I was a teenager, I decided to take a gap year before going to university. I had already done loads of research online and decided to go to a Greek island to pick olives. I had calculated that I could earn enough money to travel cheaply to Asia. Although the people were wonderful, by the end of the olive harvest I felt I was a bit cut off on such a small island, so I bought a plane ticket and set off to Malaysia.

While I was in Malaysia, I decided to become an English teacher. I knew right away that teaching was what I wanted to do for the rest of my life. A short while later, I graduated with a degree in teaching. After just 10 years, I opened my very first English-language school.

7.9 LISTEN TO THE AUDIO AND ANSWER THE QUESTIONS

 Top travel writer Maria Soames is talking about how she first became interested in travel writing.

Which country did Maria first travel to?

Vietnam ☐

Indonesia ☑

Cambodia ☐

① Which animals did Maria want to see?

Chameleons ☐

Kangaroos ☐

Komodo dragons ☐

② What job does Maria do, besides writing?

Tour guide ☐

Travel rep ☐

Magazine editor ☐

③ Where did Maria record her experiences?

Diary ☐

Notebook ☐

Blog ☐

④ Which of the following hasn't Maria written?

Travel guides ☐

Newspaper articles ☐

Travel blog ☐

⑤ What reason does Maria not give for liking her job?

Meeting people ☐

Material for writing ☐

Good pay ☐

Aa 7.10 MATCH THE DEFINITIONS TO THE PHRASAL VERBS

go to a place of departure with someone to say goodbye	take off
❶ stop someone from going somewhere and isolate them	see somebody off
❷ pause a journey in one place before continuing	stop off
❸ start flying	set off
❹ start a trip	cut off

Aa 7.11 LOOK AT THE PICTURES AND USE THE PHRASAL VERBS FROM 7.10 TO COMPLETE THE SENTENCES

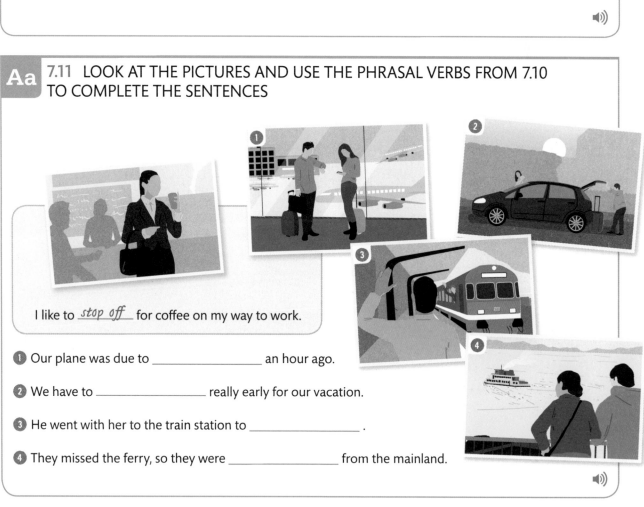

I like to _stop off_ for coffee on my way to work.

❶ Our plane was due to _____ an hour ago.

❷ We have to _____ really early for our vacation.

❸ He went with her to the train station to _____ .

❹ They missed the ferry, so they were _____ from the mainland.

Narrative tenses

When telling a story, even if you're just talking about something that happened recently, you need to use a variety of tenses so that the story can be understood easily.

⚙ **New language** The past perfect continuous
Aa Vocabulary Travel adjectives and idioms
🧩 **New skill** Talking about a variety of past actions

8.1 KEY LANGUAGE NARRATIVE TENSES

You can use different past tenses to show when past actions or states overlap, or to say which took place first.

PAST SIMPLE

The past simple describes actions or states that happened in a specific finished time period.

A specific finished time period ("last summer") is specified, so the the past simple is used.

Last summer, we flew to London. There's so much to do there!

PAST CONTINUOUS

The past continuous describes an action that began before, and possibly continued after, another past action.

While we were walking around the city, we took some photos in front of Big Ben.

You often use the past simple and the past continuous together to say that one action interrupted a longer one.

PAST PERFECT

The past perfect describes an action or state that happened before something else in the past.

This action happened before something else in the past (the trip abroad), so the past perfect is used.

Fortunately, we had looked up all the best places to go beforehand.

NOW

8.2 FILL IN THE GAPS BY PUTTING THE VERBS IN THE PAST SIMPLE OR PAST CONTINUOUS

We ___were flying___ (fly) over France when we ___saw___ (see) the Alps for the first time.

① I _____ (walk) down the road when someone _____ (ask) me to take their photo.

② Someone _____ (talk) during the tour until we _____ (tell) them to be quiet.

③ I _____ (stop) twice to take photos while I _____ (drive) through the country.

④ We _____ (decide) to order some champagne while we _____ (eat) lunch.

⑤ We were lost and our feet _____ (ache) before we finally_____ (find) a map shop.

🔊

8.3 COMPLETE THE SENTENCES USING THE PAST PERFECT, SPEAKING OUT LOUD

Our friend **told** us the city tour was great, so we went on it.

We went on the city tour because ___our friend had told us it was great.___

① We **walked** all around the city and my feet really ached by the end of the day.

My feet really ached by the end of the day because _____

② We **spent** a long time planning the trip and it was perfect.

The trip was perfect because _____

③ We **crossed** over the wrong bridge and got completely lost.

We got completely lost because _____

④ Our tour guide **recommended** a great show, so we went to see it.

We went to see a great show because _____

🔊

8.4 KEY LANGUAGE THE PAST PERFECT CONTINUOUS

You use the past perfect continuous to describe an action or activity that was happening before another moment in the past.

He had been learning English for two years before he went to London.

TWO YEARS BEFORE   PAST   NOW

8.5 HOW TO FORM THE PAST PERFECT CONTINUOUS

SUBJECT	"HAD"	"BEEN"	PRESENT PARTICIPLE	REST OF SENTENCE
He	had	been	learning	**English for two years.**

8.6 FILL IN THE GAPS BY PUTTING THE VERBS INTO THE PAST PERFECT CONTINUOUS

They _____*had been flying*_____ (fly) for ages, so she decided to walk around the aisles.

❶ We _____ (wait) for at least an hour when the taxi finally arrived.

❷ I eventually went to the pharmacy because I _____ (not feel) well for days.

❸ We went to see the movie because they _____ (promote) it for months.

❹ The streets were beautiful and white because it _____ (snow) all night.

38

8.7 READ THE ARTICLE AND ANSWER THE QUESTIONS

Travel Underground is on TV on Fridays.
True ☐ **False** ☐ **Not given** ☑

1 Travel Underground is a one-off documentary.
True ☐ **False** ☐ **Not given** ☐

2 The city was rediscovered by accident.
True ☐ **False** ☐ **Not given** ☐

3 Derinkuyu is Turkey's deepest underground city.
True ☐ **False** ☐ **Not given** ☐

4 People used the city as a place to stay safe.
True ☐ **False** ☐ **Not given** ☐

What's on TV tonight?

Tonight, 9pm

This week, the Travel Underground series visits Turkey and tells the remarkable story of Derinkuyu in Cappadocia. Back in 1963, a resident had been knocking a wall down in his house, but stopped when something caught his eye. He decided to keep on digging, and it was soon obvious that he had discovered something incredible. This documentary charts the fascinating history of Derinkuyu, the deepest underground city in Turkey. Far below the surface, Derinkuyu had been a place of safety for many peoples for hundreds of years.

8.8 LISTEN TO THE AUDIO AND MARK THE CORRECT SUMMARY

1 The Underground Cities tour lasts for one day. You need to pack your own lunch, and you can't take too much luggage with you. ☐

2 The tour lasts for two days, so you need to take lots of luggage with you and an overnight bag. There is a traditional lunch included. ☐

3 The tour takes place over two days. You get a chance to explore by yourself, but you shouldn't take a lot of luggage. ☐

4 The tour starts in the underground city, with a lunch on the second day. It's just a short tour, so there's no need for an overnight bag. ☐

Aa 8.9 MATCH THE DEFINITIONS TO THE PHRASES USED IN 8.8

make a decision on the spot

bright and early

1 very early in the morning → play it by ear

2 far from central or popular areas

travel light

3 take few things with you on a trip

off the beaten track

08 ✓ CHECKLIST

✿ The past perfect continuous ☐ **Aa** Travel adjectives and idioms ☐ ✦ Talking about a variety of past actions ☐

09 Giving advice and opinions

When you want to give advice or make recommendations, you can use a variety of modal verbs. You can vary the strength of your advice by using different modals.

⚙ **New language** Modals for advice and opinion
Aa Vocabulary Recommendations
🧩 **New skill** Giving advice and opinions

9.1 KEY LANGUAGE MAKING RECOMMENDATIONS

One of the most common ways of recommending something or making a suggestion is to use modal verbs. When you offer advice, you often also give your opinion about a topic.

TIP
You can add emphasis by putting "really" in front of "should," "ought to," and "must."

General suggestion.

You { **could / might** } **visit the park. It's nice.**

Stronger suggestion.

You { **should / ought to** } **visit the castle. It's great.**

Very strong suggestion.

You must visit the palace. It is beautiful!

🔊

⚙ 9.2 MARK THE SPEECH BUBBLES THAT INCLUDE RECOMMENDATIONS

 My son is going to Paris next week. You went last year, didn't you? ☐

Yes, I did! He should visit the Tuileries Garden; it's beautiful. ☑

2 You really must try the new Italian restaurant on Main Street. ☐

I'm going there at lunch time! Why don't you come with me? ☐

1 It's such a sunny day! You could go to the park later if you have time. ☐

I have to go shopping. I'll definitely try to go if I finish early. ☐

3 What should I do for my birthday this year? I can't believe I'll be 30! ☐

You ought to have a big party with all your friends. It would be great! ☐

🔊

9.3 FILL IN THE GAPS USING THE RECOMMENDATIONS FROM THE PANEL

The food in the restaurant is fresh and homemade. The selection at breakfast was just awesome. _____ *You should definitely eat there.* _____

1 Everything about this hotel, from the dark interior to the hard stares of the grumpy staff, was unwelcoming. _____

2 The hotel's employees are wonderful. They did everything to make our honeymoon perfect. _____

3 Not bad, although the furniture in the hotel was falling apart. The walls were very thin and it was quite noisy. _____

4 I paid for a room with a view of the ski slopes, but all I could see was the wall of the building across from us. _____

5 Outstanding! I can understand the rave reviews for this great place. Our balcony overlooked the ocean. _____

> You should tell them if it's a special occasion.   You could ask to change rooms if this happens.
>
> You might want to bring earplugs.   ~~You should definitely eat there.~~
>
> You must ask for a room with an ocean view!   They ought to hire a new receptionist!

◀))

9.4 LISTEN TO THE AUDIO AND MARK WHETHER JEFF LIKED OR DISLIKED EACH ACTIVITY

Like ☐ Dislike ☑

2 Like ☐ Dislike ☐

4 Like ☐ Dislike ☐

1 Like ☐ Dislike ☐

3 Like ☐ Dislike ☐

5 Like ☐ Dislike ☐

9.5 KEY LANGUAGE GIVING ADVICE

You can also use modals to give advice based on facts. These can highlight the negative consequences of ignoring the advice.

You $\begin{Bmatrix} \text{should} \\ \text{ought to} \end{Bmatrix}$ wear a hat. It's very sunny.

General advice.

You **must** wear a hat or you'll get sunburned.

Strong advice; there are negative consequences if it is not followed.

9.6 OTHER WAYS TO GIVE ADVICE

You can also give advice using the phrases "If I were you..." and "You had better..." (usually contracted to "You'd better...").

This is a fixed phrase for giving advice as if you were the listener.

If I were you, I would wear a hat.

You'd better wear a hat.

This is used to give very strong advice. It may even suggest a threat.

TIP
You might hear people say, "If I was you..." but this is incorrect in formal English.

9.7 SAY THE SENTENCES OUT LOUD, CHOOSING THE CORRECT WORDS

The open air concert hall is amazing. You really ought to / ~~might~~ see it.

1 That snake is poisonous. You **must** / could go to the doctor about that bite or it'll get worse.

2 We might / **had better** go back to the boat. It's leaving soon and we don't want to miss it.

3 Perhaps you must / **could** go to France this summer. That would be nice.

4 Everyone says the castle is stunning and that we **must** / could see the view from the tower.

9.8 READ ANNE'S POSTCARD AND MARK WHAT SHE LIKED AND DISLIKED

The airline	Like ☐	Dislike ☑

1. The beach resort — Like ☐ Dislike ☐
2. The hotel staff — Like ☐ Dislike ☐
3. The food — Like ☐ Dislike ☐
4. The pyramids — Like ☐ Dislike ☐
5. The camel ride — Like ☐ Dislike ☐
6. The weather — Like ☐ Dislike ☐

Hi Sara,

I'm writing from the airport. If I were you, I'd avoid flying with CheapAir. There were so many delays! The resort was nice, and the staff were wonderful, but the trip itself seemed to really drag on. The food wasn't very good either. The highlights for me were the excursions. The pyramids were amazing and then yesterday I had a great time riding camels. It was much too hot though. You really must try to visit one day, though I'm not sure I'd go again! You should have dinner with us once we're back. I have loads of photos to show you.

Lots of love, Anne

9.9 WRITE A POSTCARD RECOMMENDING A TRIP USING THE PROMPTS

Hi _____
I'm traveling back tonight. I can't believe my trip is over already!
I really enjoyed _____
_____

The town was _____
_____

You really should _____
_____

Lots of love,
_____

---

10 Making predictions

When you talk about a future event, you might need to say how likely it is that the event will happen. There are a number of ways that you can do this.

🔧 **New language** Degrees of likelihood
Aa Vocabulary Idioms about time
🧩 **New skill** Talking about possibilities

10.1 KEY LANGUAGE DEGREES OF LIKELIHOOD

You can use different constructions to show how likely you think something is to happen. These range from certainty that it won't happen to certainty that it will happen.

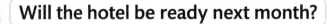

Will the hotel be ready next month?

No, the hotel definitely won't be ready by then.
No, the hotel won't be ready by then.

The hotel probably won't be ready by then.
The hotel is unlikely to be ready by then.

The hotel might be ready by then.

It's likely that the hotel will be ready by then.
The hotel will probably be ready by then.

Yes, the hotel will be ready by then.
Yes, the hotel will definitely be ready by then.

🔊

10.2 MATCH THE STATMENTS TO THE CORRECT PREDICTIONS

There are lots of delays today.

1 I don't have much money.

2 He's worked so hard for his exams.

3 She's a talented young pianist.

4 Look at the line outside the stadium.

5 You don't have a very good voice.

6 My sister loves to travel.

7 Joe goes running every day.

We probably won't get tickets.

He'll pass them all, no problem.

She'll probably go to Australia one day.

Our train will definitely be delayed too.

She might be famous one day.

He might be running a marathon soon.

I definitely won't go on vacation this year.

You definitely won't ever be in an opera.

10.3 LISTEN TO THE AUDIO AND MATCH THE PICTURES TO THE PHRASES

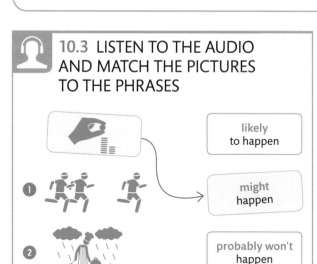

likely to happen

might happen

probably won't happen

unlikely to happen

definitely will happen

10.4 LISTEN TO THE AUDIO AND MARK THE STRESSED SYLLABLES

u n s u r p r i s i n g l y

1 f u n d a m e n t a l l y

2 e s s e n t i a l l y

3 s u r p r i s i n g l y

4 p r e d i c t a b l y

5 f o r t u n a t e l y

6 i n t e r e s t i n g l y

7 l u c k i l y

8 u n f o r t u n a t e l y

PROPERTY

HOUSE PRICES ON THE RISE

A normal goal for many young people is to fly the nest and move into a house of their own. In many tourist areas, however, this is becoming a very unlikely goal for young local people. In resorts around the world, tourists are buying properties either as short-term investments or to live in part-time. As people from the cities (or wealthy countries) compete to buy the properties, it is only a matter of time until the prices rise. These prices are unlikely to be affordable for young local people. This makes it more difficult for them to remain in their own towns if they want to live independently.

In the long run, there is a cost to society and communities. Marisa Cali lives in a picturesque village on a Greek island. "Many of the houses in the village are now empty most of the year. There are fewer people around. It's not like it used to be, but I guess it's the shape of things to come for many island villages."

Some local governments are insisting that a percentage of all new homes built in such areas must be affordable for locals. Other governments are charging higher fees for overseas buyers. So far, these policies have had little impact on the situation.

What does "flying the nest" mean?

"Flying the nest" means leaving your parents' home.

❶ What two reasons are mentioned for buying second homes?

_____

❷ What problem are many local young people facing in tourist areas?

_____

❸ How has Marisa Cali's village changed?

_____

❹ What two things are some local governments doing to counter this problem?

_____

10.6 FILL IN THE GAPS USING THE IDIOMS IN THE PANEL

He's broken his arm, but, thankfully, there's no [*long-term*] injury.

1 This is only a [   ] solution. We'll have to fix the fence properly soon.

2 OK, we'll order pizza tonight, but [   ] we need to sort out a meal plan.

3 I don't understand this new digital system, but I know it's [   ].

4 It was [   ] before the company hit its targets.

| the shape of things to come | ~~long-term~~ | only a matter of time | in the long run | short-term |

---

10 ⊘ CHECKLIST

⚙ Degrees of likelihood ☐   **Aa** Idioms about time ☐   🧩 Talking about possibilities ☐

↻ REVIEW THE ENGLISH YOU HAVE LEARNED IN UNITS 7–10

NEW LANGUAGE	SAMPLE SENTENCE	☑	UNIT
PHRASAL VERBS	He filled the customs form in. She always comes up with exciting plans.	☐	7.1, 7.3, 7.6
NARRATIVE TENSES	As we were walking home, we saw a juggler. We had already exchanged our money.	☐	8.1
THE PAST PERFECT CONTINUOUS	He had been learning English for two years before he went to London.	☐	8.4
MAKING RECOMMENDATIONS	You must visit the palace. It is beautiful!	☐	9.1
GIVING ADVICE	You should wear a hat. It's very sunny. If I were you, I would wear a hat.	☐	9.5 9.6
DEGREES OF LIKELIHOOD	The hotel's unlikely to be ready by next month. It will definitely be ready by then.	☐	10.1

11 Vocabulary

11.1 FAMILY AND RELATIONSHIPS

I look up to my older brother.

look up to somebody
[have respect and admiration for someone]

You're lucky that you take after your intelligent mother.

take after somebody
[have characteristics of a parent or relative]

They brought up their children to be polite and respectful.

bring up somebody / bring somebody up
[care for a child and teach them how to behave]

It is important to grow up in a caring environment.

grow up
[develop from a child to an adult]

She got along with her colleagues.

get along with somebody / get on with somebody
[have a positive relationship with somebody]

My siblings fell out with each other for a few years.

fall out with somebody
[stop being friends with somebody, often after an argument]

We fell in love while we were traveling across Europe together.

fall in love with somebody
[begin to love somebody]

I broke up with him after a big argument.

break up with somebody
[end a romantic relationship]

They drifted apart after they stopped working for the same company.

drift apart
[slowly become less friendly or close to somebody]

I made friends with her a long time ago.

make friends with somebody
[become friendly with a person]

We've been close friends for more than 20 years.

close friend
[a friend who you know very well]

I am really surprised by how much we have in common.

have something in common
[share an interest or opinion]

My sister gave birth to a baby girl a few months ago.

give birth to somebody
[have a child]

Curly hair runs in the family.

run in the family
[be a common feature of a family]

We used to fight a lot, but we see eye to eye nowadays.

see eye to eye with somebody
[agree with or have similar opinions to somebody]

As soon as I met Tom, we just clicked.

click with somebody
[like somebody quickly and easily]

We bumped into her teacher in the supermarket.

bump into somebody
[meet someone unexpectedly]

My dad is putting his foot down about doing chores.

put your foot down
[be strict about something]

Our parents taught us to stick up for each other at school.

stick up for somebody
[speak out in support of somebody]

I think the world of my first grandchild.

think the world of somebody
[have a very high opinion of somebody]

12 Using discourse markers

Discourse markers can be used to show a relationship between two sentences, or parts of a sentence. This can be cause, effect, emphasis, contrast, or comparison.

⚙ **New language** Linking information
Aa **Vocabulary** Family history
🧩 **New skill** Talking about relationships

12.1 KEY LANGUAGE INFORMAL LINKING DISCOURSE MARKERS

Some discourse markers are mostly used in informal writing and speech.

> **TIP**
> To emphasize the relationship between words when speaking, you can add stress to the discourse marker.

I like listening to music, { **but** / **though** } my mother hates it.

Shows contrast.

He's a talented swimmer, { **like** / **just as** } his great-grandfather was.

Shows comparison.

Staying in touch is easy, { **because** / **since** / **as** } we all have smartphones.

Shows result.

We grew up together, so we tell each other everything.
We are very close. As a result, we know everything about each other.

Shows effect.

All my siblings are tall, { **especially** / **particularly** } my older sister.

Shows emphasis.

12.2 REWRITE THESE PAIRS OF SENTENCES USING THE DISCOURSE MARKERS TO CONNECT THEM

> Julie likes her older brother. She doesn't see him very often. [but]
> _Julie likes her older brother, but she doesn't see him very often._

❶ All my siblings love playing football. My brother loves it the most. [especially]

_____

❷ We are all quite interested in our family history. We've made a family tree. [so]

_____

❸ I love talking to my aunt. She has lots of interesting stories from her travels abroad. [because]

_____

❹ My grandmother thinks I should get married. I am not as traditional as she is. [but]

_____

❺ We don't have big family gatherings very often. My grandparents live abroad. [since]

_____

 12.3 LISTEN TO THE AUDIO AND MATCH THE PAIRS OF PICTURES

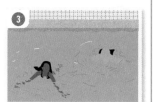

12.4 KEY LANGUAGE FORMAL LINKING DISCOURSE MARKERS

Some discourse markers are used most often in formal writing and speaking situations.

Shows contrast.

The castle was built in 1272, $\left\{ \begin{array}{c} \textbf{whereas} \\ \textbf{yet} \end{array} \right\}$ **the town is modern.**

Shows comparison.

His talk was popular and his book was $\left\{ \begin{array}{c} \textbf{similarly} \\ \textbf{equally} \end{array} \right\}$ **well-liked.**

Shows reason.

International video calls are popular $\left\{ \begin{array}{c} \textbf{due to} \\ \textbf{owing to} \end{array} \right\}$ **global internet access.**

Shows result.

Many foreigners settled there. $\left\{ \begin{array}{c} \textbf{Hence} \\ \textbf{Therefore} \end{array} \right\}$ **, the population is bilingual.**

Shows emphasis.

He is known for his research, $\left\{ \begin{array}{c} \textbf{primarily} \\ \textbf{notably} \end{array} \right\}$ **into royal families.**

12.5 FILL IN THE GAPS USING FORMAL DISCOURSE MARKERS

James won many medals, _____*notably*_____ one for bravery.

1. Elizabeth had two children, _____ Mary had none.

2. The two elderly sisters were _____ wealthy.

3. The father left the army _____ a serious arm injury.

4. James and Tom were identical twins. _____ , they looked alike.

12.6 SAY EACH SENTENCE OUT LOUD, USING THE MOST APPROPRIATE DISCOURSE MARKER

I like sandwiches, ~~whereas~~ / but the rest of my family are big pizza fans.

1 You have failed to respond to our messages. So / Hence , your subscription has been canceled.

2 My friends say I take after my dad, owing to / because we both like mountain biking.

3 After a successful book tour, the professor's lectures were equally / like well-received.

4 I really love my aunts, notably / especially Meera, because she's so funny.

12.7 READ THE ADVERTISEMENT AND ANSWER THE QUESTIONS

It is less difficult to explore your family history than it used to be.
True ☑ False ☐

1 You have to go to the library to use the service.
True ☐ False ☐

2 J.W.'s great-grandfather died in battle.
True ☐ False ☐

3 N.H. enjoys socializing more than her parents.
True ☐ False ☐

4 The service has an annual $20 fee.
True ☐ False ☐

GENEALOGY OK

It has never been easier to research your family's history. Millions of family records, including births, deaths, marriages, as well as military and emigration records, are now available online. As a result, you can now find your ancestors from the comfort of your home. All of this and more can be discovered if you join our Genealogy OK club for only $20 a month.

Here are two of our members' stories:

"I thought that all my family were pacifists, like me. It turns out that my great-grandmother was a spy, and her young husband was a heroic soldier who died in combat." - J.W.

"I've always wondered where I get my party animal personality, since my mother and father are quite quiet. I've discovered that my great-grandmother and her sister were well-known socialites in years gone by." - N.H.

12 ✓ CHECKLIST

⚙ Linking information ☐   **Aa** Family history ☐   Talking about relationships ☐

13 Past habits and states

When you talk about habits or states in the past you can use "used to" or "would." English often uses these forms to contrast the past with the present.

⚙ **New language** "Used to" and "would"
Aa Vocabulary Family values
🧩 **New skill** Contrasting the past with the present

13.1 KEY LANGUAGE "USED TO"

You can use "used to" with an infinitive to talk about past habits.

Refers to a past habit.

We used to play tennis every day, but now we prefer golf.

PAST   NOW

You can also use it to talk about fixed states at some indefinite time in the past.

Refers to a past state.

We used to live in London before we moved to Sydney.

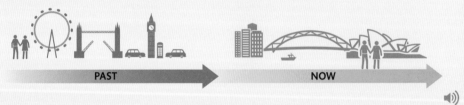

PAST   NOW

13.2 FURTHER EXAMPLES "USED TO"

"Used" becomes "use" in the question and negative forms.

Did you use to ride a scooter when you were a student?

I didn't use to believe in ghosts until I visited a haunted house.

13.3 ANOTHER WAY TO SAY "USED TO" WITH HABITS

You can also use "would" to talk about past habits. It is a little bit more formal.

When I was little, we would go for a picnic every Saturday.

Whenever there was soccer on TV, we just wouldn't do our homework.

13.4 ⚠ COMMON MISTAKES "USED TO"

You cannot use "used to" when you're talking about definite time frames
in the past, or if you said you did something a certain number of times.

We used to play lots of board games when I was young.

**We used to play lots of
board games yesterday.**

**We used to play board
games twenty times.**

◀))

13.5 FILL IN THE GAPS USING THE WORDS IN BRACKETS

Whenever my uncle visited, he _____*would bring*_____ (would / bring) presents for us all.

1. My mother _____ (use to / walk) five miles to school and back.

2. I _____ (not / use to / like) using the internet, but now I think it's great!

3. _____ (do) you _____ (use to / eat) your lunch at school?

4. My grandmother's house _____ (not / use to / have) electricity.

5. Whenever I had a toothache, my dad _____ (would / take) me to a scary dentist.

◀))

13.6 REWRITE THE HIGHLIGHTED PHRASES, CORRECTING THE ERRORS

When my grandmother tells me about how things **did used to be**, I realize how lucky I was as a child. I **use to complain** about having to walk to school in the rain, whereas she **would to walk** five miles to school in all types of weather, including snow! I **used to got upset** when a teacher told me off in class. I had usually done something really bad, but my grandmother **didn't used to do** anything bad. She **used to wrote** with her left hand, but back then, teachers **will be punish** you just for that!

used to be

1. _____

2. _____

3. _____

4. _____

5. _____

6. _____

13.7 LISTEN TO THE AUDIO AND ANSWER THE QUESTIONS

  Rui and Livia are having a debate about changing family values.

What does Rui say about young people?

They don't watch movies any more ☐

They watch movies on their own ☑

They don't go to the movies any more ☐

❶ What does Livia say about families?

They don't watch movies together ☐

They still watch movies on the TV ☐

They go to the movies together ☐

❷ What beneficial internet content does Livia mention?

Documentaries and old movies ☐

Documentaries and news archives ☐

Documentaries and new movies ☐

❸ Where does Rui think young people used to get their values from?

Older family members ☐

Movies ☐

The Internet ☐

❹ What does Livia say young people think about honesty?

It's very important to them ☐

It's not that important any more ☐

It's important for adults to be honest ☐

❺ What does Livia say is important in today's world?

Understanding historical values ☐

Communicating with other people ☐

Understanding other people's values ☐

Aa 13.8 READ THE CLUES AND WRITE THE ANSWERS IN THE CORRECT PLACES ON THE GRID

❶ Agreeing with or tolerating something

❷ Telling the truth

❸ What a person believes is right or wrong

❹ Wanting more things than you really need

❺ The qualities of someone's personality

❻ To say or do something that stops another person's actions

| values | ~~acceptance~~ | interrupt |
| character | greedy | honesty |

1. a c c e p t a n c e

◀))

56

13.9 READ THE BLOG POST AND WRITE ANSWERS TO THE QUESTIONS AS FULL SENTENCES

Researching my roots

HOME | ENTRIES | ABOUT | CONTACT

A long lost brother

A few years ago, my grandfather told me about a brother who he hadn't seen in a very long time. They lost touch over 50 years ago while they were both serving in the army overseas. I decided that I would try to find my great-uncle, the brother who my grandfather used to talk about so fondly.

I was in the library when I met a man called Robert who was also researching his family history. His grandfather also had a brother he hadn't seen for 50 years. The more we talked, the more similarities we had. Our grandfathers had both become teachers after they left the army. We realized after talking for an hour that our grandfathers were brothers. Astonishingly, they lived less than 20 miles apart from each other, and even used to live on the very same street! Last week my grandfather and my great-uncle met again for the first time in half a century.

When did the author's grandfather and great-uncle lose touch?

They lost touch over 50 years ago while they were both serving in the army overseas.

① Why did the author and Robert start talking?

_____

② What similarities did the author's grandfather and Robert's grandfather have?

_____

③ Why was it surprising that the author's grandfather and great-uncle hadn't met in 50 years?

_____

④ What happened last week?

_____

---

13 ✅ CHECKLIST

⚙ "Used to" and "would" ☐   **Aa** Family values ☐   ꜛ Contrasting the past with the present ☐

14 Comparing and contrasting

Using "as... as" is a very flexible way to make comparisons. You can use it to compare and contrast quantities and qualities of people, objects, situations, and ideas.

⚙ **New language** "As... as" comparisons
Aa Vocabulary Adjective–noun collocations
🧩 **New skill** Comparing and contrasting

14.1 KEY LANGUAGE "AS... AS" COMPARISONS

You can use "as... as" with an adjective to compare things that are similar and "not as... as" or "not so... as" to contrast things that are different.

Lisa is as tall as Marc.

Penny is not { as / so } tall as Marc.

14.2 FURTHER EXAMPLES "AS... AS" COMPARISONS

You can modify the "as... as" structure to make it more detailed or to add emphasis.

Emphasizing equality.

Bottled water is just as expensive as coffee.

Comparing similarity.

The girls were almost as loud as the boys.

This has a very similar meaning to "almost as" but contrasts the difference rather than comparing the similarity.

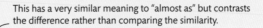

The movie is not quite as good as the book.

Specific degree of difference.

The bike is half as long as the car.

Emphasizing difference.

The mouse is nowhere near as big as the bird.

14.3 LOOK AT THE PICTURES AND MAKE A MODIFIED "AS... AS" COMPARISON, SPEAKING OUT LOUD

The cat is _not as_ big _as_ the dog.

3
The phone is _____ expensive _____ the laptop.

1
The giraffe is _____ tall _____ the house.

4
The baby is _____ old _____ the man.

2
The flower is _____ large _____ the tree.

5
The pizza is _____ wide _____ the plate.

14.4 KEY LANGUAGE "AS... AS" COMPARISONS WITH ADVERBS

You can also use the "as... as" structure with adverbs, often followed by expressions of ability or possibility.

I don't visit as often as my sister.

We sang as loudly as possible.

He arrived as early as he could.

The boys study as hard as the girls.

14.5 LISTEN TO THE AUDIO AND ANSWER THE QUESTIONS

Which is more expensive?
The soup ☐ **The steak** ☑

1 Which is funnier?
The old video ☐ **The new video** ☐

2 Which is faster?
The motorcycle ☐ **The car** ☐

3 Which is bigger?
The old house ☐ **The new house** ☐

4 Who is smarter?
Simon ☐ **Andrew** ☐

5 How frequently does Akiko visit now?
More often ☐ **Less often** ☐

14.6 READ THE ARTICLE AND ANSWER THE QUESTIONS

The young baby's father is called...
Sam ☐ **Zach** ☐ **Jon** ☑

❶ The mother of the baby is...
a teacher ☐ **a lawyer** ☐ **unemployed** ☐

❷ The person on parental leave from work is...
Sam ☐ **Zach** ☐ **Jon** ☐

❸ When Samantha walks to work it takes...
35 mins ☐ **40 mins** ☐ **45 mins** ☐

❹ Samantha does not walk to work if the weather is...
cold ☐ **windy** ☐ **rainy** ☐

❺ Most days Samantha walks to work...
alone ☐ **with a friend** ☐ **with her family** ☐

❻ Her friends and family think her decision is...
stupid ☐ **good** ☐ **bad** ☐

FAMILY LIFE

A different approach

The surprise benefits of shared parental leave
by Samantha Pope

The new "shared parental leave" law is great for my family. As a lawyer I earn twice as much as my husband, Jon, who is a teacher. This meant that we were going to pay a high price for me taking a career break at this time. I returned to work quite soon after our baby, Zach, was born, and Jon has taken parental leave from his work to be at home.

Of course, I still share lots of time with Zach. Because Jon is a heavy sleeper, I wake up to do nighttime duties. This does make me a bit tired, but a strong coffee in the morning and a quick walk to work (unless there's heavy rain) normally wakes me up. In the morning, Jon and Zach usually walk with me through the park. We were surprised to discover that this 40-minute walk is actually almost as quick as me driving the car in heavy traffic at rush hour.

I was worried that my friends and family would have a low opinion of me going back to work as soon as I did, but in the end everyone agreed with us.

14.7 FILL IN THE GAPS USING THE WORDS IN THE PANEL TO CREATE COLLOCATIONS

> **TIP**
> Words that collocate with an adjective often collocate with its opposite. For example, "heavy rain" and "light rain."

Every time I walk to work I get caught in [*heavy* rain] .

❶ Thankfully, our baby is a [sleeper] and only wakes once a night.

❷ The commute to work takes ages, even when there is [traffic] .

❸ Feeling sick every day is a [price] to pay for going on a cruise.

❹ I only really wake up in the morning after a [coffee] .

❺ My mother has a [opinion] of anyone who doesn't work hard.

[~~heavy~~   strong   high   low   heavy   light]

🔊

14.8 FILL IN THE GAPS USING THE WORDS IN THE PANEL

Alex and Sue are both chefs. Sue owns a café and Alex works in a famous restaurant. Sue's cooking is ___*just as*___ good _____ Alex's, maybe even better, although his cooking is mostly savory and she has a sweet tooth. Unfortunately, just because her food costs _____ much _____ his, some people do not have as _____ an opinion of her skills. Her café is seen as somewhere with _____ prices to grab a bite to eat, not somewhere to wine and dine people. Sue says this is a small price to pay for owning her own business. Some people just like to go out of their way to pay _____ much _____ they should for a three-course meal in Alex's restaurant, rather than enjoy a delicious piece of cake or pastry in Sue's café.

as	half as	high	as	twice as	low	as	~~just as~~

Aa 14.9 MATCH THE DEFINITIONS TO THE PHRASES

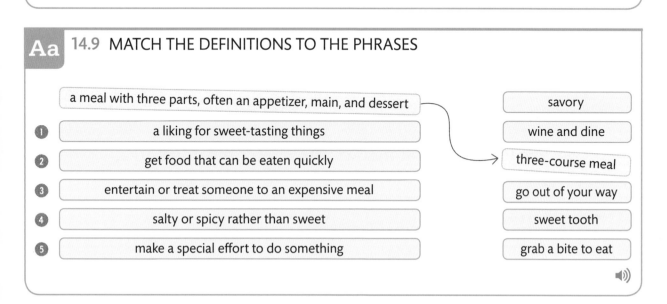

a meal with three parts, often an appetizer, main, and dessert → three-course meal

savory

1. a liking for sweet-tasting things

wine and dine

2. get food that can be eaten quickly

three-course meal

3. entertain or treat someone to an expensive meal

go out of your way

4. salty or spicy rather than sweet

sweet tooth

5. make a special effort to do something

grab a bite to eat

14 ✓ CHECKLIST

⚙ "As... as" comparisons ☐   **Aa** Adjective–noun collocations ☐   🧩 Comparing and contrasting ☐

15 Two comparatives together

You can use two comparatives in a sentence to show the effect of an action. You can also use them to show that something is changing.

🔧 **New language** Two comparatives together
Aa Vocabulary Age and population
🧩 **New skill** Expressing cause, effect, and change

15.1 KEY LANGUAGE TWO COMPARATIVES TOGETHER

You can make comparisons that show cause and effect by using two comparatives in one sentence.

The harder I train, the stronger I get.

Implies that training causes you to get stronger.

🔊

15.2 FURTHER EXAMPLES TWO COMPARATIVES TOGETHER

The worse the children behave, the angrier the teacher gets.

The louder the cat meows, the louder the dog barks.

🔊

15.3 HOW TO FORM TWO COMPARATIVES TOGETHER

"THE"	COMPARATIVE EXPRESSION	SUBJECT	VERB	"THE"	COMPARATIVE EXPRESSION	SUBJECT	VERB
The	harder	I	train,	the	stronger	I	get.

15.4 REWRITE THE SENTENCES, PUTTING THE WORDS IN THE CORRECT ORDER

The | terrified | he | more | drives | become. | faster | the | I

The faster he drives, the more terrified I become.

1. longer | went | the | more | The | the | film | on | bored | I | became.

_____

2. quicker | it | more | the | rained | The | the | vegetables | grew.

_____

3. me | more | not | The | she | the | to | laugh | told | more | I | laughed.

_____

4. a | it | dessert | The | contains | is | for | sugar | more | the | worse | you.

_____

15.5 REWRITE THE SENTENCES, CORRECTING THE ERRORS

I've noticed that the less I sleep, grumpier I am.
I've noticed that the less I sleep, the grumpier I am.

1. The louder my music is, the more angrier my mother gets.

_____

2. The young the skier is, the less frightened of falling they are.

_____

3. The annoyed my teacher gets, more I giggle nervously.

_____

4. Faster the car went, louder the passengers screamed.

_____

15.6 ANOTHER WAY TO USE TWO COMPARATIVES TOGETHER

Double comparatives that end with "the better" can be made shorter by losing the subjects and the verbs.

How do you like your tea?

The stronger the better.

Can I bring my brother along?

Sure! The more the merrier.

This expression means people are welcome.

15.7 MATCH THE QUESTIONS TO THE CORRECT ANSWERS

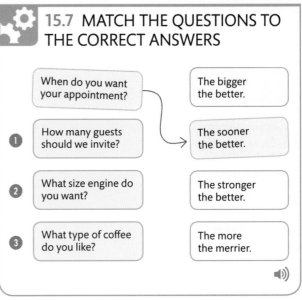

When do you want your appointment? — The sooner the better.

The bigger the better.

1 How many guests should we invite?

2 What size engine do you want? — The stronger the better.

3 What type of coffee do you like? — The more the merrier.

15.8 KEY LANGUAGE TWO COMPARATIVES TOGETHER

A comparative can be repeated to show that something is changing.

The weather is getting colder and colder.

The repetition emphasizes that the change is ongoing.

15.9 READ THE ARTICLE AND ANSWER THE QUESTIONS

People are living longer than they used to.
True ✓ False ☐ Not given ☐

1 There are fewer babies being born these days.
True ☐ False ☐ Not given ☐

2 Pensions and social care will cost nations more.
True ☐ False ☐ Not given ☐

3 A younger workforce is more experienced.
True ☐ False ☐ Not given ☐

4 Retired people have more time to do charity work.
True ☐ False ☐ Not given ☐

YOUR HEALTH

We're all living longer and longer

Life expectancy has risen around the world and older people make up a larger and larger proportion of the population in many countries.

An aging population can cause challenges such as increasing pension and social care costs.

However, there are also potential benefits. The older a workforce is, the more skills and experience it has. Also, as people live longer after retirement, they can offer more time to good causes such as volunteering for charity.

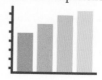

15.10 LISTEN TO THE AUDIO AND WRITE ANSWERS TO THE QUESTIONS IN FULL SENTENCES

A radio station is reporting
on aging populations.

> What two reasons are mentioned for people living longer?
> _The news report mentions improved healthcare and improved standards of living._

❶ What economic issue do aging populations lead to?

_____

❷ In the first suggested solution, who is responsible for people's care in old age?

_____

❸ In the second suggested solution, who is responsible for people's care in old age?

_____

❹ What is the third suggested solution?

_____

15 ✓ CHECKLIST

✿ Two comparatives together ☐   **Aa** Age and population ☐   Expressing cause, effect, and change ☐

↻ REVIEW THE ENGLISH YOU HAVE LEARNED IN UNITS 12–15

NEW LANGUAGE	SAMPLE SENTENCE	☑	UNIT
INFORMAL LINKING DISCOURSE MARKERS	I like listening to music, but my mother hates it.	☐	12.1
FORMAL LINKING DISCOURSE MARKERS	The castle is ancient, whereas the town is modern.	☐	12.4
"USED TO" AND "WOULD"	We used to live in London before we moved to Sydney. Whenever my uncle visited, he would bring us presents.	☐	13.1, 13.3
"AS... AS" COMPARISONS	Lisa is as tall as Marc.	☐	14.1
TWO COMPARATIVES TOGETHER	The harder I train, the better I get. The weather is getting colder and colder.	☐	15.1, 15.6, 15.8

16 Vocabulary

16.1 STUDYING

My daughter took a year off **before starting university.**

take a year off (US) / take a year out (UK)
[have a year away from education or work]

My brother enrolled in **an accounting course this week.**

enrol in (US) / enrol on (UK)
[register to start something]

The college provides housing for undergraduates.

undergraduate
[someone studying for a first degree at college or university]

She is a graduate **student of biochemistry.**

graduate (US) / postgraduate (UK)
[study carried out following graduation from a first degree]

When I was a freshman, **everything seemed so exciting.**

freshman (US) / fresher (UK)
[a student in their first year at college or university]

Make sure you plan ahead. You have to write four essays this semester.

semester (US) / term (UK)
[a period of time in an academic calendar, during which classes are held]

I will be the first person in my family to get a degree.

get a degree
[be awarded a qualification after college or university]

It is very important to attend classes **regularly and keep notes.**

attend classes
[go to lessons or lectures]

I was so nervous before I took my driving test, **but I passed!**

take a test / take an exam
[answer questions or perform actions to show how much you know about something]

My tutors give me regular feedback on **my projects.**

give someone feedback on something
[provide comments and advice on how somebody is doing something]

I worked late last night to meet the deadline for this report.

meet a deadline
[finish something within a given time]

He's so unreliable! He's always missing deadlines for projects.

miss a deadline
[fail to finish something within a given time]

We have continuous assessment, not final exams.

continuous assessment
[grading based on work done over a long period]

You can't draw a comparison between then and now.

draw a comparison between
[point out similarities between things]

The essay asked us to compare the similarities between the countries.

compare similarities
[consider and describe how things are alike]

We looked at two pictures and contrasted the differences.

contrast differences
[consider and describe how things differ from each other]

Their views on this subject are polar opposites.

polar opposite
[completely different]

There is a clear distinction between these projects.

clear distinction
[an obvious difference]

For twins, their interests are strikingly different.

strikingly different
[surprisingly not alike]

Your hard work has made a world of difference this year.

a world of difference
[a significant level of difference]

17 Taking notes

Discourse markers can help you to organize language to make it easier for the listener or reader to follow. Listening for them is very useful when taking notes.

🔧 **New language** Organizing information
Aa Vocabulary Academic life
🧩 **New skill** Taking notes

17.1 KEY LANGUAGE FORMAL ORGANIZING DISCOURSE MARKERS

Some discourse markers indicate what is coming next. They help organize paragraphs and longer passages of formal text.

TIP
Discourse markers often go at the beginning of a clause or sentence.

Sequencing markers can help you order information.

First, it is important to consider which courses you want to study.

Some markers introduce new or additional points.

Moreover, you should bear in mind where you want to study.

Other markers highlight examples.

For instance, you should consider if you want to study abroad.

Conclusion markers are used when summing up.

In conclusion, several factors will affect your choice of college.

🔊

Aa 17.2 READ THE LEAFLET AND PUT THE DISCOURSE MARKERS IN CATEGORIES

WHY STUDY ABROAD?

First, it is easier to learn a foreign language abroad. You can enjoy other aspects of the country's culture such as the food and music. Second, you can get a global perspective on your subject. Additionally, universities abroad may specialize in different subjects. Furthermore, your university base may act as a springboard for further travel in the region. For example, a Korean base could lead to more Asian travel. Overall, there are many cultural and educational reasons to study abroad. To sum up, study abroad opens doors.

SEQUENCING
first
Second

EXAMPLES
such as
for example

ADDING
additionally
furthermore

CONCLUDING
overall
To sum up

🔊

17.3 CROSS OUT THE INCORRECT WORDS IN EACH SENTENCE

Some universities are known globally,
for example / ~~secondly~~ Yale and Oxford.

1 Others, additionally / such as Sydney University and Toronto, are renowned for their stunning historical buildings.

2 Moreover / To sum up, there are newer universities like Moscow and Xiamen that have equally impressive buildings.

3 For instance / Next, Moscow State University is incredibly impressive at night.

4 Third / Additionally, a number of modern university buildings in Australia are spectacular.

5 Such as / Overall, there are some amazing educational buildings around the world.

6 To sum up / First, it can be worth your time to look at educational buildings, even if you are visiting as a tourist.

🔊

17.4 LISTEN TO THE AUDIO AND ANSWER THE QUESTIONS

A talk is being given about Welcome Week, when college students arrive for the first time.

Classes start on Monday in two weeks.
True ☐ **False** ☐ **Not given** ☑

1 Clubs are free to join during Welcome Week.
True ☐ **False** ☐ **Not given** ☐

2 You will need your ID to register.
True ☐ **False** ☐ **Not given** ☐

3 You can find all the books on your book list in the library.
True ☐ **False** ☐ **Not given** ☐

4 Your library card can be used in the cafeteria.
True ☐ **False** ☐ **Not given** ☐

5 You should tell your academic department about accommodation problems.
True ☐ **False** ☐ **Not given** ☐

17.5 KEY LANGUAGE INFORMAL ORGANIZING DISCOURSE MARKERS

You can use a number of general discourse markers to move from one topic to another in conversational English.

Here, "Right" gets attention before saying something important.

Right, let's get started...

Here, "OK" acknowledges that you have heard the other speaker.

... OK, and are you happy with your choice?

Here, "So" indicates that you are reaching a conclusion.

... So, I think we agree overall.

🔊

17.6 KEY LANGUAGE THE ZERO CONDITIONAL

You can use the zero conditional to talk about things that are generally or always true.

If you study every day, you learn more quickly.

"When" can sometimes be used instead of "if."

When you sign up for a club, you meet new people.

"Unless" means "if... not." (If you don't have a lot of money, don't join every club.)

Unless you have a lot of money, don't join every club.

17.7 MATCH THE BEGINNINGS OF THE SENTENCES TO THE CORRECT ENDINGS

When you join the photography club ———————→ you can exhibit your own work.

you can join the historical society.

1 You must pay to play tennis

unless you need more time to think.

2 If you are a history student,

unless you join the club.

3 If you join the water sports club,

4 You can join today

you can learn how to sail.

17.8 FILL IN THE GAPS USING THE WORDS IN THE PANEL

If you try to write every word, you _____*get*_____ lost very quickly.

1 If you hear _____ markers, use them to help organize your notes.

2 When you take notes, _____ a simple shorthand with symbols and abbreviations.

3 If your handwriting is messy, try to _____ sure it is readable.

4 Unless you record every lecture, try to _____ your notes soon after.

discourse

review

make

~~get~~

use

70

Before start the course... more information on taking notes at university. Spoken already about tips and advice but a little about passive and active note-taking differences. If have handout and listen to lecture and underline something = not actively engaging in the lecture. Recording lecture/ borrowing friend's notes = not engaging in the lecture. Trying to write every word from lecture = passively note-taking.

1 ☐

Passive and active note-taking: June 17

Passive note-taking examples:
1. Underlining
2. Recording
3. Borrowing notes
4. Writing down everything

Doesn't save time in the end because can't remember what said.

2 ☐

Lecture notes from June 17

- Passive note-taking is "not actively engaging in the lecture"

- If you "sit and record the lecture or borrow your friend's notes then you are not fully engaging"

- It is still passive note-taking "even if you try to write down every word from the lecture".

3 ☐

 17.10 LISTEN TO THE THE REST OF THE LECTURE AND WRITE NOTES AS YOU LISTEN

Active note-taking examples: _____

_____

_____

_____

_____

_____

17 ✓ CHECKLIST

⚙ Organizing information ☐   **Aa** Academic life ☐   🧩 Taking notes ☐

18 Speaking approximately

English has a number of useful phrases to describe approximate quantities and amounts. You can use them when a number is unknown or roughly accurate.

🔧 **New language** Generalization
Aa Vocabulary Approximate quantity phrases
🧩 **New skill** Talking about numbers

18.1 KEY LANGUAGE APPROXIMATE QUANTITIES

If you have specific figures, it may be useful to give them. However, you may need to use more general terms if you do not have the figures or you want to avoid repetition.

3 out of 15 students live off campus.

In some cases, students live off campus.

"Some" is a very unspecific word. The only numbers it could not mean in this example are none, one, or 15.

🔊

18.2 FURTHER EXAMPLES APPROXIMATE QUANTITIES

A minority is less than half, but often refers to much less than half.

In a minority of cases,
In a few cases,
} employers provide funding for education.

> **TIP**
> "Minority" and "majority" are often qualified, for example "small minority" or "vast majority."

"Most" and "majority" refer to more than half.

In most cases,
In the majority of cases,
} students can contact their professors online.

These unspecific references could mean a majority or minority of cases.

In some cases,
In a number of cases,
} students can live in dorms on campus.

🔊

18.3 LISTEN TO THE AUDIO AND NUMBER THE INFOGRAPHICS IN THE ORDER THEY ARE MENTIONED

A ☐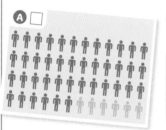

B ☐1

C ☐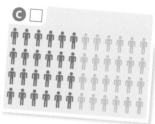

D ☐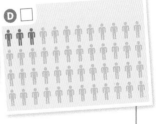

18.4 **KEY LANGUAGE** APPROXIMATE STATISTICS

You can make statistics more general by modifying them
with words such as "approximately," "well," or "just."

 Approximately **half of the students are from Europe.**

 Just under **a third of the assessment consists of coursework.**

 Well over **50 percent of the course is online.**

🔊

18.5 CROSS OUT THE INCORRECT WORDS IN EACH SENTENCE

52% Approximately / ~~well over~~ half of the students are male.

❶ **97%** The vast majority / minority of the lecture halls have wireless internet access.

❷ **27%** Just / well over a quarter of classes are recorded for students to listen to online.

❸ **85%** After one week, most / some people know their way around campus.

❹ **4%** Only a huge / tiny minority of our students do not have smartphones.

❺ **72%** Well over / under half of our students eat a hot meal on campus.

❻ **67%** Just over / under two-thirds of our professors can speak two languages.

🔊

18.6 KEY LANGUAGE SURPRISING NUMBERS

Certain expressions are used to show that a particular number or quantity is surprising.

This indicates that €100 is a surprisingly large amount of money.

Other universities charge as much as €100 for this service.

This indicates that $5 is a surprisingly small amount of money.

For as little as $5 per semester, you can join the club.

This indicates that 25 is a surprisingly large number of events.

There are as many as 25 free student events each month.

This indicates that 2 is a surprisingly small number of days.

The library is generally closed for as few as 2 days a month.

18.7 READ THE LEAFLET AND ANSWER THE QUESTIONS

Just over 50 percent of the courses are international standard.
True ☐ False ☑

1 Undergraduates also learn important research skills.
True ☐ False ☐

2 You must join a club to use the sports facilities.
True ☐ False ☐

3 You can join a club that encourages the discussion of political issues.
True ☐ False ☐

4 Over 50 percent of the students live on campus.
True ☐ False ☐

5 The university does not provide any graduate-level courses for students.
True ☐ False ☐

Why study with us?

Academic Excellence We are one of the top 20 colleges in the country in terms of teaching quality, with the vast majority of our courses rated as international standard. Our undergraduates come from all over the world, attracted by our outstanding teaching and research guidance.

Superb Facilities We strive to ensure that you have a first-class student experience. Our excellent sports facilities are open to all and include an Olympic-size swimming pool. For those interested in the arts, we have a successful drama department, an art gallery, and a multiscreen cinema. We have as many as 40 different sport, cultural, political, and volunteering clubs to choose from.

Accommodation In most cases, our students prefer to live on campus. In other cases, however, students may wish to live off campus. Our friendly accommodation team can also help with this.

Careers Our Career Development Center can help with your present and future career choices. Approximately half our students continue to pursue a graduate-level course with us. Our dedicated team can help you make the best choice for your future.

18.8 KEY LANGUAGE QUESTIONING GENERALIZATIONS

One polite way of showing that you disagree with a generalization is to question it. Use questions like "Is that so?," "Really?," "Is that right?," and "Are you sure?" before challenging a generalization.

I've been told that the campus is very unwelcoming and quiet.

Is that so? My experience has not been like that at all.

You can disagree with the comment after your question.

18.9 RESPOND TO THE AUDIO, SPEAKING OUT LOUD AND QUESTIONING THE GENERALIZATIONS WITH FACTS FROM THE LEAFLET IN 18.7

All the students come from the same country.

Is that right? _I read that there were students from all over the world there._

① There isn't much to do there.

Really? _____

② The accommodation is really poor.

Is that so? _____

③ They don't offer you any advice for after you have graduated.

Are you sure? _____

---

18 ✓ CHECKLIST

⚙ Generalization ☐   **Aa** Approximate quantity phrases ☐   🧩 Talking about numbers ☐

19 Changing emphasis

There are a number of ways that you can change emphasis in English. One way is to use a less common grammatical structure, such as the passive voice.

⚙ **New language** The passive voice
Aa Vocabulary Online learning
🧩 **New skill** Changing sentence emphasis

19.1 KEY LANGUAGE THE PASSIVE VOICE

In a passive sentence, the emphasis is taken away from the agent (the person or thing doing the action), and put on the action itself (or the person or object receiving it).

The focus is on the many people.

Many people studied the book.

The subject of the active verb is the "people."

The book was studied by many people.

The focus is on the book.

The subject of the passive verb is the "book."

19.2 WHEN TO USE THE PASSIVE VOICE

The passive is used when the agent is obvious, unknown, or unimportant. It is also useful when describing a process where the result of the action is important.

The agent is not specified because the verb obviously refers to the police.

Hopefully, the thief will be arrested soon.

The agent is not specified because it is unknown.

Sarah's laptop was stolen from the library.

The agent is not specified because it is the process that is important, not who did it.

The posters are printed on good quality paper.

19.3 HOW TO FORM THE PASSIVE VOICE

To form the passive, use "be" with the past participle. Use "by" when you want to show the agent.

Use different forms of "be" for the past, continuous, future, and perfect forms of the passive.

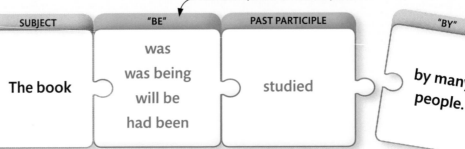

SUBJECT	"BE"	PAST PARTICIPLE	"BY"
The book	was was being will be had been	studied	by many people.

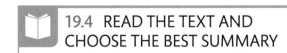 **19.4 READ THE TEXT AND CHOOSE THE BEST SUMMARY**

The rise of online learning

Massive Open Online Courses (MOOCs) are open to anyone, anywhere, and often have subscriptions in the thousands. Millions of people around the world are currently taking part in MOOCs and studying everything from digital photography through to engineering and science. The courses are free, though you may have to pay for a certificate to prove that you have taken the course.

1 Millions of people are being enrolled onto each MOOC. ☐

2 MOOCs are being taken online by millions of people. ☐

3 MOOCs will be being taken by thousands of people. ☐

 19.5 CROSS OUT THE INCORRECT WORDS IN EACH SENTENCE

Many of the students could ~~affect~~ / be affected by the changes.

1 English is spoken / speaks by millions of people across the world.

2 Online courses are studying / are being studied by a variety of students.

3 The courses are paying for / are being paid for by a number of universities.

4 Certificates can be printed out / can print out at home by participants.

5 Some exams can be taken / take in several different languages.

 19.6 REWRITE THE SENTENCES USING PASSIVE VOICE

TIP
Remember that you can sometimes omit the agent if the meaning is still clear.

More than 400 universities across the world offer MOOCs.

MOOCs _are offered by more than 400 universities across the world._

1 People write 80 percent of the courses in English.

Eighty percent _____

2 Some universities offer credits for MOOC courses.

Credits _____

3 Some people provide technical help for the participants.

Technical help _____

4 Millions of students will take MOOCs next year.

Next year, MOOCs _____

19.7 KEY LANGUAGE NOUNS BASED ON PHRASAL VERBS

Some nouns are made from phrasal verbs, often formed by joining the verb and the particle together. When these words are spoken, the stress is usually on the verb.

The teacher asked me to hand out the exam papers.

Verb — Particle

The teacher gave us a handout containing homework tasks.

Noun

Sometimes, the noun is formed by putting the particle in front of the verb. In these cases, the spoken stress is usually on the particle.

Oh no! It was sunny and now it's pouring down.

The plural is formed by adding an "s" to the newly-formed noun.

We have a rainy season with daily downpours.

Aa 19.8 MATCH THE DEFINITIONS TO THE NOUNS

people who watch something happening without taking part		crackdown
① failure, or a sudden decline in reputation or rank		outset
② severe action taken by an authority to stop a certain activity		backup
③ extra support or help / a copy of computer data		onlookers
④ the act of signing in to a computer program or system		downfall
⑤ time or knowledge that has been put into a project		leftovers
⑥ what remains at the end of eating a meal		input
⑦ the act of registering your arrival at a hotel or airport		login
⑧ the beginning or start of something		check-in

19.9 READ THE ARTICLE AND ANSWER THE QUESTIONS

A very narrow range of courses is provided online nowadays.
True ☐ **False** ☐ **Not given** ☑

1 Business management is being studied more than any other subject online.
True ☐ **False** ☐ **Not given** ☐

2 With online courses, contributions can be posted at any time.
True ☐ **False** ☐ **Not given** ☐

3 Blended learning courses are written by university professors.
True ☐ **False** ☐ **Not given** ☐

Education Nation

HOME   ENTRIES   ABOUT   CONTACT

Online or face-to-face?

You can take a multitude of courses online nowadays: everything from online yoga through to a Master's degree in business management. But what are the pros and cons of online learning and how does it compare with the face-to-face experience? Of course one major advantage of learning online is that it is often more flexible. You can read and write whenever and wherever you like. Another bonus is that these courses are often cheaper or even free. However, because you are not in the same place as your peers, or even online at the same time, you may miss out on the camaraderie and peer support. Sometimes online learning can be a lonely experience. So, what is the solution? Well, maybe you can have the best of both worlds. With blended learning, you can have some face-to-face lessons while other course content is delivered online.

19.10 FILL IN THE GAPS USING THE WORDS IN THE PANEL, USING THE CORRECT FORM AND VOICE

My Italian class ___*is delivered*___ online, with classes on Fridays.

1 The things we learn are _____ in a weekly online exam.

2 The face-to-face lessons expand on the online course _____ .

3 From the _____ , I knew this course would be successful.

4 Lack of motivation has always been my _____ in online learning.

5 The course is _____ by language-learning experts.

6 They have made changes to make it easier to _____ to your account.

7 There has also been a _____ on security to prevent cheating.

outset
~~deliver~~
downfall
write
crackdown
log in
test
input

19 ✓ CHECKLIST

⚙ The passive voice ☐   **Aa** Online learning ☐   🧩 Changing sentence emphasis ☐

20 Things that might happen

There are many ways to talk about hypothetical future situations. You can use different structures to indicate whether you think a hypothesis is likely or unlikely.

⚙️ **New language** "What if," "suppose," "in case"

Aa Vocabulary Exams and assessment

🧩 **New skill** Talking about hypothetical situations

20.1 KEY LANGUAGE LIKELY TO HAPPEN

If a future outcome is likely to happen, you can use "what if," "suppose," and "in case" followed by the present tense to express it.

"What if" means "what would happen if a hypothetical situation occurred?"

Present tense shows the speaker believes this is likely to happen.

What if I fail my exams?
I won't be able to go to college.

20.2 FURTHER EXAMPLES LIKELY TO HAPPEN

"Suppose" refers to the consequences of a hypothetical situation.

**Suppose they assess our coursework.
We will have to keep a portfolio.**

We should start organizing our project work in case they want to see it.

"In case" refers to being prepared for the hypothetical situation.

20.3 MATCH THE SITUATIONS TO THE LIKELY CONSEQUENCES

What if we don't pass our exams?	Maybe you could apply for funding.
1 I'm going to take a water bottle	in case the exam room is hot.
2 Suppose you cannot afford to study.	Maybe we'll have to take them again.
3 I am studying really hard tonight	Maybe they will have spares.
4 What if I forget to bring a calculator?	in case we have a test tomorrow.

20.4 KEY LANGUAGE UNLIKELY TO HAPPEN

If a future outcome is possible, but unlikely to happen, you can also use "what if" and "suppose" followed by the past tense to express it. You can also use "just in case" with the present tense.

The past tense shows the speaker thinks this is unlikely to happen.

Just imagine! What if we all passed our exams with perfect scores?

20.5 FURTHER EXAMPLES UNLIKELY TO HAPPEN

"Suppose" and "supposing" are interchangeable in this context.

Suppose I got caught cheating. My parents would be furious.

"Just" is added to "in case" to talk about preparation for a situation that is less likely.

You should apply for a job just in case you fail your exams.

The verb remains in the present tense after "just in case."

 ## 20.6 MARK WHETHER THE OUTCOMES ARE LIKELY OR UNLIKELY

I've studied hard. I'm buying champagne in case I pass all my exams. **Likely** ☑ **Unlikely** ☐

① What if she notices that I've copied the essay from the internet? **Likely** ☐ **Unlikely** ☐

② Suppose I won the lottery. I could afford to study abroad. **Likely** ☐ **Unlikely** ☐

③ Suppose I write three good essays. That will be enough. **Likely** ☐ **Unlikely** ☐

④ What if I studied for 14 hours every day from now on? **Likely** ☐ **Unlikely** ☐

⑤ Suppose the examiner asks my name in French. What should I say? **Likely** ☐ **Unlikely** ☐

⑥ I'm taking 10 pencils to the exam just in case nine break. **Likely** ☐ **Unlikely** ☐

⑦ It's supposed to stop raining, but I'll bring an umbrella in case it doesn't. **Likely** ☐ **Unlikely** ☐

⑧ What if I misunderstood all the questions? That would be a disaster. **Likely** ☐ **Unlikely** ☐

20.7 KEY LANGUAGE THE FIRST AND SECOND CONDITIONALS

FIRST CONDITIONAL	SECOND CONDITIONAL

FIRST CONDITIONAL

You can use the first conditional to talk about realistic future results if a realistic condition is fulfilled.

"If" + present simple.

If you study really hard this year, you'll pass your university exams.

"Will" + infinitive.

SECOND CONDITIONAL

You can use the second conditional to predict future results if an unlikely condition is fulfilled.

"If" + past simple.

If you went to fewer parties, you would get better results.

"Would" + infinitive.

20.8 READ THE TEXT AND ANSWER THE QUESTIONS

Students do not need to remember information for exams.
True ☐ **False** ☑

❶ Students take three exams at the end of the year.
True ☐ **False** ☐

❷ The students currently have continuous assessment.
True ☐ **False** ☐

❸ The author thinks exams are a fair way to assess students.
True ☐ **False** ☐

❹ Students are told that they can encourage change.
True ☐ **False** ☐

Memorizing is not learning!

Why are you trying to remember dozens of facts, figures, and quotations? The only reason is so that you can use them in the 12 terrifyingly stressful 3-hour exams that will be the only "proof" of how much you have learned over the academic year. Suppose it didn't have to be this way? What if you had continuous assessment throughout the year that showed what you can do with the knowledge, rather than how much you can cram into your memory? This can happen if you write to the head of your academic departments and urge them to consider 21st-century modes of assessment. Make time and write today.

20.9 LISTEN TO THE AUDIO AND MARK WHETHER EACH OUTCOME IS LIKELY OR UNLIKELY

Likely ☐ Unlikely ☑

❶ Likely ☐ Unlikely ☐

❷ Likely ☐ Unlikely ☐

❸ Likely ☐ Unlikely ☐

❹ Likely ☐ Unlikely ☐

20.10 RESPOND TO THE AUDIO, SPEAKING OUT LOUD

Suppose you could live anywhere. Where would you choose?

I'd live in my hometown to be near my family.

1 If you could meet any historical leader, who would it be?

2 Supposing you were ruler of the world, what would you do?

3 What will you do next if you pass the exam?

---

20 ✓ CHECKLIST

⚙ "What if," "suppose," "in case" ☐   **Aa** Exams and assessment ☐   🧩 Talking about hypothetical situations ☐

♲ REVIEW THE ENGLISH YOU HAVE LEARNED IN UNITS 17–20

NEW LANGUAGE	SAMPLE SENTENCE	☑	UNIT
ORGANIZING DISCOURSE MARKERS	First, **it is important to consider which courses you want to study.**	☐	17.1
MAKING GENERALIZATIONS	In some cases, **students live off campus.**	☐	18.1
THE PASSIVE VOICE	**The book** was studied **by many people.**	☐	19.1
NOUNS FORMED FROM PHRASAL VERBS	**The teacher gave us a** handout.	☐	19.7
LIKELY AND UNLIKELY SITUATIONS	What if **I fail my exams?** What if **we all** passed **with top grades?**	☐	20.1, 20.4

21 Vocabulary

21.1 WORKING

It is difficult to work a nine-to-five job when you have young children.

nine-to-five
[a job with regular hours]

We've built a positive working environment for our staff.

working environment
[the conditions in which you work]

Our employees are qualified and also have hands-on experience.

hands-on experience
[the knowledge and skill gained through doing something yourself]

Have you ever held a position in management?

hold a position
[have a job]

My career really took off after I got that first big deal.

take off
[suddenly begin to have more success]

Her chosen career path meant she worked abroad a lot.

career path
[progression within a profession, in a job or through a series of jobs]

I worked my way up from the bottom of the career ladder.

bottom of the career ladder
[a position with the lowest level of responsibility or compensation]

I'm going to college so I don't have to get a dead-end job.

dead-end job
[a position without many prospects]

He was fired for stealing goods from the warehouse.

be fired
[be forced to leave your job for doing something wrong]

Many people were laid off from the factory.

laid off / made redundant (UK)
[made to leave a job because there is not enough work available]

I'm stepping down to let another person do the job.

step down
[stop doing a job voluntarily]

We had to tackle this problem head-on before it got worse.

tackle something head-on
[deal with something directly]

We've set our sights on being number one in our industry.

set your sights on something
[aim to achieve a particular goal]

You need to work hard to get ahead in this industry.

get ahead
[make more progress than others]

We took on three new members of staff this year.

take somebody on / take on somebody
[employ somebody]

I'm sorry I didn't answer your email. I was snowed under.

be snowed under
[have too much work to do]

She must have her hands full with those four children.

have your hands full
[be busy with a task or many tasks]

I can't come out because I'm up to my eyes with work.

be up to your eyes / ears
[be so busy that you can't take on anything else]

He always goes the extra mile to ensure deliveries are on time.

go the extra mile
[do more than you are required to do]

The deal involved give and take on both sides.

give and take
[compromise]

22 Job applications

In English, prepositions can only be followed by a noun phrase or a gerund. This is particularly important when talking about the order of events.

⚙ **New language** Prepositions and gerunds
Aa Vocabulary Job applications
🧩 **New skill** Writing a résumé and cover letter

22.1 KEY LANGUAGE PREPOSITIONS AND GERUNDS

If you want to use a verb after a preposition, it has to be a gerund, which is the "-ing" form of a verb.

After graduating, I worked in a hospital.

Preposition   Gerund

22.2 FURTHER EXAMPLES PREPOSITIONS AND GERUNDS

Instead of applying for a job, I went to college.

After seeing the job listing, I wrote a cover letter.

22.3 FILL IN THE GAPS USING THE WORDS IN THE PANEL

Since _____attending_____ some training sessions, I feel more confident about my work.

❶ _____ seeing that job listing, I thought I would never find my perfect job.

❷ After _____ as an engineer, I volunteered in Cambodia.

❸ _____ working in a low-paid job, I decided to train as an accountant.

❹ Without _____ my exams, it would be difficult to have a decent career.

| qualifying | ~~attending~~ | Instead of | passing | Before |

22.4 READ THE COVER LETTER AND ANSWER THE QUESTIONS

The job was advertised in the local job center.
True ☐ **False** ☐ **Not given** ☑

① Alice's degree was in Social Media Marketing in the 21st Century.
True ☐ **False** ☐ **Not given** ☐

② Her degree was a mixture of theory and practical training.
True ☐ **False** ☐ **Not given** ☐

③ Alice did some voluntary work while studying.
True ☐ **False** ☐ **Not given** ☐

④ A project Alice did was similar to this job.
True ☐ **False** ☐ **Not given** ☐

⑤ Alice is very creative, but less interested in details.
True ☐ **False** ☐ **Not given** ☐

⑥ Alice would be happy to start on a low salary.
True ☐ **False** ☐ **Not given** ☐

Dear Mrs. Evans,

I'm writing to apply for the Social Media Marketing Assistant post advertised in Social Journal. Please find attached a copy of my résumé for your consideration.

I have recently completed a degree in Digital Marketing, which has prepared me well for this position and has made me very enthusiastic about working in this area. As well as providing a strong theoretical grounding, it required a great deal of practical research and initiative. One of the courses, Social Media Marketing in the 21st Century, was particularly relevant to this position. As part of a project for this course, I developed and managed a social media campaign for a soft drinks company.

I have a keen interest in following developments in digital marketing, and am very creative as well as having a good eye for detail and accuracy.

I would be able to take the position immediately. Thank you for taking the time to consider my application, and I look forward to hearing from you in the near future.

Yours sincerely,

A Williams

Alice Williams

22.5 MATCH THE DEFINITIONS TO THE PHRASES

has a very close connection	take the position
① sharp and enthusiastic	post
② be good at noticing small things	is particularly relevant
③ job	keen
④ soon	have an eye for detail
⑤ start the job	in the near future

🔊

George Brandani

275 Main Street
Minneapolis, MN 55401
george@brandani.com
612-555-1746

I am an award-winning, experienced head barista who has managed teams of up to five colleagues. I have in-depth knowledge of the coffee industry and am certified in current hygiene and health and safety regulations.

EMPLOYMENT HISTORY

Coffee Galore
HEAD BARISTA • June 2013–Present
Coffee Galore is an independent, but very highly rated and vibrant coffee shop. I was part of the initial team that established the inviting, friendly, coffee-drinking experience.

Duties:
- Train and manage one full-time and three part-time baristas
- Order and control stock of foods and beverages
- Ensure maximum sales by devising promotions
- Ensure compliance with hygiene and safety regulations

Coffee Time Out
BARISTA • July 2011–June 2013
Part of a large team of baristas in a well-known chain with strict customer service and hygiene standards.

Duties:
- Make and serve up to 250 coffee drinks per day
- Provide a clean and welcoming environment for the customers

Awards
Creative Barista Champion

Qualifications
I hold current certificates in food hygiene and first aid, as well as being a trained fire warden.

Education
Elmwood High School • 2007–2011
High school diploma

Interests
I am passionate about coffee and like to spend my free time visiting places where it is grown, such as Costa Rica and Colombia. I am also a quiz master for the local quiz league.

George helped set up the Coffee Galore coffee shop.
True ✓ **False** ☐ **Not given** ☐

❶ George has worked in coffee shops since he left high school.
True ☐ **False** ☐ **Not given** ☐

❷ George does not like his boss in his current job.
True ☐ **False** ☐ **Not given** ☐

❸ George has only ever worked for small coffee shops.
True ☐ **False** ☐ **Not given** ☐

❹ George is trained to deal with medical emergencies.
True ☐ **False** ☐ **Not given** ☐

❺ All of George's hobbies are related to coffee.
True ☐ **False** ☐ **Not given** ☐

22.7 LISTEN TO THE AUDIO AND ANSWER THE QUESTIONS

HR executive, Janice Streatham, has recorded a podcast giving out tips on how to write a good résumé.

What does Janice say is the most important thing to get right on your résumé?

School qualifications	☐
Employment record	☐
Contact details	☑

① If you left school early and did unpaid work, what should you emphasize on your résumé?

School qualifications	☐
Work experience and skills	☐
Interests and hobbies	☐

② What should you do if you spent a year abroad before starting work or college?

Leave a gap in your résumé	☐
Say what you were doing	☐
Say you were doing something else	☐

③ How long should your résumé be?

About four sides of paper	☐
At least two sides of paper	☐
Less than two sides of paper	☐

22.8 MARK THE MORE FORMAL SENTENCE IN EACH PAIR

I spent ages working in retail even though I didn't really like it.	☐
I worked in retail for many years, then looked for a career change.	☑

① The job was quite challenging in terms of improving the consumer experience. ☐
The shop floor was a real nightmare and my boss wasn't very nice at all. ☐

② I went with my mates on holiday to Vietnam and we did some volunteer stuff. ☐
I traveled to Vietnam where I volunteered for a number of educational projects. ☐

③ I did loads of courses about what to do in a fire and how to write risk assessments. ☐
I am a qualified fire warden and am trained in writing risk assessments. ☐

④ I have an in-depth knowledge of real estate due to having eight years' experience. ☐
I know lots of things about selling houses because I've been doing it for ages. ☐

22 ✓ CHECKLIST

⚙ Prepositions and gerunds ☐   **Aa** Job applications ☐   🧩 Writing a résumé and cover letter ☐

23 Asking polite questions

In English, asking questions directly can sometimes be seen as impolite. It is very common for English speakers to make their questions more indirect.

🔧 **New language** Direct and indirect questions
Aa Vocabulary Job interviews
🧩 **New skill** Asking questions politely

23.1 KEY LANGUAGE POLITE OPEN QUESTIONS

If an indirect question contains "to be," this verb comes after the subject.

What are your career goals?

⬇

Could you tell me what your career goals are?

└─ Polite questions usually start with one of these phrases.

The auxiliary verb "to have" also comes after the subject in indirect questions.

What have you designed before?

⬇

I was wondering what you have designed before.

The auxiliary verb "to do" does not appear in indirect questions.

Why do you enjoy working in fashion?

⬇

I'd like to know why you enjoy working in fashion.

 ## 23.2 REWRITE THE DIRECT QUESTIONS AS INDIRECT QUESTIONS

| What are your strengths? | = Could you tell me _what your strengths are?_ |

1 When are you available? = I was wondering _____

2 Why have you applied for this job? = I'd like to know _____

3 What is our best-selling product? = Do you have any idea _____

4 Who was your last manager? = I'm curious to know _____

23.3 KEY LANGUAGE POLITE YES / NO QUESTIONS

An indirect, more polite, way of asking yes/no questions is to use "if" or "whether."

Have you worked in a café before?

Could you tell me if you have worked in a café before?

"If" can be replaced by "whether," to make the question more formal.

23.4 REWRITE THE DIRECT QUESTIONS AS INDIRECT QUESTIONS USING "IF" OR "WHETHER"

Have you ever led a team? = Could you tell us *if you have ever led a team?*

1 Do you like working with animals? = We were wondering _____

2 Have you applied for other jobs? = Would you mind telling us _____

3 Do you have any computer skills? = Could you tell me _____

4 Do you have relevant experience? = We'd like to know _____

23.5 REWRITE THE INDIRECT QUESTIONS, PUTTING THE WORDS IN THE CORRECT ORDER

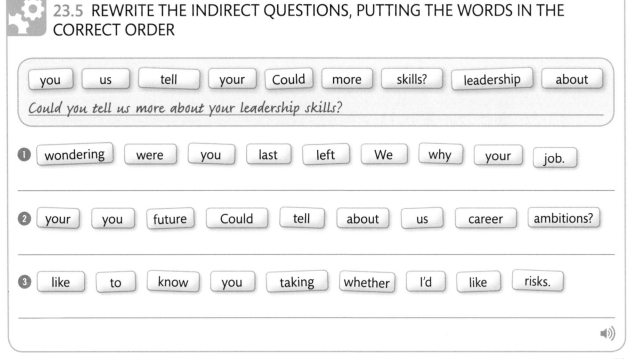

| you | us | tell | your | Could | more | skills? | leadership | about |

Could you tell us more about your leadership skills?

1 | wondering | were | you | last | left | We | why | your | job. |

_____

2 | your | you | future | Could | tell | about | us | career | ambitions? |

_____

3 | like | to | know | you | taking | whether | I'd | like | risks. |

_____

23.6 READ THE ARTICLE AND ANSWER THE QUESTIONS

Wear whatever you want to the interview.
True ☐ **False** ☑

1 You shouldn't wear your interview outfit before the interview.
True ☐ **False** ☐

2 You will probably be asked questions about the company.
True ☐ **False** ☐

3 You should learn detailed answers by heart.
True ☐ **False** ☐

4 You should think of questions to ask the interviewer.
True ☐ **False** ☐

Top Tips for Job Interviews

1 Dress well for the interview. Try on your interview outfit so that you feel comfortable wearing it.

2 Know the company and the job. You will be expected to talk about both of them.

3 Think of potential questions and your answers. Don't learn answers by heart, but think about possible points you could make.

4 Think of questions to ask the interviewer. It's a great opportunity to make yourself look interesting and interested.

5 Be calm and confident. You've got something they like to get this far!

23.7 KEY LANGUAGE STALLING TECHNIQUES

If you need extra time to think about a difficult question before answering it, you can start your response with a stalling phrase that indicates you are considering the question.

| **Would you be happy to work on weekends?** | **Well, I do have two children.** | **What are your strengths?** | **Good question. I have excellent computer skills.** |

| **Why should we hire you?** | **Let's see... I think my experience would be very useful.** |

23.8 LISTEN TO THE AUDIO AND ANSWER THE QUESTIONS

Sunaina is interviewing Rhodri for a job at her company.

What does Rhodri say about Alphomega?

Its reputation is not that good ☐
Its reputation is growing ☐
It's a well-respected company ☑

① Why does Rhodri say that, as a new graduate, he would benefit the company?

He is clever and so learns things easily ☐
He has learned new techniques and skills ☐
He will not have developed bad habits ☐

② Why didn't Sunaina ask about Rhodri's strengths?

She had already read about them ☐
She thought he might not tell the truth ☐
She thought it might be boring ☐

③ What did Rhodri say was his greatest weakness?

He used to be very critical of himself ☐
He gets bored easily because he's so smart ☐
He is honest when he shouldn't be ☐

④ Why had Rhodri researched Alphomega Marketing so thoroughly?

He knew he was coming for an interview ☐
It was part of his final-year project ☐
It was part of his second-year project ☐

23.9 RESPOND TO THE AUDIO, SPEAKING OUT LOUD USING STALLING TECHNIQUES

What is your proudest career moment?

Good question. *I think it'd be when I was promoted to senior manager.*

① When have you worked as part of a team?

Well, _____

② What do you know about our company?

Actually, _____

③ Where do you see yourself in five years?

Let's see. _____

④ Why do you think we should hire you?

Good question. _____

---

23 ✓ CHECKLIST

⚙ Direct and indirect questions ☐   **Aa** Job interviews ☐   👣 Asking questions politely ☐

24 Complex verb patterns

There are several different patterns that verbs can follow, including whether they can be followed by an infinitive or a gerund.

⚙ **New language** Verb + infinitive / gerund
Aa Vocabulary World of work
🧩 **New skill** Using complex verb patterns

24.1 KEY LANGUAGE VERB + INFINITIVE PATTERNS

Some verbs are followed by an infinitive.

VERB + INFINITIVE

He managed to finish the report just in time.

Other verbs must have an object before an infinitive.

VERB + OBJECT + INFINITIVE

My computer enables me to work on two screens at once.

 ## 24.2 CROSS OUT THE INCORRECT PHRASE IN EACH SENTENCE

I was delighted when the HR department ~~offered me~~ / offered to improve my salary.

1 The new product launch caused the profits to rise / to rise the profits, which was excellent news.

2 I recently lost my job, but I managed me / managed to find a new one quite quickly.

3 The employees were furious, so they threatened the boss / threatened to not work yesterday.

4 I always get scared when my boss invites me to / invites to me her office. It's never good news.

5 Sometimes it can be good to volunteer you / volunteer to do extra work. It'll impress your boss.

6 On Fridays, my manager sometimes allows me / allows to leave early to enjoy the weekend.

24.3 KEY LANGUAGE VERB + GERUND PATTERNS

Some verbs are usually followed by a gerund instead of an infinitive.

VERB + GERUND

I really enjoy working at the zoo. It's a lot of fun.

Some verbs can be followed by an object and a gerund.

VERB + OBJECT + GERUND

Hayley heard the boss interviewing the new secretary.

🔊

 ## 24.4 FILL IN THE GAPS USING THE WORDS IN THE PANEL

I remember ___*mentioning*___ some changes to you briefly, so here's a little more information.

1. Over the years we have enjoyed _____ the market when it comes to the environment.

2. An auditor has advised us _____ some of our policies in order to improve further.

3. One change we would like _____ is to no longer supply disposable cups.

4. We're sure that you will approve of us _____ to become more environmentally friendly.

5. The change will prevent our company _____ up to 25,000 cups each year.

6. Bringing your own mug will enable us _____ to this new initiative.

7. We hope that you approve of the company _____ a change like this. It's for a great cause.

8. I'll send another quick memo on Friday to remind you _____ your own mug to work.

to stick	leading	throwing away	~~mentioning~~	to make
trying	to bring	making	to change	

🔊

24.5 KEY LANGUAGE VERBS THAT NEED A PREPOSITION

Some verbs need to be followed by a specific preposition before an object. Different verbs are followed by different prepositions.

VERB + PREPOSITION

The head chef used to shout at **the staff to encourage them to work harder.**

24.6 FURTHER EXAMPLES VERBS THAT NEED A PREPOSITION

 The café was counting on **the new menu to impress its customers.**

 The head chef appealed to **the manager to hire more kitchen staff.**

 The café advertised for **another chef to join the team.**

 24.7 CROSS OUT THE INCORRECT WORDS IN EACH SENTENCE

> They planned for / ~~at~~ / ~~on~~ / ~~to~~ a babysitter to look after their son while they went to a dinner party.

1 He appealed for / at / on / to the audience, asking them to stop booing the actors in the play.

2 She always shouts for / at / on / to him when he doesn't take the dog for a walk.

3 You should wait for / at / on / to Jane to arrive before talking to Max about this important issue.

4 I'm sure that I can count for / at / on / to you to support your boss at this difficult time.

5 I've arranged for / at / on / to the doctor to see you tomorrow morning at 10am.

6 My children never listen for / at / on / to me when I tell them what to do.

24.8 READ THE ARTICLE AND WRITE ANSWERS TO THE QUESTIONS AS FULL SENTENCES

YouToPrint

HOME | ABOUT | CONTACT

WELCOME!

Here you can find out more about the YouToPrint company history, where we are now, and our exciting plans for the future. We began designing and printing documents and cards for businesses 20 years ago.

Last year, we streamlined our processes by putting the client in charge of design, while we focused on providing the quality materials and printing. While this meant that we had to let go of a few of our staff, we made a number of economies which we could then pass on to our clients in the form of cheaper prices.

We will shortly be revealing our SmartUBiz cards. You only need to tap these cards on a smartphone to be taken directly to a website. Those websites can be changed by the client at any time, so the business card is always up to date.

What information can you find on this page of the YouToPrint website?

You can discover more about the company's history, and also its present and future plans.

---

❶ What part of the process did YouToPrint do 20 years ago that they don't now?

_____

❷ What did the company focus on when the clients started designing the products?

_____

❸ How did the clients benefit when a number of people were let go?

_____

❹ How do SmartUBiz cards work?

_____

---

24 ✅ **CHECKLIST**

⚙️ Verb + infinitive / gerund ☐   **Aa** World of work ☐   🧩 Using complex verb patterns ☐

25 Double object verbs

Some verbs can be followed by both a direct object and an indirect object. Sentences using these verbs can be ordered in a number of different ways.

🛠 **New language** Double object verbs
Aa Vocabulary New businesses
🧩 **New skill** Talking about starting a business

25.1 KEY LANGUAGE DOUBLE OBJECT VERBS WITH NOUNS

The direct object is the person or thing that an action happens to. The indirect object benefits from the same action. If the indirect object is the focus, it comes after the direct object plus "to" or "for."

The indirect object can also come before the direct object. In this case, no preposition is needed.

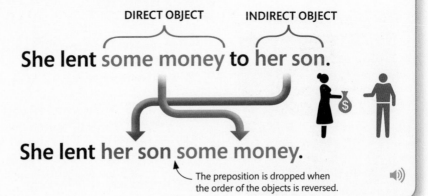

DIRECT OBJECT   INDIRECT OBJECT

She lent some money to her son.

She lent her son some money.

The preposition is dropped when the order of the objects is reversed.

25.2 KEY LANGUAGE DOUBLE OBJECT VERBS WITH PRONOUNS

If the direct object is a pronoun, it must come before the indirect object.

She lent it to her son. ✓
She lent her son it. ✗

If the indirect object is a pronoun, it can come before or after the direct object.

She lent him some money. ✓
She lent some money to him. ✓

25.3 REWRITE THE SENTENCES CORRECTING THE ERRORS

He bought a house his daughter.
He bought a house for his daughter.

❶ Barbara gave it me.

_____

❷ We gave to them some candy.

_____

❸ James passed to me the documents.

_____

25.4 KEY LANGUAGE VERBS WITH "TO" OR "FOR"

Some verbs can take either "to" or "for," depending on the context.
"To" is usually used when there is a transfer of something, whereas
"for" is used when someone benefits from something.

He sold the house to the family.
[The family bought the house.]

He sold the house for the family.
[He sold the house on behalf of the family.]

25.5 CROSS OUT THE INCORRECT WORD TO MAKE THE PAIRS OF SENTENCES MATCH

The brothers bought the business.	= She sold the business to / ~~for~~ the brothers.

1. The students received the homework. = The teacher gave homework to / for the students.

2. The speech was promoting the business. = He made a speech to / for the business.

3. He passed on his knowledge. = He gave advice to / for them.

4. A charity worker is collecting money. = He's collecting money to / for the charity.

25.6 READ THE ARTICLE AND ANSWER THE QUESTIONS

The museum has recently been built.
True ☐ **False** ☐ **Not given** ☑

1. Hugh Walker won an award at the ceremony.
True ☐ **False** ☐ **Not given** ☐

2. People have donated money to help save the museum.
True ☐ **False** ☐ **Not given** ☐

3. Walker is still in charge of the building.
True ☐ **False** ☐ **Not given** ☐

16 ART AND CULTURE

SAVE THE MUSEUM

Historian Hugh Walker last night gave an emotional speech to the audience at the Heritage Awards held in the newly renovated museum. He thanked all the people who had donated money to the "Save the Museum" campaign. He thanked them for preserving the historic museum for the benefit of thousands of future history enthusiasts. Walker, who bought the building five years ago, gave it to the charity to run last year.

25.7 LISTEN TO THE AUDIO AND CORRECT THE SENTENCES

Colin is talking to his friend about starting his new business.

Colin still has quite a lot of paperwork to do.
Colin has finished all of the paperwork.

❶ The business will start trading next year.

_____

❷ Starting a business is expensive, but Colin has lots of money.

_____

❸ Lots of companies have made walking map apps.

_____

❹ If it fails, he will really regret opening the business.

_____

25.8 LISTEN AGAIN AND FILL IN THE GAPS USING THE IDIOMS BELOW

I've been planning to start my own map shop for years, and finally I've done all the paperwork and all the

_____ red tape _____ is out of the way. We don't formally open until next month, but I'm getting

everything ready now so we can really _____ . It hasn't been cheap though. Starting a

business is very expensive and I don't have a _____ to buy thousands of maps. The

walking map app is the _____ though. Not many people do those yet and I hope to

have _____ by the end of next year. Of course, it might all go horribly wrong, but

_____ , eh?

| cornered the market | ~~red tape~~ | ace up my sleeve | blank check |
| nothing ventured, nothing gained | | hit the ground running | |

25.9 REWRITE THE HIGHLIGHTED PHRASES, CORRECTING THE ERRORS

opening Saturday

1. _____
2. _____
3. _____
4. _____
5. _____
6. _____
7. _____

Colin's Maps will be openning Saturday!

For all you're map needs.

We are 20 years' experience in the map industry and have always moved with the times. Now, however, we are a head of the times. Colin's Maps will be lunching the new walking and leisure map app for your digital devices soon. This app will be aviable for all smartphones and tablets and you will be able to make digital notes on it as you walk or later, once you youve returned home.

We also have a enormous stock of traditional paper and waterproof maps.

Stop in to see us!

---

25 ✓ CHECKLIST

⚙ Double object verbs ☐   **Aa** New businesses ☐   🧩 Talking about starting a business ☐

♻ REVIEW THE ENGLISH YOU HAVE LEARNED IN UNITS 22–25

NEW LANGUAGE	SAMPLE SENTENCE	☑	UNIT
PREPOSITIONS AND GERUNDS	After graduating, I worked in a hospital.	☐	22.1
INDIRECT QUESTIONS	Could you tell me what your career goals are? I'd like to know if you've worked in a café before?	☐	23.1 23.3
STALLING TECHNIQUES	Good question, I think I'd have to check first.	☐	23.7
COMPLEX VERB PATTERNS	He managed to finish writing the report just in time. She likes her boss telling her what's happening.	☐	24.1 24.3
VERBS WHICH NEED A PREPOSITION	The café advertised for another chef to join the team.	☐	24.5
DOUBLE OBJECT VERBS	She lent some money to her son. She lent him some money.	☐	25.1
VERBS WITH "TO" OR "FOR"	He sold the store to the family. He sold the store for the family.	☐	25.4

26.1 MEETING AND PRESENTING

You will need to attend the finance meeting **tomorrow.**

attend a meeting
[go to a meeting]

I'd like you to give a presentation on your research.

give a presentation
[present a formal talk for a group of people]

The CEO has put forward an agenda for tomorrow's meeting.

put forward an agenda
[suggest what will be discussed in a meeting]

Our falling profits will be on the agenda **today.**

on the agenda
[included in a list of things to discuss]

OK, now you've all been introduced, let's get down to business.

get down to business
[start working or doing something that you have to do]

John is ill and so he will be absent **from the meeting.**

absent
[not present]

We've arranged a conference call **with our French and German managers.**

conference call
[a telephone call with a number of people at the same time]

Sanjay has been on the board of directors **for three years.**

board of directors
[a group of people who manage a business or organisation]

On the one hand it is affordable, but on the other hand it is not durable.

**on the one hand /
on the other hand**
[something to consider / a contrasting thing to consider]

Let's look at **last year's sales figures for this product.**

look at
[begin to consider or discuss]

Can we have a show of hands for those who agree with the idea?

show of hands
[a vote performed by raising hands to show agreement with a proposal]

It took hours to reach a consensus.

reach a consensus
[arrive at a position of agreement]

We reached a unanimous agreement on the plan.

unanimous
[when everyone is in agreement]

So, to sum up, we need to increase sales in this area.

sum up
[conclude]

Shall we set a date for the next meeting?

set a date
[agree on a date in the future]

I think we're finished unless there is any other business?

any other business (AOB)
[any matter discussed in a meeting that is not on the agenda]

I will take questions at the end of the presentation.

take questions
[listen to and answer questions]

We can't discuss replacing the printers because we've run out of time.

run out of time
[have no time left for something]

Maria will take the minutes of the meeting today.

take the minutes
[write the record of what was said during a meeting]

Let's start by reviewing the minutes of last month's meeting.

review the minutes
[look again at the written record of a past meeting]

27 Reflexive pronouns

Reflexive pronouns show that the subject of a verb is the same as its object. They can also be used in other situations to add emphasis.

🔧 **New language** Reflexive pronouns
Aa Vocabulary Workplace language
🧩 **New skill** Talking about work issues

27.1 KEY LANGUAGE REFLEXIVE PRONOUNS

Reflexive pronouns in English are formed by adding the suffix "-self" or "-selves" to simple pronouns.

 I left myself a reminder about the meeting.

 Sarah sees herself as a natural team leader.

 We pride ourselves on our customer service.

 Not a single person let themselves down today.

🔊

27.2 HOW TO FORM

I ➡	myself
you ➡	yourself
he ➡	himself
she ➡	herself
it ➡	itself
we ➡	ourselves
you ➡	yourselves
they ➡	themselves

🔊

27.3 CROSS OUT THE INCORRECT WORDS IN EACH SENTENCE

> You made ~~itself~~ / yourself sound good in your application.

① We had to run the meeting ourselves / yourselves.

② Do you ever send meeting reminders to myself / yourself?

③ I taught herself / myself how to play the guitar.

④ Do you and Priya see yourself / yourselves as team players?

⑤ He put himself / herself forward for a big promotion.

⑥ The company promotes itself / ourselves online.

🔊

27.4 KEY LANGUAGE USING REFLEXIVE PRONOUNS FOR EMPHASIS

Sometimes reflexive pronouns are not essential to the grammar of the sentence, but can be used to add emphasis in different ways.

The company director gave the talk.

This sentence makes sense without a reflexive pronoun.

Adding the reflexive pronoun at the end of the clause emphasizes that the action was not delegated.

The company director gave the talk himself.

[The company director gave the talk, rather than getting someone else to do it.]

Adding the reflexive pronoun directly after the subject emphasizes its importance.

The company director himself gave the talk.

[The company director, who is an important person, gave the talk.]

27.5 FILL IN THE GAPS WITH THE MOST APPROPRIATE REFLEXIVE PRONOUNS

The CEO ___himself___ came in to discuss his views about the merger.

1 I'm very impressed that they planned this conference _____ !

2 I spent all evening doing research for this presentation _____ .

3 The area is traditional, but the city _____ is full of modern offices.

4 Nobody helped us. We won this contract _____ .

5 I couldn't believe it! The Queen _____ presented the award.

6 Marta writes summaries for her boss. He can't write them _____ .

7 It's very important that you fix these problems _____ , Jacob.

8 The company founders _____ will be making the final decision.

105

27.6 KEY LANGUAGE REFLEXIVE COLLOCATIONS

Many collocations contain reflexive pronouns. They often follow the pattern verb plus reflexive pronoun plus preposition.

Try to tear yourself away from the computer as often as possible.

27.7 FURTHER EXAMPLES REFLEXIVE COLLOCATIONS

The managers don't concern themselves with minor issues.

Remember to behave yourselves when you are in public.

She still has to familiarize herself with company policy.

Are you leaving early today? Enjoy yourself!

"You" is the implied subject in this imperative phrase.

> **TIP**
> Sometimes the subject is not included, but is implied by the reflexive pronoun.

27.8 FILL IN THE GAPS USING THE REFLEXIVE PHRASES FROM THE PANEL

STRANGE CIRCUMSTANCES
CEO leaves coworkers mystified following surprise resignation

Steven Strange, CEO of AngloEuroCorp, left the company in unusual circumstances last week. Acting CEO Don Black was called into the CEO's office by Strange, who said, "You should _familiarize yourself_ with this office and _____ at home." Another employee commented on Strange's odd behavior: "He usually _____ from our meetings because he didn't _____ with day-to-day matters. Last Friday was different. Mr. Strange _____ away from his office and attended the weekly meeting. He even thanked us for our hard work!" As he left, Strange supposedly announced: "Go home early and _____ !"

~~familiarize yourself~~
concern himself
make yourself
tore himself
absented himself
enjoy yourselves

106

27.9 LISTEN TO THE AUDIO, THEN MATCH THE DEFINITIONS TO THE PHRASAL VERBS

have too much work to do	stay behind
❶ do things you haven't had time to do	knock off
❷ decide or agree to do something	be snowed under
❸ deal with a problem or situation	take on
❹ finish work	catch up
❺ remain somewhere after others have left	sort out

27.10 REWRITE THE SENTENCES CORRECTING THE ERRORS

I think I've taken up too many clients. I'm always rushing to meetings!

I think I've taken on too many clients. I'm always rushing to meetings!

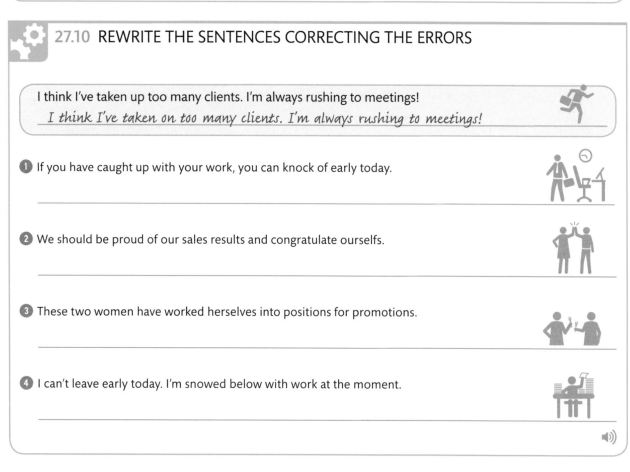

❶ If you have caught up with your work, you can knock of early today.

_____

❷ We should be proud of our sales results and congratulate ourselfs.

_____

❸ These two women have worked herselves into positions for promotions.

_____

❹ I can't leave early today. I'm snowed below with work at the moment.

_____

28 Meeting and planning

Many verbs can be followed by another verb.
This can be a "to" infinitive ("want to eat") or
a gerund ("enjoy cooking").

🔧 **New language** Combining verbs
Aa Vocabulary Office tasks
🧩 **New skill** Taking part in meetings

28.1 KEY LANGUAGE VERBS FOLLOWED BY "TO" OR "-ING" (NO CHANGE IN MEANING)

Some verbs can be followed by a gerund (an "-ing" form)
or a "to" infinitive, with little or no change in meaning.
You can often use both forms interchangeably.

Emails are really awkward. I prefer { meeting / to meet } **in person.**

I like { working / to work } **in an open-plan office with a team.**

28.2 MATCH THE BEGINNINGS OF THE SENTENCES TO THE CORRECT ENDINGS

> **TIP**
> These verbs can all be
> followed by "to" or
> "-ing" with no change
> in meaning.

Oh no. It's James! Once he **starts** ——→ talking, he never stops.

① He was fired because he **continued** — to run for the bus.

② How would you **propose** — being cold and wet.

③ I was so late that I **began** — writing to people by hand.

④ Let's go inside. I really **can't stand** — to ignore his duties.

⑤ I have to say that I **prefer** — to raise the money?

28.3 KEY LANGUAGE VERBS FOLLOWED BY "TO" OR "-ING" (CHANGE IN MEANING)

Some verbs change their meaning depending
on the form of the verb that follows them.

He stopped to talk to her in the office before lunch.

[He was walking around the office, and he stopped
so that he could talk to her.]

She stopped talking to him and rushed to a meeting.

[She was talking to him, and she stopped
in order to do something else.]

28.4 FURTHER EXAMPLES VERBS FOLLOWED BY "TO" OR "-ING" (CHANGE IN MEANING)

In general, the infinitive is used to describe an action that comes
after that of the main verb. The gerund is often used for an action
that happens before, or at the same time as, that of the main verb.

VERB + INFINITIVE	VERB + GERUND
She forgot to send the email, so her team never received the update. [She did not send the email.]	**She forgot sending the email, so she sent it a second time.** [She forgot that she had already sent the email.]
He went on to write the report once the meeting had finished. [He finished a meeting and then wrote the report.]	**He went on writing the report all evening. It took hours.** [He was writing the report, and continued to do so.]
I regret to tell you the unhappy news. Your flight has been delayed. [I have to tell you unhappy news, and I am sorry about this.]	**I regret telling you the unhappy news. I can see it has upset you.** [I wish I hadn't told you the unhappy news because you are very upset now.]
Did you remember to meet David? Your meeting was scheduled for today. [You were supposed to meet David. Did you remember to do that?]	**Did you remember meeting David? I'd forgotten that we had already met him.** [You had met David before. Did you remember that?]

28.5 CROSS OUT THE INCORRECT WORDS IN EACH SENTENCE

We regret to inform / ~~informing~~ you that the hotel will be closed for refurbishment.

1 I hope you remembered to put / putting the advertisement for the grand reopening in the newspaper?

2 Unfortunately, when the hotel reopened, they had forgotten advertising / to advertise, so it was empty.

3 I'll never forget to see / seeing the manager's face when there were no guests at the party.

4 Do you remember to plan / planning the grand opening party with Ceri last year?

5 Do you regret to ask / asking Tim to promote the reopening?

6 After the initial failure, the refurbished hotel went on to be / being a huge success.

7 Now it's famous and successful, the hotel will probably go on being / to be popular for many years.

28.6 FILL IN THE GAPS BY PUTTING THE VERBS IN THE PANEL INTO THE CORRECT FORMS

I hope you ___remembered___ to finish your assignment from last week.

1 I need to _____ spending so much money on food at work.

2 My dad says he could never _____ meeting Elvis, even though it was a long time ago.

3 If I'm not busy tonight, I'd absolutely _____ to go to dinner with you.

4 My boss _____ talking on the phone to video calls.

5 Thanks for the offer. If you don't mind, I'd like to _____ to do my work instead.

6 After the book was published, he _____ to write an award-winning screenplay.

7 I _____ to inform you that the meeting has been postponed.

8 It looks like it will be expensive to get catering. I _____ making the food ourselves.

| propose | continue | ~~remember~~ | go on | love | prefer | regret | forget | stop |

Should you have meetings to hand out information?
Yes ☐ No ✓

1 Should you only have a meeting when it is needed?
Yes ☐ No ☐

2 Should you ask participants to set meeting objectives?
Yes ☐ No ☐

3 Should you use written objectives to help manage the meeting?
Yes ☐ No ☐

4 Should you share the agenda on the day of the meeting?
Yes ☐ No ☐

5 Should you stop meetings to ask people why they are late?
Yes ☐ No ☐

6 Should you start late if some attendees are not yet present?
Yes ☐ No ☐

7 Should you talk to latecomers after the meeting has finished?
Yes ☐ No ☐

98 BUSINESS WORLD

HOW TO RUN EFECTIVE MEETINGS
Top tips from our experts

1 Make sure the meeting you propose having is necessary. Could a notice or email be used to hand out information more effectively? Remember many people can't stand attending unnecessary meetings. If you only have meetings when necessary, then participants will prepare properly and take them more seriously.

2 Remember to set objectives for meetings. This serves a number of purposes. First, everyone knows why the meeting is being held and so will see it as potentially useful. Second, if a participant starts bringing up unrelated topics, you can refer back to the objective.

3 Make sure everyone knows the meeting's objectives by sharing an agenda at least a few days before the meeting. Some people prefer to assign a pre-meeting task to ensure that the agenda is read.

4 Begin talking on time to show respect to those attendees who arrived on time. Don't stop to talk to latecomers. Deal with them later.

29 Qualifying descriptions

There are many ways to qualify or add further detail to adjectives. Some types of adjectives can only be modified in certain ways.

🔧 **New language** Non-gradable adjectives
Aa Vocabulary Qualifying words
🧩 **New skill** Adding detail to descriptions

29.1 KEY LANGUAGE NON-GRADABLE ADJECTIVES

Most adjectives can be modified with grading adverbs, such as "slightly," "very," and "extremely." Non-gradable adjectives cannot be modified in this way. These adjectives tend to fall into three categories: extreme, absolute, and classifying.

Gradable adjectives like "good" can be modified with grading adverbs like "extremely" and "very."

Her arguments were extremely good.

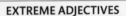

Her arguments were fantastic!

Non-gradable adjectives like "fantastic" cannot be modified by grading adverbs.

EXTREME ADJECTIVES

Extreme adjectives are stronger versions of gradable adjectives, such as "awful," "hilarious," "fantastic," or "terrifying."

Her presentation was awful.

The sense of "extremely" is already incorporated here.

ABSOLUTE ADJECTIVES

Absolute adjectives cannot be graded because they describe fixed qualities or states, such as "unique," "perfect," or "impossible."

She has a unique presenting style.

It is not possible for something to be more or less unique.

CLASSIFYING ADJECTIVES

Classifying adjectives are used to say that something is of a specific type or class, such as "American," "nuclear," or "medical."

The audience was American.

🔊

29.2 WRITE THE ADJECTIVES FROM THE PANEL IN THE CORRECT CATEGORIES

EXTREME	ABSOLUTE	CLASSIFYING
awful	*unique*	*organic*

unknown   ~~awful~~   digital   dead   enormous   right   ~~organic~~   wrong

chemical   industrial   superb   tiny   ~~unique~~   disgusting   electronic

29.3 MARK THE SENTENCES THAT ARE CORRECT

This new product is great. It's extremely perfect for kids. ☐
This new product is great. It's perfect for kids. ☑

1. Have you seen this very amazing designer watch? ☐
   Have you seen this amazing designer watch? ☐

2. This new software is so slow. It's slightly awful. ☐
   This new software is so slow. It's awful. ☐

3. Because it runs on solar power, it's extremely cheap. ☐
   Because it runs on solar power, it's extremely cheaply. ☐

4. The instructions for this product are very impossible. ☐
   The instructions for this product are impossible. ☐

5. The numbers on the watch are tiny! ☐
   The numbers on the watch are slightly tiny! ☐

6. I need to replace my computer. It's extremely broken. ☐
   I need to replace my computer. It's broken. ☐

29.4 KEY LANGUAGE NON-GRADING ADVERBS

Some adverbs can be used to qualify non-gradable adjectives. These are called "non-grading adverbs," and often mean "entirely" or "almost entirely." They cannot usually be used with gradable adjectives.

Her presentation was absolutely awful!

She has a totally unique presenting style.

She had a completely American audience.

29.5 FURTHER EXAMPLES NON-GRADING ADVERBS

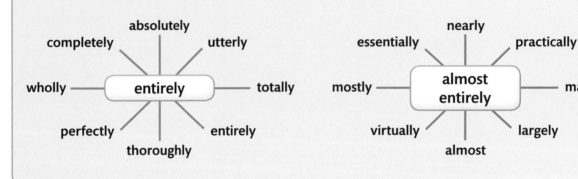

absolutely
completely · utterly
wholly — **entirely** — totally
perfectly · entirely
thoroughly

nearly
essentially · practically
mostly — **almost entirely** — mainly
virtually · largely
almost

29.6 CROSS OUT THE INCORRECT WORD IN EACH SENTENCE

If this new design is really popular, it will be an absolutely huge / ~~big~~ bonus for the company.

① It is incredibly / perfectly important to know a lot about the product you are trying to sell.

② Did you see that slightly / completely digital presentation by the marketing team?

③ Don't you think that this kind of product is extremely useful / excellent for teenagers?

④ To copy and then sell someone else's invention as your own is slightly / utterly wrong.

⑤ From the initial product design to marketing is a rather / completely long process.

⑥ The new designer in my department is absolutely / really fantastic.

⑦ I think the food at the conference was bad. I felt extremely sick / boiling this morning.

⑧ I have to say that I think it was an absolutely superb / okay presentation.

29.7 KEY LANGUAGE "REALLY," "FAIRLY," AND "PRETTY"

A few adverbs can be used with both gradable and non-gradable adjectives. They are "really" (meaning "very much"), and "pretty" and "fairly" (both meaning "quite a lot but not very").

TIP
Note that "fairly" can have a negative connotation and so is not normally used to suggest something is very good or necessary.

Gradable

What you need is a really { good / brilliant } **idea.**

Non-gradable

You need to be fairly { confident / certain } **it works.**

Inventing a new product is pretty { difficult / impossible } **.**

29.8 LISTEN TO THE AUDIO AND ANSWER THE QUESTIONS

Two business partners, James and Maria, have just watched several presentations from product developers. They are discussing which products to invest in.

What did James think of the presentations?
Liked them a lot	✓
Hated them	☐
Liked them a little	☐

❶ What did Maria think about how the smartwatch looked?
Liked it a lot	☐
Hated it	☐
Liked it a little	☐

❷ What did they both think about the smartwatch functionality?
Really good	☐
Really bad	☐
Not very good	☐

❸ What did they think about the cardboard coffee capsules idea?
Liked it a lot	☐
Hated it	☐
Liked it a little	☐

❹ What did Maria think about how the coffee machine looked?
Liked it a lot	☐
Hated it	☐
Didn't like it very much	☐

❺ What did James think of the air freshener?
Liked it a lot	☐
Hated it	☐
Didn't like it very much	☐

29.9 KEY LANGUAGE "QUITE"

You can use "quite" with both gradable and non-gradable adjectives. In US English, it usually means "very." In UK English, it weakens gradable adjectives to mean "not very," but strengthens non-gradable adjectives to mean "very" or "completely."

Her invention is quite incredible.
[Her invention is absolutely fantastic.]

Her idea was quite good.
[Her idea was really good.] (US)
[Her idea was good, but not great.] (UK)

29.10 READ THE PRODUCT REVIEWS AND ANSWER THE QUESTIONS

GAVAC

PRODUCT DESCRIPTION:
The 2-in-1 Gavac is a cordless, lightweight vacuum cleaner. It can be used as an upright vacuum cleaner, or the bottom can easily be detached and used as a handheld cleaner for those difficult-to-reach places. It charges overnight and the battery lasts for up to 15 minutes.

REVIEWS:
Don, Liverpool: This machine is quite useless. It takes all night to charge the battery. It works well for five minutes and then has less and less power until it finally stops after 10 minutes. It takes me three days to vacuum my house!

Marta, London: This cleaner is quite frustrating. I bought it because the description says that it easily changes to a handheld cleaner. It takes about a minute to get the sections apart and then 5 more to put them back together again!

Owen, Cardiff: It's quite lightweight, but only because it is made from awful, cheap materials that break quickly. Do not buy.

The vacuum cleaner does not weigh very much.
True ✓ False ☐

1 It takes 15 minutes to charge the vacuum cleaner.
True ☐ False ☐

2 Don says the vacuum works well for ten minutes.
True ☐ False ☐

3 Marta says it is difficult to put the parts back together.
True ☐ False ☐

4 Owen agrees that the Gavac cleaner is lightweight.
True ☐ False ☐

5 Overall, the reviews are quite positive about the Gavac.
True ☐ False ☐

HOME SHOPPING TODAY

New gadgets for your home

Inventions and innovations to make your home life easier and more comfortable. Order now for next-day delivery!

Envirocaff

The Envirocaff is a coffee machine like no other. Not only does it look absolutely amazing, but it also makes fantastic-tasting coffee every time. Unlike any other machine, the coffee capsules are made entirely from cardboard and can be recycled. Great coffee that doesn't cost the earth.
$85 for the machine
$5.99 / 12 coffee capsules

Blingtech3000

This sleek, fashionable watch face can be combined with a number of different designer straps from traditional leather through to modern rubber. The software is cutting edge and ensures all the functionality you would hope for from a smartwatch: email alerts, a fitness suite, and, of course, a watch. $259

AirFresh 4ever

This everlasting air freshener will bring all the smells of the countryside into your home forever! Unlike our rivals' products, there are no costly refills. There is just a great fragrance to make your house smell fresh forever. Enjoy AirFresh in three incredible fragrances: Country, Sea, and Highland fragrances. $24.99

Coz-E-Slip

The amazing new self-warming slippers. You can choose when to heat them up by using the timer or you can use the completely self-regulating thermostat option and have cozy, toasty, ready-to-go slippers at any time of day. Stay warm this winter with Coz-E-Slip.
$45.99 / batteries not included

The Envirocaff makes coffee that is ___remarkably tasty___ .

1. The coffee capsules are _____ .

2. The Blingtech3000 is an _____ timepiece.

3. The Blingtech3000's software is _____ .

4. Most air freshener refills are _____ .

5. Coz-E-Slip slippers have a _____ thermostat.

6. The slippers are supposed to be _____ .

wholly recyclable

utterly stylish

~~remarkably tasty~~

extremely expensive

totally automatic

incredibly comfortable

absolutely state-of-the-art

---

29 ✓ CHECKLIST

⚙ Non-gradable adjectives ☐   **Aa** Qualifying words ☐   🧩 Adding detail to descriptions ☐

30 Expressing purpose

There are a number of ways to express the purpose of, or reason for, an action. You use different expressions to describe the purpose of an object.

⚙ **New language** "In order to," "so that"
Aa **Vocabulary** Language of apology
🧩 **New skill** Expressing purpose

30.1 KEY LANGUAGE "IN ORDER TO"

You can use "in order to" to talk about the purpose of an action.

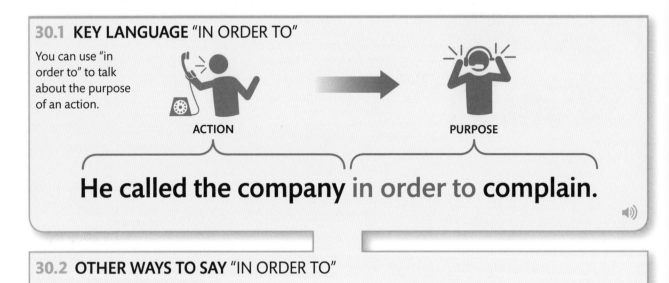

ACTION

PURPOSE

He called the company in order to complain.

30.2 OTHER WAYS TO SAY "IN ORDER TO"

Here "so as to" means exactly the same as "in order to."

He called the company so as to complain.

Base form of verb.

In informal speech, "in order" and "so as" are often dropped.

He called the company to complain.

30.3 MATCH THE BEGINNINGS OF THE SENTENCES TO THE CORRECT ENDINGS

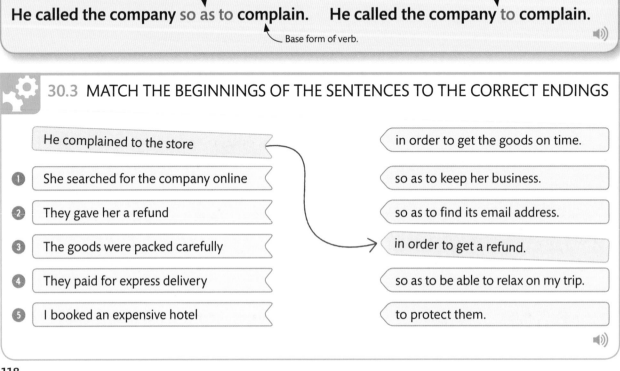

He complained to the store — in order to get a refund.

1. She searched for the company online — so as to find its email address.

2. They gave her a refund — so as to keep her business.

3. The goods were packed carefully — to protect them.

4. They paid for express delivery — in order to get the goods on time.

5. I booked an expensive hotel — so as to be able to relax on my trip.

in order to get the goods on time.

so as to keep her business.

so as to find its email address.

in order to get a refund.

so as to be able to relax on my trip.

to protect them.

30.4 KEY LANGUAGE "SO THAT"

"So that" has a similar meaning to "in order to" and "so as to," but is less formal.

He complained so that he would get a refund.

"So that" is followed by subject + verb.

"So that" is often followed by modal verbs such as "can," "could," and "would."

30.5 FURTHER EXAMPLES "SO THAT"

He reported the problem so that it could be fixed in other machines.

If the main verb is in the past, the verb after "so that" usually refers to the past.

They check goods for damage so that customers don't receive broken items.

If the main verb is in the present tense, the verb after "so that" usually refers to the present or future.

30.6 LISTEN TO THE AUDIO AND ANSWER THE QUESTIONS

Peter works in the customer service department for a home appliance company. He is talking to a customer about an order.

The customer bought the product in a store.
True ☐ **False** ☐ **Not given** ✓

❶ The customer is happy with what she received.
True ☐ **False** ☐ **Not given** ☐

❷ The product arrived broken.
True ☐ **False** ☐ **Not given** ☐

❸ The company tries to pack the product well.
True ☐ **False** ☐ **Not given** ☐

❹ The customer number is MN80.
True ☐ **False** ☐ **Not given** ☐

❺ The replacement will arrive the same day.
True ☐ **False** ☐ **Not given** ☐

❻ The replacement will arrive at 3pm.
True ☐ **False** ☐ **Not given** ☐

❼ Peter offers 25 percent off the next purchase.
True ☐ **False** ☐ **Not given** ☐

30.7 REWRITE THE SENTENCES, JOINING THEM WITH THE GIVEN EXPRESSION OF PURPOSE

> I always go to Austria on vacation. I like to go skiing. [so that]
> _I always go to Austria on vacation so that I can go skiing._

1 Last year we had to complain. We wanted to get a bigger room. [in order to]

_____

2 I usually go to the same resort. I like staying in the same hotel. [so that]

_____

3 He bought the latest model. He wanted to impress his friends. [to]

_____

4 I pack very carefully. I don't want to forget anything. [so as not to]

_____

5 I went to the top of the highest mountain. I wanted to race down. [so that]

_____

6 I went to a hospital. I needed to get an X-ray of my leg. [in order to]

_____

🔊

30.8 KEY LANGUAGE GENERAL PURPOSE

Sometimes you may want to talk about why something exists or what it is used for. You can describe a general purpose by using "to" and "for."

"TO" INFINITIVE — You can use this watch **to track** your heart rate.

↳ You can use a "to" infinitive when the subject of the sentence is a person.

"FOR" + GERUND — The device is perfect **for improving** your health.

This structure commonly answers the question "What is it (used) for?"

"FOR" + NOUN — It is designed **for people** who love technology.

🔊

30.9 FILL IN THE GAPS USING "FOR" OR "TO"

This form is ___for___ complaining about product quality and customer service.

1 Special "outlet" stores are known _____ selling excess goods at reduced prices.

2 This process is for customers who want _____ complain about the products they have received.

3 People are employed _____ check the quality of the goods before they are sent to stores.

4 These notes are here _____ help you complete the form and submit your complaint.

5 There is a telephone number _____ unhappy customers who wish to make further complaints.

6 I think a large number of people only complain _____ get refunds.

7 This new product is _____ busy people who want to make their lives simpler.

30 ✓ CHECKLIST

⚙ "In order to," "so that" ☐   **Aa** Language of apology ☐   🧩 Expressing purpose ☐

↻ REVIEW THE ENGLISH YOU HAVE LEARNED IN UNITS 27–30

NEW LANGUAGE	SAMPLE SENTENCE	☑	UNIT
REFLEXIVE PRONOUNS	I left myself a reminder about the meeting. The company director gave the talk himself.	☐	27.1, 27.4
VERBS FOLLOWED BY "TO" OR "-ING" (NO CHANGE IN MEANING)	I prefer to meet in person. I prefer meeting in person.	☐	28.1
VERBS FOLLOWED BY "TO" OR "-ING" (CHANGE IN MEANING)	He stopped to talk to her in the office. She stopped talking to him and rushed off.	☐	28.3
GRADABLE AND NON-GRADABLE ADJECTIVES	Her arguments were extremely good. Her arguments were fantastic!	☐	29.1
NON-GRADING ADVERBS	Her presentation was absolutely awful!	☐	29.4
"REALLY," "FAIRLY," "PRETTY," "QUITE"	What you need is a really good idea. Her invention is quite brilliant.	☐	29.7, 29.9
"IN ORDER TO," "SO THAT"	He called the company in order to complain. He complained so that he could get a refund.	☐	30.1, 30.4

31.1 ENVIRONMENTAL CONCERNS

Factory emissions contribute to global warming.

global warming
[the increase in the Earth's temperature]

The protesters wanted to raise awareness of climate change.

climate change
[changes in the Earth's weather patterns]

Carbon dioxide is a well-known greenhouse gas.

greenhouse gases
[gases that cause the greenhouse effect, heating up the Earth]

Coal and oil are fossil fuels, which produce carbon dioxide.

fossil fuels
[fuels based on oil, coal, and gas]

This process consumes a lot of fuel.

consume
[use a supply of something, such as fuel or energy]

Flying less will help reduce your carbon footprint.

reduce your carbon footprint
[lower the level of carbon dioxide produced by your actions]

We need new laws if we are going to tackle pollution.

tackle pollution
[deal with the problem of pollution]

It is essential that we start using more types of alternative energy.

alternative energy
[energy that does not use fossil fuels]

Wind and solar are fairly green energy sources.

green energy sources
[types of energy that do not damage the environment]

It is more economical to use renewable energy.

renewable energy
[energy from sources that do not run out]

These big cars can be very harmful to the environment.

harmful to the environment
[causing damage to the environment]

Polluted rivers have dire consequences for local wildlife.

dire consequences
[very bad results]

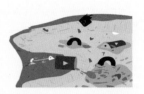

Some people use solar power to heat their water.

solar power
[energy created using sunlight]

A lot of the houses here have solar panels on their roofs.

solar panel
[equipment needed to turn sunlight into electricity]

Here we use turbines to turn wind power into electricity.

wind power
[energy created using the wind]

This wind farm has been running for eight years.

wind farm
[a place with many turbines for generating wind power]

After years of poaching, the white rhino is endangered.

endangered
[at risk of extinction]

Dinosaurs have been extinct for millions of years.

extinct
[no longer existing]

It's terrible to see the destruction of the rainforests.

destruction
[the act of damaging something so badly that it cannot survive or be repaired]

As the planet heats up, it will undergo irreversible change.

irreversible change
[permanent change that cannot be undone]

32 Conditional tenses

You can use the third conditional to describe an unreal past, or events that did not happen. This is useful for talking about regrets you have about the past.

⚙ **New language** The third conditional
Aa **Vocabulary** Environmental threats
🧩 **New skill** Talking about an unreal past

32.1 KEY LANGUAGE THE THIRD CONDITIONAL

SECOND CONDITIONAL

The second conditional is used to describe unreal situations in the present.

**If I lived in New York,
I would go running in Central Park.**

THIRD CONDITIONAL

Use the third conditional to describe unreal situations in the past.

**If we had left earlier,
we would have caught the train.**

🔊

32.2 HOW TO FORM THE THIRD CONDITIONAL

"IF"	"HAD" + PAST PARTICIPLE	"WOULD / COULD / MIGHT"	"HAVE" + PAST PARTICIPLE
If	we had left earlier,	we would	have caught the train.

The "if" clause is the unreal past condition.

Using different modals varies the certainty of the imagined result.

The conditional clause is the unreal result.

32.3 ANOTHER WAY TO SAY THE THIRD CONDITIONAL

The past perfect continuous can also follow "if" in the third conditional.

If you'd been wearing a coat, you would have stayed warm.

We would've caught the train if we'd left on time.

Often "have" is contracted when spoken.

Sentences in the third conditional can be reordered without a comma so the "if" clause is second.

🔊

32.4 FILL IN THE GAPS BY PUTTING THE VERBS IN THE CORRECT TENSES TO MAKE SENTENCES IN THE THIRD CONDITIONAL

If he ___had asked___ (ask) me to marry him, I ___would have said___ (would / say) yes.

1 If I _____ (choose) the trip, we _____ (would / go) to Spain.

2 If we _____ (arrive) earlier, we _____ (would/ not miss) the show.

3 I _____ (could / help) them if they _____ (call) me earlier.

4 If we _____ (stop) eating earlier, we _____ (might / not feel) so sick.

5 She _____ (would / pass) her exam if she _____ (work) a bit harder.

6 If you _____ (shut) the door, we _____ (might / not be) so cold.

🔊

32.5 KEY LANGUAGE FORMAL INVERSION

You can make the third conditional more formal by inverting the subject and "had," and dropping "if."

If you had attended **the meeting, you would have met the manager.**

Had you attended **the meeting, you would have met the manager.**

This is used more in formal and academic written English.

🔊

32.6 LISTEN TO THE AUDIO AND MARK THE THINGS THAT ACTUALLY HAPPENED

32.7 PRONUNCIATION CONTRACTED FORMS

In spoken English, you will often hear the contracted forms of "would have," "could have," and "might have." The vowel sound before the final "v" is a lazy "uh" sound.

would've

could've

might've

🔊

32.8 SAY THE SENTENCES OUT LOUD USING THE CONTRACTED FORMS

They would have taken my car if I had not paid the bill.

They would've taken my car if I hadn't paid the bill. 🗣

1 I might have worked harder if I had been paid more.

🗣

2 If more people had voted for him, he would have won.

🗣

3 If you had left earlier, we would have arrived on time.

🗣

4 She might have finished on time if she had started sooner.

🗣

🔊

32.9 REWRITE THE SENTENCES CORRECTING THE ERRORS

If Jack had visited sooner, he will have seen us.

If Jack had visited sooner, he would have seen us. 🥾

1 If you'll have kept the fire alight, we wouldn't have been so cold.

2 You might slept better if you had brought a sleeping bag!

3 If she'd wore her boots, she wouldn't have had such wet feet.

4 If they'd keep the river clean, the fish not might have died.

🔊

32.10 READ THE ARTICLE AND ANSWER THE QUESTIONS

There are only a few rhinos left in Java.
True ✓ False ☐

① The last Javan rhino in Vietnam died of old age.
True ☐ False ☐

② It is important to protect the rhinos' habitat.
True ☐ False ☐

③ Rhinos naturally live in tropical forests.
True ☐ False ☐

④ It is quite cheap to buy rhino horn.
True ☐ False ☐

⑤ Rhino horn is mostly used in cooking.
True ☐ False ☐

⑥ The leaflet says there is nothing that readers can do.
True ☐ False ☐

CONSERVATION WEEKLY

Save the Javan rhino

In 2010, the last surviving Javan rhino in Vietnam was killed for its horn. How can we make sure that the same does not happen to the few remaining rhinos on Java? What can we do differently?

Firstly, if the rhinos' habitat had been better protected, the rhinos would have had a much greater chance of survival.

Not only does their natural tropical rainforest habitat provide a place for the rhinos to live and find food but it also acts as a place to hide from hunters and poachers.

We also need to stop the market in rhino horns. Prices are so high that poachers take huge risks to get them. Had we persuaded more people not to use rhino horn in traditional medicines, we might have saved that last Javan rhino in Vietnam. We must do all we can to stop the illegal trade in rhino horn.

Go to our website for more information.

 ## 32.11 LISTEN TO THE AUDIO AND MARK THE CORRECT SUMMARY

① In the 1930s more than three-quarters of Java was covered in forest. The Javan tiger was classified as endangered in 1976 and now it is nearly extinct. The population of its main food source, the Rusa deer, has also declined. ☐

② In the 1930s nearly a quarter of Java was covered in forest. The Javan tiger was last seen in the wild in 1976 and is now classified as extinct. The population of its main food source, the Rusa deer, has also declined. ☐

③ In the 1930s more than half of Java was covered in forest. The Javan tiger was last seen in the wild in 1952 and is now classified as extinct. The population of its main food source, the Rusa deer, has increased significantly. ☐

32.12 KEY LANGUAGE "I WISH"

PRESENT REGRETS

You can express regrets about the present in a similar way to the second conditional by using "I wish."

The snow is amazing!
I wish I knew **how to ski.**

"Wish" + past
has present meaning.

PAST REGRETS

You can also use "I wish" to express regrets about the past in a similar way to the third conditional.

My camera has no power.
I wish I'd charged **the battery.**

"Wish" + "had" + past participle
has past meaning.

32.13 ANOTHER WAY TO SAY "I WISH"

PRESENT REGRETS

You can express stronger regrets about the present by using "if only" and the past tense.

These mountains are incredible!
If only I knew **how to ski.**

PAST REGRETS

You can express stronger regrets about the past by using "if only" with "had" and the past participle.

I really wanted to take pictures.
If only I'd charged **the battery.**

 ## 32.14 CROSS OUT THE INCORRECT WORDS IN EACH SENTENCE

There wasn't much wildlife. I wish I **had seen** / ~~saw~~ more animals!

1. I wish we **weren't** / **hadn't been** outdoors right now.

2. I think about the trip a lot. I wish I **took** / **had taken** more photos.

3. I feel sick. If only I **had eaten** / **ate** fewer of those berries.

4. The bus has broken down! If only the driver **had known** / **knew** how to fix it.

5. I'm so exhausted! If only I **sleep** / **'d slept** a little more.

32.15 FILL IN THE GAPS TO MAKE "I WISH" AND "IF ONLY" SENTENCES

I was so hot in the sun today. I wish _____I had remembered my hat!_____ (remember / hat).

1. I missed the bus again. I wish _____ (set / alarm).

2. I caught a huge fish yesterday. If only _____ (take / photo).

3. I can't afford those boots. If only _____ (not spend / money).

4. I was so cold last winter. I wish _____ (buy / coat).

32.16 READ THE ARTICLE AND COMPLETE THE SENTENCES

I wish I'd _____gone_____ sailing with him.

1. He wished he'd _____ the fishermen from killing the seal.

2. He thought, if only he'd _____ something to protect the seals.

3. If I hadn't helped, I know I would've _____ guilty forever.

4. If he'd seen me become a campaigner, he'd have _____ very proud.

WHY ARE YOU A CAMPAIGNER?

My grandfather was a sailor and explored the world by sea. He'd tell me stories of his adventures. He never asked me to go sailing with him, though I would have loved to. Once, in the 1930s, he saw fishermen killing a Caribbean monk seal. He wanted to stop the fishermen, and always felt bad that he did not do anything. After about 20 years, he read that the very last Caribbean monk seal had been killed. He always regretted not doing anything to protect these seals. Many years later when I was in Greece, I saw a leaflet about the endangered Mediterranean monk seal. I knew I had to help or else I'd feel guilty forever. Unfortunately my grandfather never knew I became a campaigner. He'd be very proud.

33 Past regrets

You can use "should have" or "ought to have" to talk about past mistakes. They both signal that you wish you had done something differently in the past.

⚙ **New language** "Should have" and "ought to have"
Aa Vocabulary Time markers
🏃 **New skill** Expressing regret about the past

33.1 KEY LANGUAGE "SHOULD HAVE" AND "OUGHT TO HAVE"

You use "should have" or "ought to have" to express regret about something that did not happen in the past. "Ought to" is less common than "should" and usually sounds more formal.

This bill is so big. I { **should have** / **ought to have** } **used less electricity.**

🔊

33.2 FURTHER EXAMPLES "SHOULD HAVE" AND "OUGHT TO HAVE"

Perhaps I ought to have used energy-saving light bulbs.

The negative form "ought not to have" is grammatically correct, but it is rarely used.

I shouldn't have fallen asleep with the TV on.

🔊

⚙ 33.3 FILL IN THE GAPS USING "SHOULD HAVE" OR "SHOULDN'T HAVE"

We ___*shouldn't have*___ damaged the environment. It's becoming a long-term problem.

① People _____ thrown things in the river. The fish population has declined dramatically.

② Factories _____ reduced pollution in accordance with environmental agreements.

③ Companies _____ used fewer vehicles in order to lower their carbon footprint.

④ Factories _____ released pollution into the water. It has poisoned the ecosystem.

33.4 REWRITE THE SENTENCES CORRECTING THE ERRORS

> You really should have not watched a horror film on your own.
> *You really shouldn't have watched a horror film on your own.*

1 I ought have gone to bed earlier last night. I'm feeling really exhausted now.

_____

2 We really shouldn't to have eaten so much at lunchtime. I'm feeling sleepy now.

_____

3 You should drove more carefully on the wet road. You could have had an accident.

_____

4 Should have I bought this desktop computer, or would the laptop have been better?

_____

🔊

33.5 READ THE ARTICLE AND ANSWER THE QUESTIONS

> Humans intentionally introduce non-native species.
> **True** ✓ **False** ☐

1 New species are introduced to help other animals.
True ☐ **False** ☐

2 Sometimes no animals hunt the introduced species.
True ☐ **False** ☐

3 The Small Indian Mongoose is not native to Mauritius.
True ☐ **False** ☐

4 The mongooses killed the rats on Mauritius.
True ☐ **False** ☐

5 The mongooses also killed all the local animals.
True ☐ **False** ☐

THE ENVIRONMENT

MONGOOSE MADNESS
Mongooses wreak havoc on Mauritius.

One surprising environmental problem caused by humans is the introduction of non-native species of animals to solve local problems.

The new species is supposed to eat the animal that is causing a problem for humans. The difficulties arise when there are no predators for this newly introduced species or when it decides to feed on plants and animals that we do want. For example, the Small Indian Mongoose was introduced to Mauritius and should have dealt with an ever-growing rat population. The mongooses killed the rats, but then they also killed many local animals which then became extinct on the island.

33.6 VOCABULARY TIME MARKERS

| | 1980s | | 1990s | |

Initially, the factories were quite small.

[At first, the factories were quite small.]

During the 1980s, people invested money in the factories.

[At some point in the 1980s, people invested in the factories.]

Throughout the 1990s, the factories grew in size.

[From the beginning to the end of the 1990s, the factories grew in size.]

33.7 LISTEN TO THE AUDIO AND NUMBER THE PICTURES IN THE ORDER THEY ARE DESCRIBED

 Ⓐ ☐

 Ⓑ ①

 Ⓒ ☐

 Ⓓ ☐

 Ⓔ ☐

Aa 33.8 LISTEN AGAIN AND FILL THE GAPS USING THE WORDS FROM 33.6

_____Initially_____ , Easter Island was expansively forested.

❶ _____ the rise of a new civilization, the islanders built statues to honor their ancestors.

❷ _____ this time, the islanders were cutting down lots of trees.

❸ _____ his visit, the first European explorer noticed that there weren't many trees.

❹ The ship HMS Blossom visited in 1825, and _____ , the statues had been toppled over.

❺ An airport was built in 1987 and _____ , lots of tourists have visited Easter Island.

2004 **2005**

Pollution peaked in 2004.
By that time many trees had died.

[At the start of 2004, many
trees had already died.]

Following new laws in 2005,
pollution levels dropped.

[After new laws were passed in
2005, pollution levels dropped.]

Since then, there have been
some signs of a recovery.

[From that point onward, there
has been a slight recovery.]

33.9 READ THE ARTICLE AND ANSWER THE QUESTIONS

Humans are producing less waste now
than they used to.
True ☐ **False** ☐ **Not given** ☑

❶ Radioactive waste is the most
widespread problem.
True ☐ **False** ☐ **Not given** ☐

❷ All the waste is poured into rivers.
True ☐ **False** ☐ **Not given** ☐

❸ The kind of waste humans produce
has changed over time.
True ☐ **False** ☐ **Not given** ☐

❹ Modern plastics can be difficult to
dispose of effectively.
True ☐ **False** ☐ **Not given** ☐

THE PROBLEM WITH POLLUTION
Pollution levels rising across the globe.

The growing human population is producing more and more waste, ranging from sewage and smog to radioactive fuel. Dealing with all this waste is a huge problem. Much of it is just dumped, pumped into the atmosphere, or even poured into rivers and oceans. The resulting pollution is damaging nature.

One of the main issues is the kind of waste humans are now producing. Until the mid-20th century, most of the waste was buried and it just slowly decayed. Nowadays, however, modern plastics make up a large portion of what we throw away. These plastics are almost indestructible by any natural process, so they just pile up, creating huge heaps of waste.

33 ✓ CHECKLIST

⚙ "Should have" and "ought to have" ☐ **Aa** Time markers ☐ 🧩 Expressing regret about the past ☐

34 Actions and consequences

Unlike many parts of speech, prepositions often have little meaning in themselves, but work to change the meaning of the words around them.

⚙ **New language** Dependent prepositions
Aa Vocabulary Actions and consequences
🧩 **New skill** Changing sentence stress

34.1 KEY LANGUAGE DEPENDENT PREPOSITIONS

Some words need to go with specific "dependent" prepositions.

I am late for my meeting!

"Late" could not be paired with any other preposition in this context.

We agreed about the idea.

He's really afraid of flying.

There was an increase in sales.

🔊

Aa 34.2 FILL IN THE GAPS USING THE DEPENDENT PREPOSITION PHRASES IN THE PANEL

Recently, there has been a [*lack of*] energy in the team.

1 Please make sure you [ ] help if you need it.

2 Who is giving the lecture? I have never [ ] him.

3 My brother and I are always [ ] current affairs.

4 The global, [ ] natural resources is worrying.

5 Thank you so much! I am so [ ] all you have done.

6 When you're stressed, it is good to [ ] problems.

7 The [ ] the economic crisis is enormous.

8 Most of the population [ ] climate change.

9 All of the scientific evidence [ ] one direction.

Panel:
- decline in
- talk about
- arguing about
- grateful for
- ~~lack of~~
- knows about
- heard of
- points in
- ask for
- effect of

🔊

34.3 FILL IN THE GAPS WITH THE CORRECT PREPOSITIONS

Have you ever heard __of__ Esperanto?

1 Why do they always argue _____ everything?

2 There was a decline _____ the number of birds.

3 There's a lot to be grateful _____ .

4 This demonstrates a real lack _____ talent.

5 How do I ask _____ directions in Greek?

6 I don't think we'll ever agree _____ this.

7 I really don't want to be late _____ work.

8 My mother is very afraid _____ heights.

9 What is the long-term effect _____ this?

34.4 KEY LANGUAGE WORDS WITH MORE THAN ONE DEPENDENT PREPOSITION

Some words can pair with more than one preposition. The change in preposition often changes the meaning of the phrase.

He talked to the teacher.
[He had a conversation with the teacher.]

He talked about the teacher.
[He had a conversation with someone else about the teacher.]

34.5 LISTEN TO THE AUDIO AND CROSS OUT THE INCORRECT PREPOSITIONS

Technology is a great way to increase interest in / ~~interest with~~ the environment.

1 I'm so bored with / bored about their constant fighting about policies.

2 They've made a new app for / of children to learn about the Earth.

3 Do you have any objection to / objection for this environmental policy?

4 I often worry to / worry about the future of our planet.

5 You need to apologize to / apologize for them to / for the things you said.

6 Do you think a policy like this is suitable with / suitable for a country like ours?

34.6 PRONUNCIATION SENTENCE STRESS

You can change the meaning of a sentence by emphasizing different words as you say it.

The <u>journalist</u> called the mayor today.

[Her assistant didn't make the call.]

The journalist <u>called</u> the mayor today.

[She didn't email.]

The journalist called the <u>mayor</u> today.

[She didn't call the mayor's secretary.]

The journalist called the mayor <u>today</u>.

[She didn't call yesterday.]

34.7 UNDERLINE THE WORDS YOU NEED TO STRESS AND SAY EACH SENTENCE OUT LOUD

The minister changed the policy <u>content</u> this afternoon.

[Not just the policy title.]

1 What do you think of the new statistics in this report?

[I know what everyone else thinks.]

2 These carbon emissions are extremely harmful to the environment.

[I know you think they aren't.]

3 It's is very important that we think of our children's futures.

[Not just their present state.]

4 We need to find solutions sooner rather than later.

[It is not optional.]

93 ENVIRONMENT NEWS WEEKLY

GROWTH AND DECAY

The complex effects of urbanization in a rapidly changing world

Urbanization (the population shift from rural areas to towns and cities) has been happening for centuries. However, the rate and extent of population shift has reached astonishing levels. Some Asian cities, such as Osaka, Jakarta, Mumbai, Seoul, and Beijing, already have populations of more than 20 million people.

What are the environmental ___consequences___ of urbanization on such a massive scale? One major effect of urbanization is the creation of "urban heat islands." Rural areas can remain cooler _____ the sun evaporating the moisture from the vegetation and the soil. However, in the cities there is much less soil and vegetation. _____ , the sun beating on the buildings and roads _____ to an increase in temperatures. Additional heat from vehicles, factories, and cooling units also increases temperatures. This heat then _____ changes in local weather patterns.

Not only is there increased air pollution, but also higher levels of rainfall, _____ in flooding within the cities themselves and also downstream. Another _____ of urbanization is the increased consumption of food, energy, and durable goods. This has a far-reaching _____ on levels of natural resources.

causes   impact   ~~consequences~~   due to   Consequently   consequence   leads   resulting

---

34 ✔ CHECKLIST

⚙ Dependent prepositions ☐   **Aa** Actions and consequences ☐   🧩 Changing sentence stress ☐

35 Few or little?

The words used to describe quantities vary according to a number of factors, including whether you are talking about something countable or uncountable.

⚙ **New language** "Few," "little," "fewer," "less"

Aa Vocabulary Nature and environment

🧩 **New skill** Describing quantities

35.1 KEY LANGUAGE "FEW" FOR SMALL NUMBERS

Use "few" with a plural countable noun to say that there are not many of something. It emphasizes how small the number is. You use "a few" to mean "some." It emphasizes that the number, though small, is enough.

| few = not many |

There are few rare birds here. We probably won't see any.

| a few = some |

There are a few rare birds here. We might see one.

🔊

35.2 KEY LANGUAGE "LITTLE" FOR SMALL AMOUNTS

Use "little" with an uncountable noun to say that there is not much of something. It emphasizes how small the amount is. You use "a little" to mean "some." It emphasizes that the amount, though small, is enough.

TIP
You can add "very" to "few" and "little" to mean "almost none."

| little = not much |

I have little money left. I can't afford to visit the wildlife park.

| a little = some |

I have a little money left. Should we visit the wildlife park?

🔊

35.3 OTHER WAYS TO USE "LITTLE" AND "FEW" FOR SMALL QUANTITIES

Informally, you can use "a (little) bit of" instead of "a little."

↓

There's a little bit of the park that we haven't seen yet.

"Little" and "few" can also be used as pronouns to mean "not much / many."

↓ ↓

Little can be done when few are willing to contribute.

🔊

35.4 CROSS OUT THE INCORRECT WORDS IN EACH SENTENCE

 I'm so excited. I've got ~~few~~ / a few hours to explore the city tonight.

 ❶ I'm afraid we have little / a little time to catch the train. We must hurry.

 ❷ That cake is delicious. I'll have little / a little bit more.

 ❸ Sadly, there are few / a few examples of this quality craftmanship left.

 ❹ Great! We have little / a little spare money. Should we go out for dinner?

 ❺ Wow! Look at all these monkeys! I think there are few / a few different species here.

 ❻ Unfortunately, I have few / a few friends. It's quite lonely here.

35.5 LOOK AT THE PICTURES AND FILL IN THE GAPS USING "(A) FEW" OR "(A) LITTLE"

There is ___little___ water left in the bottle. I'm so thirsty!

❶ Great! There are _____ magazines to choose from.

❷ Sadly, there are _____ fish in my aquarium.

❸ There is very _____ cake left, I'm afraid.

❹ It should be OK. We have _____ time left.

❺ The café is closing soon. There are so _____ customers.

35.6 KEY LANGUAGE "QUITE A FEW" AND "QUITE A BIT (OF)" FOR BIG QUANTITIES

The phrases "quite a bit of" and "quite a few" are understatements that actually mean "a lot" or "many."

| quite a few = many | **The park has been open for** quite a few **years.** |

| quite a bit of = a lot of | **They collected** quite a bit of **money for charity.** |

35.7 FILL IN THE GAPS USING "(A) FEW" AND "(A) LITTLE"

Ninety-year-old Ken Wilson has finally decided to have ___*a little*___ time off after volunteering at his local wildlife park for 30 years. Ken started volunteering _____ years after he retired from teaching. He says, "I started making coffee for people in the little visitor center, but I've had quite _____ different roles since then."

Ken has been a guide, he's surveyed butterflies, and he even managed to get his hands dirty quite _____ times clearing up litter. What does he like so much about the park? "Well, there are _____ green places left like this in big cities. For _____ or no money, a family can explore all day and learn _____ about local wildlife. It's _____ bit of calm in a busy world."

What will he do now? "I'd like quite _____ days sitting in the park doing nothing." After three decades looking after the wildlife, it's time for Ken to take _____ break.

35.8 KEY LANGUAGE "FEWER" AND "LESS"

Confusion between "less" and "fewer" is very common. Remember to use "less" with uncountable nouns and "fewer" with plural countable nouns.

"Issues" is a plural countable noun.

There are fewer issues with electric cars these days.

It would be great to use less fuel.

"Fuel" is an uncountable noun.

35.9 FURTHER EXAMPLES "FEWER" AND "LESS"

There are fewer whales in the oceans nowadays.

We need to spend less money.

"Money" is uncountable, but currencies like "dollars" are countable.

Fewer people enjoy gardening these days.

There is much less traffic today.

35.10 MATCH THE BEGINNINGS OF THE SENTENCES TO THE CORRECT ENDINGS

People are spending much less ──────────┐   volunteers than last year.

① Protesters have demanded fewer   wildlife near big factory sites.

② The charity has fewer ──────────────→ money on organic food than expected.

③ The new light bulbs use far less   electricity than the old ones.

④ Unsurprisingly, there is much less   pollution in the capital city.

⑤ Since the new traffic laws, there is a lot less   harmful emissions by 2025.

35.11 KEY LANGUAGE "FEWER THAN" AND "LESS THAN"

Use "less than" when talking about amounts, distances, time, and money. Use "fewer than" for groups of people or things.

There are fewer than 3,500 tigers in the wild.

Baby elephants weigh less than 300 pounds.

35.12 FURTHER EXAMPLES "FEWER THAN" AND "LESS THAN"

The charity survives with fewer than 20 volunteers.

Charity workers are paid less than $10 an hour.

There are fewer than 50 tickets left for the charity concert.

You can donate less than the recommended amount.

35.13 LISTEN TO THE AUDIO AND ANSWER THE QUESTIONS

A local radio news station is reporting about an environmental campaigner's recent success.

	True	False
Environmental campaigner Rachel Roberts is 70 years old.	☐	☑
❶ The proposal was to build houses on the site of the lake.	☐	☐
❷ Rachel's family used to have family picnics near Lake Lucid.	☐	☐
❸ There were only modern pictures at the photography exhibition.	☐	☐
❹ After 25 days, the exhibition had raised just under $3,000.	☐	☐
❺ People have come to visit the lake from other countries.	☐	☐
❻ The plans for the bypass are delayed, but are still going ahead.	☐	☐

35.14 FILL IN THE GAPS IN THE SUMMARY OF 35.13, USING THE PHRASES IN THE PANEL

___Few___ people would have believed the government would change their minds.

1 Rachel also had the help of _____ friends during her campaign.

2 Rachel knew that _____ people held the same opinion as her.

3 The area is home to _____ 500 plant and animal species.

4 The photography exhibition raised $25,000 in _____ a week.

5 _____ people sent messages of support via social media sites.

6 Making Lake Lucid a popular tourist site will only take _____ years.

| ~~Few~~ | a few | more than | quite a few | less than | Quite a few | a few |

🔊

---

35 ✓ CHECKLIST

⚙️ "Few," "little," "fewer," "less" ☐   **Aa** Nature and environment ☐   🧩 Describing quantities ☐

↻ REVIEW THE ENGLISH YOU HAVE LEARNED IN UNITS 32–35

NEW LANGUAGE	SAMPLE SENTENCE	☑	UNIT
THE THIRD CONDITIONAL	If we had left **earlier**, we would have caught **the train**.	☐	32.1
"I WISH" AND "IF ONLY"	I wish **I knew how to ski.** If only **I'd charged the battery.**	☐	32.12, 32.13
"SHOULD HAVE" AND "OUGHT TO HAVE"	**This bill is so big, I** should have **used less electricity.**	☐	33.1
DEPENDENT PREPOSITIONS	I am late for **my meeting!**	☐	34.1, 34.4
"FEW" AND "LITTLE"	**There are** few **rare birds here.** **I have** little **money left.**	☐	35.1, 35.2
"FEWER" AND "LESS"	**There are** fewer **issues with electric cars.** **It would be great to use** less **fuel.**	☐	35.8

36.1 TRADITION, LUCK, AND SUPERSTITION

I **told a white lie** and said the
dress looked good on her.

tell a white lie
[say something that is not true to avoid
upsetting someone]

She always **drops hints** about
the presents she wants.

drop a hint
[say something indirectly]

Varinder **started a rumor**
that Sonia stole some money.

start / spread a rumor
[to start / continue saying things
that may or may not be true]

Paulo loves to **gossip**. He's always
talking behind people's backs.

gossip
[talk about other people,
often in a negative way]

I **have a sneaking suspicion** that he
won't come to the party tonight.

have a sneaking suspicion
[have a persistent idea about
something with little evidence]

I don't **believe in** ghosts.

believe in something
[think that something exists
or is true]

I haven't ever broken a bone.
Knock on wood!

knock on wood (US)
touch wood (UK)
[wish for good luck, or avert bad luck]

Close your eyes and
make a wish.

make a wish
[hope for something to happen]

I **have serious misgivings**
about this new policy.

have serious misgivings / doubts
[have a strong feeling that something
is not right]

She was such a **tattletale** at school.

tattletale (US) / telltale (UK)
[somebody who tells an authority
figure when another person has
done something wrong]

The best type of publicity is word of mouth.

word of mouth
[information or news transmitted by people telling other people]

I want you to tell me the truth, not another fairy tale.

fairy tale
[a traditional story with magic, or a story designed to mislead others]

That story about the haunted hotel is just an urban myth.

urban myth
[a modern story which is untrue but believed by many]

A black cat is seen as both a good and bad omen.

good / bad omen
[a positive / negative sign about something that will happen]

Winning that car was a real stroke of luck.

a stroke of luck
[a single piece of good fortune]

Winning that game was just beginner's luck.

beginner's luck
[have good fortune the first time you do something]

This is a game of pure luck.

pure luck
[good fortune with no skill involved]

I've just read a book about Chinese folklore.

folklore
[stories, sayings, and traditions from a certain area or culture]

That generation has a different set of beliefs to ours.

set of beliefs
[a group of values]

She has an unshakable belief in the goodness of people.

unshakeable belief
[a firm and unchangeable conviction]

37 Past possibility

You can use a variety of language to talk about possible events in the past, and to indicate whether you agree or disagree with speculation.

⚙ **New language** "Might / may / could" in the past
Aa Vocabulary Urban myths
🧩 **New skill** Talking about past possibility

37.1 KEY LANGUAGE PAST POSSIBILITY

You can use this construction to talk about something that you think possibly happened in the past.

The copier isn't working. It { **might** **may** **could** } **have run out of paper.**

[He thinks it is possible that the copier has run out of paper.]

You can use this construction to talk about something that possibly did not happen in the past.

You { **might not** **may not** } **have plugged it in properly.**

[He thinks it is possible that the printer wasn't plugged in properly.]

"Could not" can only be used when the speaker is certain that something did not happen.

You couldn't have changed the ink properly earlier.

[He is certain that the ink wasn't changed properly.]

🔊

37.2 CROSS OUT THE INCORRECT WORDS IN EACH SENTENCE

 I feel a bit sick. I might / ~~may not~~ / ~~could not~~ have eaten something bad.

❶ It was raining, so I could / might not / could not have gone sunbathing even if I had wanted to.

❷ Look at him! Do you think he might / may not / could not have won the lottery?

❸ If I had left the house a little earlier, I may / might not / could not have missed the bus.

❹ I don't know where she is. She could / may not / could not have gone for a run. She loves exercise.

37.3 LISTEN TO THE AUDIO AND WRITE ANSWERS TO THE QUESTIONS IN FULL SENTENCES

 Sophie is telling her friend about an urban myth that she's heard.

What is an urban myth?
An urban myth is a modern story that isn't true, but lots of people think it is.

❶ How did Sophie's opinion change about about her brother's story?

_____

❷ Why were the golfers celebrating?

_____

❸ What did they do after they knocked over the kangaroo?

_____

❹ What did the kangaroo do when it woke up?

_____

❺ Why couldn't the golfers continue driving home?

_____

37.4 KEY LANGUAGE REPORTED SPEECH

In reported speech, the main verb often changes tense to a past form. You may also need to change a time or place reference.

I don't believe these ghost stories.

The present simple "don't" becomes past simple "didn't."

He said that he didn't believe those ghost stories.

"These" is replaced by the more distant "those."

In reported open questions, the subject comes before the verb and you don't use a question form.

What are you reading?

I asked her what she was reading.

In reported closed questions (with a yes / no answer), you use "if" or "whether."

Are you enjoying it?

I asked her { if / whether } **she was enjoying it.**

37.5 REWRITE THE SENTENCES USING REPORTED SPEECH

Amal has bought a book about ghosts.

Amal said _____that she had bought a book about ghosts._____

❶ Amal's reading a scary story.

Amal mentioned _____

❷ Amal's finished the book.

Amal told me _____

❸ Are you going to the movies?

I asked her _____

❹ What kind of movie are you going to see?

I asked her _____

❺ Did you enjoy it?

I asked her _____

37.6 READ THE EMAIL AND ANSWER THE QUESTIONS

> Carl went to New Zealand before Australia.
> **True** ☐ **False** ☐ **Not given** ☑

❶ Last week Sophie visited their father.
True ☐ **False** ☐ **Not given** ☐

❷ Their father had received an email from the bank.
True ☐ **False** ☐ **Not given** ☐

❸ The email looked genuine.
True ☐ **False** ☐ **Not given** ☐

❹ The police have found the email scammers.
True ☐ **False** ☐ **Not given** ☐

❺ Their father cannot get the money back.
True ☐ **False** ☐ **Not given** ☐

✉ ⌄ ✕

To: Carl Underwood

Subject: Update from home

Hi Carl,

Your Australian vacation photos look great. I'm just writing to keep you up to date with events while you're away.

I've been looking after Dad and I went to see him last week. I'm afraid he looked quite a sorry sight. He said that he'd received an email asking for his bank details. He sent them and then someone stole money out of his account!

At first sight, the email really looked like one from his bank, but it turned out to be fake.

Well, I saw red and called the police and the bank immediately, and luckily they agreed to refund his money. I've told him to call me if another email like that arrives! Other than that, everything is fine here.

Keep having fun!

Sophie

↩ ↩↩   📎 🗑

37.7 FILL IN THE GAPS USING THE IDIOMS IN THE PANEL

> The detectives said they were [*looking into*] the case.

❶ I was so angry that I just [   ] and shouted.

❷ The poor dog had been left in the cold and was a very [   ].

❸ The watch looked genuine [   ], but it wasn't.

❹ I'll just have to [   ] about my English test results.

> at first sight   saw red   ~~looking into~~   sorry sight   wait and see

🔊

---

37 ✓ CHECKLIST

⚙ "Might / may / could" in the past ☐   **Aa** Urban myths ☐   🧩 Talking about past possibility ☐

149

38 Speculation and deduction

You can use modal verbs to describe past events with varying degrees of certainty. These constructions are useful for speculating about events you haven't witnessed.

⚙ **New language** More uses for modal verbs
Aa Vocabulary Phrasal verbs with "out"
🧩 **New skill** Speculating and making deductions

38.1 KEY LANGUAGE MODAL VERBS FOR SPECULATION AND DEDUCTION

When you're speculating about the past and you're sure something happened, use "must have" with the past participle.

He just disappeared. Aliens must have abducted him.
↑ The speaker is sure.

When you're not sure whether something happened or not, replace "must" with "may," "might," or "could."

They { might / may / could } **have taken him to another planet.**
↑ The speaker is unsure.

If you are sure something did not happen, use "can't" or "couldn't."

Hold on! It { can't / couldn't } **have been aliens, they don't exist.**
↑ The speaker is sure it is not possible.

🔊

 ## 38.2 MATCH THE PAIRS OF SENTENCES TOGETHER

He drove his car into the water! — He couldn't have seen the "flood" sign.

He must have hurt his legs.

It could have been the delivery man.

They may have had a party last night.

She might have passed her exam.

It can't have rained all week.

1. He's walking with crutches.
2. Those teenagers look very tired today.
3. The plants are all dry and dead.
4. Someone's left the gate open again.
5. The girl next door looks really happy.

 🔊

38.3 REWRITE THE SENTENCES, CORRECTING THE ERRORS

She broke her arm falling off a horse. It might have hurt.
She broke her arm falling off a horse. It must have hurt.

1 The ground is dry so it can't rained last night.

_____

2 She ate two more slices of cake, so it could have tasted nice.

_____

3 A police car just drove past. There might have was a robbery.

_____

4 He doesn't have any money. He can't not have bought that car himself.

_____

5 They were in the same store as us. They have might buy the same coat.

_____

38.4 CROSS OUT THE INCORRECT WORDS IN EACH SENTENCE

 He had a brand new waterproof coat on. He must / ~~might~~ / ~~can't~~ have stayed dry.

1 I missed a call. It must / may / couldn't have been Diego, he said he might call.

2 I haven't checked my emails yet, so she must / might / can't have replied already, I'm not sure.

3 After the run, he drank a whole bottle of water. He must / might / can't have been really thirsty.

4 She loved both dresses, but she must / might / can't have bought both, as they were too expensive.

5 She hadn't slept for two days. She must / might / can't have been exhausted.

38.5 DESCRIBE WHAT EACH PERSON MUST HAVE DONE, SPEAKING OUT LOUD

> *He must have scored a goal.*

| passed her driving test | eaten too much candy | ~~scored a goal~~ |
| won the lottery | slept through his alarm | failed their exams |

38.6 LISTEN TO THE AUDIO AND MARK THE CORRECT SUMMARY

 A radio host is talking about the unsolved mystery of the SS *Ourang Medan*.

1 The ship sent out a call saying that most of the crew had passed out. The *Silver Star* went to check out the ship and found that everyone on board was dead except the dog, which had passed out. ☐

2 The ship sent out a call saying that a few of the crew were dead. The *Silver Star* went to check out the ship and the sailors freaked out when they saw the dead crew. However, the dog was still alive. ☐

3 The ship sent out a call saying that most of the crew were dead. The *Silver Star*'s crew went to check out the ship and found that everyone on board, including the dog, had died with their eyes still open. ☐

38.7 FILL IN THE GAPS USING THE PHRASAL VERBS IN THE PANEL

I was so scared on the roller coaster ride that I nearly _____*passed out*_____.

1 Every month my company _____ a newsletter to all its customers.

2 Every time my sister sees a spider, she _____ and starts screaming.

3 Should we go to the movie theater and _____ what's showing?

4 He isn't like anyone else. He really _____ from the crowd.

5 I can't _____ what this guy's written. His handwriting is awful.

| passed out | sends out | stands out | check out | work out | freaks out |

38.8 READ THE ARTICLE AND ANSWER THE QUESTIONS

Lateral thinking puzzles give you a lot of information.
True ☐ **False** ☑

1 Pete lives on the 10th floor of the apartment building.
True ☐ **False** ☐

2 Pete always gets out of the elevator at the right floor for his apartment.
True ☐ **False** ☐

3 Pete doesn't like walking, but he sometimes climbs two flights of stairs.
True ☐ **False** ☐

4 The article tells you the solution to the puzzle about Pete.
True ☐ **False** ☐

GAMES AND PUZZLES

Lateral Thinking Puzzles

With a lateral thinking puzzle, you are given an unusual situation and a little information. Your task is to discover the explanation. Can you work this one out?

A young boy, Pete, lives on the 12th floor of an apartment building. Every morning he takes the elevator down to the lobby. In the evening, he gets into the elevator, and, if there's someone else there, he goes up to his floor directly. Otherwise, he goes to the 10th floor and walks up two flights of stairs to his apartment. He does this even though he hates walking. Why?

The solution to this puzzle is that the young boy is too short to reach the buttons for those floors numbered above 10.

38 ✓ CHECKLIST

⚙️ More uses for modal verbs ☐   **Aa** Phrasal verbs with "out" ☐   🧩 Speculating and making deductions ☐

153

39 Mixed conditionals

You can use different types of conditional statements to talk about hypothetical situations. Mixed conditionals use more than one of these types in the same statement.

⚙ **New language** Mixed conditionals
Aa Vocabulary Personality traits
🧩 **New skill** Talking about hypothetical situations

39.1 KEY LANGUAGE MIXED CONDITIONALS

SECOND CONDITIONAL

Use the second conditional to talk about hypothetical situations in the present.

PAST SIMPLE

If I didn't believe in astrology, I wouldn't read my horoscope.

"WOULD" + INFINITIVE

THIRD CONDITIONAL

Use the third conditional to talk about hypothetical situations in the past.

PAST PERFECT

If I had known he was an Aquarius, I would not have gone out with him.

"WOULD" + "HAVE" + PAST PARTICIPLE

MIXED CONDITIONAL

Mixed conditionals combine second and third conditionals.

If you had been born a month earlier, you would be a Virgo like me.

🔊

39.2 FURTHER EXAMPLES MIXED CONDITIONALS

Mixed conditionals are often used to express regret.

If I had finished my assignment sooner, I could be out with my friends today.

You would be starting a new school tomorrow if you hadn't failed your exams.

You can use mixed conditionals to refer to future situations.

 🔊

39.3 MATCH THE BEGINNINGS OF THE SENTENCES TO THE CORRECT ENDINGS

If you had kept on going to the gym, —————→ you would be fitter by now.

if you hadn't worked so hard at school.

1 You wouldn't be such a success today

if she hadn't had famous parents.

2 If my alarm had gone off,

you wouldn't have such great tickets.

3 She might not be such a celebrity

you would be fitter by now.

4 He would be playing today

I wouldn't be in trouble for being late.

5 If you had spent less money,

I wouldn't be managing the business today.

6 If I had given up trying,

we might not be so hungry now.

7 If we had eaten breakfast,

if he hadn't broken his leg yesterday.

39.4 FILL IN THE GAPS BY PUTTING THE VERBS IN THE CORRECT TENSE

If he _____*had not fixed*_____ (not fix) my car, I would still be walking to work every day.

1 If Clara _____ (not stay) up so late, she might not be so tired now.

2 She might not be a famous actress today if she _____ (not go) to that first audition.

3 If he _____ (keep) playing the guitar, he would be in a famous band by now.

4 If Juan _____ (listen) to all his critics, he would not be a world-famous chef today.

5 He would not be playing for a premier team if he _____ (not train) every day.

6 If she _____ (say) "yes" to your proposal, you could be married by now.

7 They would not be so confident if they _____ (see) their team training yesterday.

You have had good ideas, but you haven't used them sensibly.
True ☑ **False** ☐

❶ You need to get others to invest in your business.
True ☐ **False** ☐

❷ You should be braver in promoting your ideas at work.
True ☐ **False** ☐

❸ You should have said sorry for something yesterday.
True ☐ **False** ☐

❹ You will definitely have an exciting weekend, especially Sunday.
True ☐ **False** ☐

❺ If it's your birthday, today is a good day to care for your friends.
True ☐ **False** ☐

Aa 39.6 USE THE ADJECTIVES FROM THE PANEL TO COMPLETE THE SENTENCES

He reads lots of books and loves going to museums. He's very _intellectual_ .

❶ You need _____ staff who turn up on time and do their work.

❷ He's so _____ . He just jumped into the fire to save the kitten.

❸ My husband is really _____ . He even cries during romantic films.

❹ If he hadn't been so violent and _____ , he would not be in jail today.

❺ If she hadn't been so _____ , she might not be such a successful singer.

❻ Jane is very _____ . She can fix the car and put up shelves.

intellectual   sensitive   determined   courageous   reliable   quick-tempered   practical

🔊

IN YOUR STARS?

HOME | ENTRIES | ABOUT | CONTACT

Diana Carter (24), Scorpio (Oct 24–Nov 22)

I'm a Scorpio and I check my stars every day. I've got an app on my smartphone and it's one of the first things I read in the mornings. If the horoscope says I shouldn't do something, I won't. For example, if it says "Don't travel," then there's no chance of me getting on a plane that day. I know that, logically, it's very unlikely that anything will happen, but I don't want to take the risk. I'm a typical Scorpion because I'm quite passionate about things, but I'm also a little obsessive. I guess that's why I have to check my stars every day!

Richard Davis (22), Sagittarius (Nov 24–Dec 22)

I'm Sagittarius, I think, but I never think about horoscopes. I think that it's all nonsense. I mean, when you read the things that they say will happen to you on a certain day, there's a fair chance that they will happen to most people on most days. Things like "You'll get some news" or "You'll talk to a stranger." I also think that, if you believe in these things, then it is inevitable that the predictions will suit what happens because you will make them fit. I mean, if you wear red because your stars tell you to, and everything is OK, then you can say that the horoscope was right. Apparently, I'm supposed to be intellectual and superficial. I'm not sure how I can be both!

> Diane reads her stars in the newspaper first thing every day.
> _Diane reads her stars on a phone app first thing every day._

1 Diane would not change her plans because of her horoscope's advice.

_____

2 Diane thinks she's a typical Scorpio because she's not very passionate about things.

_____

3 Richard thinks that things a horoscope says will happen are unlikely.

_____

4 He says it's surprising how many times horoscopes make correct predictions.

_____

---

39 ✓ CHECKLIST

⚙ Mixed conditionals ☐   **Aa** Personality traits ☐   🧩 Talking about hypothetical situations ☐

40 Adding "-ever" to question words

Adding "-ever" to question words changes their meaning. These new words modify the question words to mean "no matter" or "it doesn't matter."

⚙️ **New language** Words with "-ever"

Aa Vocabulary Chance and weather phrases

🧩 **New skill** Joining a clause to a sentence

40.1 KEY LANGUAGE QUESTION WORDS WITH "-EVER"

You can use "-ever" words as subjects, objects, or adverbs in their own clauses. They can also be used to join a clause to the rest of a sentence.

I'm still going to the game, whatever the weather's like.

[It doesn't matter what the weather is like. I'm still going.]

Here, "whichever" is an object.

We can take a taxi or walk, whichever you prefer.

[It doesn't matter to me which you choose, taxi or walking.]

Here, "whoever" is a subject.

Whoever invented the umbrella was a very clever person indeed.

[I don't know who invented the umbrella, but they were very clever.]

It always seems to rain whenever I go away.

[Any time I go away, it rains.]

I always check the forecast for wherever I'm going to be.

[I check the forecast for the place I am going to be, no matter where it is.]

Here, "however" is an adverb.

If there's a chance of rain, however small, I'll take an umbrella.

[I'll take an umbrella, no matter how small the risk of rain.]

🔊

40.2 CROSS OUT THE INCORRECT WORD IN EACH SENTENCE

~~Whoever~~ / Whatever choice you make, you know we'll support you.

1 Buy red or green peppers, however / whichever is the cheapest.

2 She moves every few years to wherever / whatever her company asks her to go.

3 I love going to concerts and watching live music, whenever / whoever is playing.

4 My mother never likes my brother's girlfriends, however / whoever nice they are.

5 The company director visits our office whenever / wherever she's in town.

6 The competition winner deserves praise, however / whoever they are.

7 The company is in a difficult situation, whichever / however way you look at it.

◀))

40.3 FILL IN THE GAPS USING THE WORDS IN THE PANEL

I'm happy to go _____wherever_____ you like for a vacation, as long as there's a beach.

1 She's an excellent cook. I'm sure _____ cake I choose will be delicious.

2 Sometimes I just can't start my car _____ I do. It's really frustrating.

3 I don't think I'll ever be a good long-distance runner, _____ hard I try.

4 During the winter months, we can visit the castle for free _____ we want.

5 I will give my full support to the next head chef, _____ it is.

| whatever | whichever | whoever | whenever | ~~wherever~~ | however |

◀))

159

40.4 READ THE EMAIL AND WRITE ANSWERS TO THE QUESTIONS AS FULL SENTENCES

✉

To: Eleri Roberts

Subject: Update from home

Hi Eleri, I hope you're having a great time in Chile! I've had an unusual week here. I got an email saying that I'd won a competition for two free bungee jumps. It was a bit of a bolt from the blue because I'd completely forgotten that I'd even entered the competition!

I was on cloud nine, so I told my sister. I thought she would be overjoyed like me, but she was so moody! You know what she's like, always wanting to get all the attention and trying to steal my thunder. Well, I asked her if she'd do it with me. I thought it would be really funny because she hates heights.

The jump was all planned for Thursday, but as I was driving to her house, she sent me a text message saying that she had the flu and so would have to take a rain check. I thought this was a bit odd because she was as right as rain the night before.

Anyway, I had already decided that I was doing this jump come rain or shine, so I went without her. I jumped off the canal bridge. It was absolutely awesome! So now I'm just going to throw caution to the wind and do a sky dive next year. I already can't wait!

Matt

↩ ⏪   📎 🗑

> Where is Eleri at the moment?
>
> *At the moment, Eleri is in Chile.*

❶ Why was the email from the adventure activity company a surprise?

_____

❷ Why wasn't Matt's sister happy about his prize?

_____

❸ Why did Matt's sister say that she couldn't do the bungee jump?

_____

❹ Where did Matt do the bungee jump?

_____

❺ What is Matt planning to do next year?

_____

She's feeling good and healthy this morning.

Go on. Throw caution to the wind.

1 She looks extremely happy this morning.

She's feeling right as rain this morning.

2 Do it and don't worry about the consequences.

You're constantly trying to steal my thunder.

3 Maybe you should accept the offer at a later date.

The party's happening come rain or shine.

4 You're always trying to take attention away from me.

She seems to be on cloud nine this morning.

5 That news is a great surprise.

Perhaps you should take a rain check.

6 It's going to take place whatever happens.

Wow! That's a bolt from the blue.

40 ✓ CHECKLIST

⚙ Words with "-ever" ☐ Aa Chance and weather phrases ☐ 🧩 Joining a clause to a sentence ☐

♻ REVIEW THE ENGLISH YOU HAVE LEARNED IN UNITS 37–40

NEW LANGUAGE	SAMPLE SENTENCE	☑	UNIT
PAST POSSIBILITY	The printer isn't working. It might have run out of paper.	☐	37.1
REPORTED SPEECH	He said that he didn't believe those ghost stories.	☐	37.4
SPECULATION AND DEDUCTION	Aliens might have taken him to another planet.	☐	38.1
MIXED CONDITIONALS	If you had been born a month earlier, you would be a Virgo like me.	☐	39.1
ADDING "-EVER" TO QUESTION WORDS	I'm still going to the game, whatever the weather's like.	☐	40.1

41 Vocabulary

41.1 MEDIA AND CELEBRITY

The newspapers always sensationalize things.

sensationalize
[make something more dramatic or exciting than it is]

I honestly think that the newspaper exploited that politician.

exploit
[use something or someone for your own gain]

He's a household name in lots of countries.

be a household name
[be known by most people]

All of the publicity has gone to her head.

go to somebody's head
[make somebody feel more important than they are]

Have you seen this morning's newspaper headline?

newspaper headline
[the large text at the top of a newspaper page]

The journalist exposed the politician's lies.

expose
[reveal something hidden]

Nowadays you can become a celebrity without being talented.

become a celebrity
[become a famous person]

My son has always wanted to have his name in lights.

have your name in lights
[be very famous]

She's always been in the public eye. Perhaps she's used to it!

be in the public eye
[be seen and well known by the public]

It seems like her love life is always headline news.

headline news
[news that is widely reported]

The internet has supported the rise of celebrity culture.

celebrity culture
[the popular culture which surrounds famous people]

His real claim to fame was that he could eat five burgers in a row.

claim to fame
[the thing that somebody or something is known for, often said jokingly]

I always vote for my favorites on talent shows.

talent show
[a competition with performances by entertainers showcasing their skills]

There are so many reality shows on TV nowadays.

reality show
[a show based on or around real-life events]

I would hate to be followed everywhere by the paparazzi.

paparazzi
[photographers who take pictures of famous people]

All the stars went to the opening night in Hollywood.

opening night
[the first night of a show or film]

The stars were all on the red carpet this evening.

red carpet
[a carpet for important guests to walk or stand on at an event]

She's had a truly meteoric rise in the film industry.

meteoric rise
[a very rapid rise, often in a career]

Join us for an exclusive interview with the stars of the movie.

exclusive interview
[an interview that no other source has obtained]

She always wears such attention-grabbing outfits.

attention-grabbing
[something designed to get your attention quickly]

42 Reporting with passives

One way to distance yourself from facts is to use the passive voice and reporting verbs. This device is commonly used in newspaper and television journalism.

⚙ **New language** Passive voice for reporting
Aa Vocabulary Reporting language
🧩 **New skill** Distancing yourself from facts

42.1 KEY LANGUAGE REPORTING WITH PASSIVES

A number of structures and reporting verbs can be used in the passive voice to distance the writer or speaker from the facts.

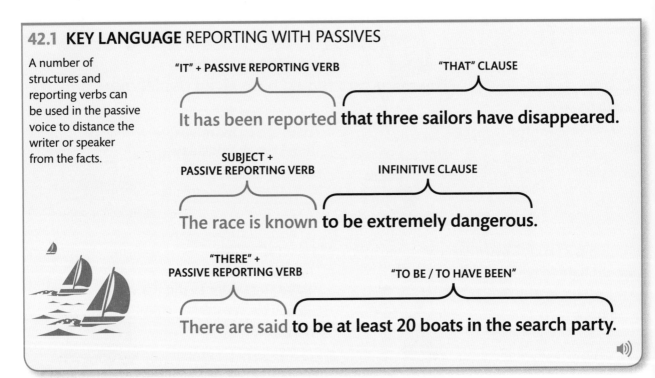

"IT" + PASSIVE REPORTING VERB **"THAT" CLAUSE**

It has been reported **that three sailors have disappeared.**

SUBJECT + PASSIVE REPORTING VERB **INFINITIVE CLAUSE**

The race is known **to be extremely dangerous.**

"THERE" + PASSIVE REPORTING VERB **"TO BE / TO HAVE BEEN"**

There are said **to be at least 20 boats in the search party.**

42.2 MATCH THE BEGINNINGS OF THE SENTENCES TO THE CORRECT ENDINGS

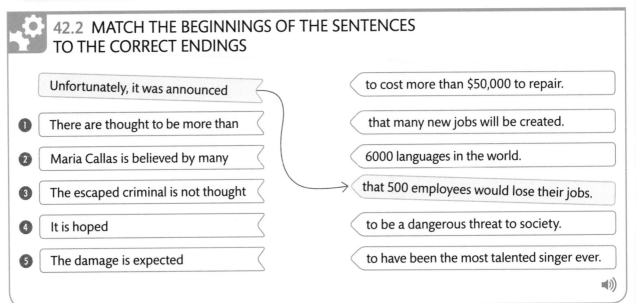

Unfortunately, it was announced ———→ that 500 employees would lose their jobs.

1. There are thought to be more than — to cost more than $50,000 to repair.

2. Maria Callas is believed by many — that many new jobs will be created.

3. The escaped criminal is not thought — 6000 languages in the world.

4. It is hoped — to be a dangerous threat to society.

5. The damage is expected — to have been the most talented singer ever.

42.3 KEY LANGUAGE MODALS IN THE PASSIVE VOICE

Modals in the present can be made passive by replacing the base form of the main verb with "be" plus the past participle.

You should tell Barbara the exciting news.
[The important thing is that you tell her the news.]

Barbara should be told the exciting news.
[The important thing is that Barbara is told the news, not who tells her.]

Modals in the past tense can be made passive by replacing "have" with "have been."

The managers should have given Daniel more time.
[The main issue is what the managers failed to do.]

Daniel should have been given more time.
[The main issue is what Daniel did not get, not the people responsible.]

42.4 FURTHER EXAMPLES MODALS IN THE PASSIVE VOICE

Modal expressing prohibition.

Phones must not be used in school.

Modal expressing desirability (the right thing to do).

Homeless youngsters should be housed here.

Extra tickets may be sold on the day.
Modal expressing possiblity.

It must have been mentioned on the news.
Modal expressing strong probability.

 ## 42.5 CROSS OUT THE INCORRECT WORDS IN EACH SENTENCE

With no exceptions, seat belts must ~~worn~~ / be worn at all times in the vehicle.

❶ I'm so sorry! You should have been / be introduced to each other earlier this evening.

❷ Thirty people are expected to have been / be awarded top prizes at the ceremony later.

❸ It would help if the school children could be given / give different instruments to try.

❹ It's been a strange tournament, and there have been / are thought to be more surprises to come.

42.6 REWRITE THE SENTENCES USING THE PASSIVE VOICE

TIP
Remember that you can sometimes omit the agent (the person or thing doing the action) if the meaning remains clear.

Industry experts must have written the report.

The report _must have been written by industry experts._

1 Somebody should have thanked the hosts of the party before we left.

The hosts _____

2 The journalist reported that 20 people were injured in the stampede.

It has _____

3 Many people think that Pelé was the best soccer player ever.

Pelé is _____

42.7 DESCRIBE THE NEWS OUT LOUD USING PASSIVE REPORTING LANGUAGE

FIVE RESTAURANTS CLOSED

Since the flood, it has been reported _that five restaurants have closed._

TORNADO DESTROYS HOMES

2 Many homes are said _____

_____

YOUTH TEAM WINS CUP

1 It has been announced that the Cup

_____

COUPLE MARRIES IN PARIS

3 This celebrity couple are reported

_____

42.8 FILL IN THE GAPS USING THE CORRECT FORM OF THE VERBS IN THE PANEL

16   THE DAILY HERALD

CRIMINAL NEGLIGENCE

The police in Longerton had a suprisingly easy arrest when a robber was foolish enough to incriminate himself.

Bank robber Mark Thomas is _____ *spending* _____ the night in jail before going to court to be

_____ tomorrow.

Last June, Mr. Thomas, dressed in a mask and hat and armed with a knife, demanded $10,000 from the

cashier of a local bank. He was _____ the money, but at this point

Mr. Thomas' planning skills must be _____ . Instead of escaping the area, Mr. Thomas

took off his hat and mask and walked into the bank next door. He tried to deposit the money and gave the

cashiers his full name, address, and bank details. Fortunately, the police had been _____

by the original bank and Mr. Thomas was quickly _____ .

He is understood to have been _____ the robbery for many months. He stated that

he had been _____ for a vacation, but it was taking too long to raise enough money.

It is _____ that he will be given a lengthy sentence, so he will have to wait even longer

for his trip abroad.

| question | sentence | ~~spend~~ | save | call | predict | arrest | plan | give |

---

42 ✓ CHECKLIST

⚙ Passive voice for reporting ☐   **Aa** Reporting language ☐   🧩 Distancing yourself from facts ☐

43 Making indirect statements

Sometimes you may wish to avoid giving definite facts or personal opinions. This is known as "hedging." Certain words and indirect statements can help you with this.

⚙️ **New language** Indirect statements
Aa Vocabulary Hedging language
🧩 **New skill** Expressing uncertainty

43.1 KEY LANGUAGE HEDGING

Hedging words and phrases can be added to a sentence to make its meaning less definite or direct.

___HEDGING VERBS___ **Polls suggest that locals dislike the new statue.**

___HEDGING ADVERBS___ **It is arguably the strangest statue around.**

___HEDGING PHRASES___ **To some extent, locals feel their views are being ignored.**

43.2 FILL IN THE GAPS USING THE HEDGING LANGUAGE IN THE PANEL

_____Often_____ people use hedging language if they do not have exact figures.

1 There are _____ five hundred employees in this factory.

2 These new figures _____ a downward trend in sales.

3 The director _____ took all of the money from the company.

4 This kind of market behavior _____ an underlying problem.

5 _____ by some that her opinions are controversial.

6 _____ they are not enjoying the film very much.

7 Academics _____ to use hedging language if something is not proven.

| allegedly   indicate   It looks like   tend   approximately   ~~Often~~   It has been said   suggests |

🔊

43.3 KEY LANGUAGE "SEEM" AND "APPEAR"

"Seem" and "appear" are words that you can use to distance yourself from a statement. This is useful if you are not sure if the statement is true.

The prisoners { seem / appear } to have vanished.

"Seem" and "appear" are often followed by another verb in the infinitive.

It { seems / appears } that the prison cell was left unguarded.

You can also use "It seems" or "It appears" followed by a "that" clause.

It would { seem / appear } that a file was used to saw the bars.

"Would" adds even more distance or uncertainty.

43.4 CROSS OUT THE INCORRECT WORDS IN EACH SENTENCE

The detectives seem / ~~suggest~~ to have found an important piece of information.

1. It appears / believes that two prisoners have escaped from the police station.

2. I don't trust her. I think it tends / looks like she is guilty of both crimes.

3. They seem / suggest to have found more important evidence to support their case.

4. I believe / indicate that the police have made a mistake and arrested the wrong man.

5. I don't know, but it would appear / tend that he stole the car when the owner was inside.

6. With a huge number of hit records, the Beatles are arguably / allegedly the best band ever.

7. After a difficult year, all our figures appear / indicate that sales are finally improving.

8. It's too soon to judge. He probably / approximately committed the crime, but we're not sure.

9. We used to go to Spain a lot. Sometimes we drove there, but we often / probably flew.

THE DAILY POST

NEWS | BUSINESS | LIFE

LATEST NEWS

Town in chaos as burglar strikes again

POSTED TUESDAY, 7:00AM

In the lastest incident in what is arguably the most unusual series of crimes in the area, the Daylight Burglar has apparently struck again. It looks like this time he has targeted cheese from victims' refrigerators. It has only been a few days since the last series of burglaries, but it seems that the Daylight Burglar's spree is not over yet. If anything, these new crimes suggest that he has no plans to stop soon.

The Daylight Burglar tends to take fairly unusual items of little value. Last week, single socks were taken from approximately 20 homes. Before that, it was teapots.

It could be said that this burglar is harmless, but that is not how the victims feel. Often, they are left traumatized by the fact that someone has broken into their homes. "It's very scary. To some extent we no longer feel safe at home. We all assume it's a local person, probably a someone we all know," said burglary victim Sasha Johnson.

It would appear that each week the burglar targets one unusual item to steal from people's homes. We believe that the police have no clue who the burglar is, but the evidence indicates that it is someone who likes tea and cheese.

WEATHER   SPORT   TRAVEL   ARTS

ADVERBS	VERBS	PHRASES
arguably	*suggest*	*it looks like*

43.6 LISTEN TO THE AUDIO AND ANSWER THE QUESTIONS

A local news station is reporting about a
popular video that has been posted online.

The report is about a video that was famous last year.	**True** ☐ **False** ☑

① The video was recorded on Sara's mother's smartphone.   **True** ☐ **False** ☐

② The video has been watched just under a million times.   **True** ☐ **False** ☐

③ The cat screeched and waved her paws at the hissing snake.   **True** ☐ **False** ☐

④ The snake, or a similar one, had been seen on other properties.   **True** ☐ **False** ☐

⑤ The animal charity said that these snakes often attack young people.   **True** ☐ **False** ☐

43.7 FILL IN THE GAPS IN THE SUMMARY USING THE HEDGING LANGUAGE IN THE PANEL

It _____*looks*_____ like three-year-old Sara Wilson is fine after her brush with a snake last week.

① An online video _____ shows her pet cat, Mini, protecting her.

② _____ that the snake was frightened away by Mini.

③ Interviews with neighbors _____ that the snake had been seen on other properties.

④ A local animal charity _____ that it would be unusual for such a snake to attack.

⑤ The charity said that these snakes _____ to be extremely shy.

⑥ They also stated that _____ these kinds of snakes are pets that have escaped.

~~looks~~	tend	often	suggested	indicate	apparently	It would appear

◀))

---

43 ✓ CHECKLIST

⚙ Indirect statements ☐   **Aa** Hedging language ☐   🧩 Expressing uncertainty ☐

44 Adding emphasis

You can add emphasis, or even a sense of drama, to a statement through grammar and pronunciation. Inversion is one effective way to do this.

⚙ **New language** Inversion after adverbials
Aa Vocabulary Media and celebrity
🧩 **New skill** Adding emphasis to statements

44.1 KEY LANGUAGE INVERSION AFTER NEGATIVE ADVERBIALS

In more formal or literary texts, inversion (when the normal order of words is reversed) is used for emphasis after negative adverbial phrases like "not only," "not since," and "only when."

In this simple sentence, the subject comes before the verb.

She is a famous singer. She is also a very good actor.

Not only is she a famous singer, but she's also a very good actor.

After the negative adverbial, the subject and the verb swap places.

44.2 FURTHER EXAMPLES INVERSION AFTER NEGATIVE ADVERBIALS

Negative adverbials are generally followed by auxiliary verb + subject.

Not since **I was a teenager** have I **enjoyed a performance so much.**
Not until **the performance was over** did he **look up at the audience.**

Where there is no auxiliary verb, "do" is used.

Only if **it stops raining** will the race **go ahead this afternoon.**
Only when **he emerged from the car** did the fans **start cheering.**
Only after **the race** did he **realize what he had achieved.**

Little do they know **how lucky they are to be successful.**
Little did they realize **how difficult fame would be.**

44.3 CROSS OUT THE INCORRECT WORDS IN EACH SENTENCE

 Not since 2003 ~~we had~~ / had we seen such a dramatic match.

 1 Little he did / did he know that someone else had already invented the same thing.

 2 Only after living there for two weeks did they / they did notice the smell.

 3 Not when / until we spoke to the manager did the company admit their mistake.

 4 Not since the children were little had we / we had been on such a fun day out.

 5 Only when / until she won the award did people start taking her writing seriously.

44.4 FILL IN THE GAPS USING THE WORDS IN THE PANEL

Not ___*since*___ the 1990 World Cup has the team reached the quarter finals.

1 _____ if the company invests more money can the project be completed.

2 _____ until the wedding day did the groom see the bride's dress.

3 Little did they _____ that the weather would be absolutely terrible for the festival.

4 Not _____ the final encore did the audience begin to leave their seats at the concert.

5 Only _____ she was paying for the album did she realize she already owned it.

6 Not _____ will you be famous, but you will also be rich beyond your wildest dreams.

7 Only _____ she got home from the party did she notice how late it was.

| ~~since~~ | Not | when | realize | after | until | Only | only |

173

44.5 KEY LANGUAGE INVERSION AFTER TIME ADVERBIALS

You can also emphasize when something happened by using inversion after time adverbials like "no sooner" and "never before."

In this simple sentence, the subject comes before the verb.

Tina had **just released an album when she starred in her first movie.**

No sooner had Tina **released an album than she starred in her first movie.**

The subject ("Tina") and the auxiliary verb ("had") swap places.

44.6 FURTHER EXAMPLES INVERSION AFTER TIME ADVERBIALS

Hardly had she **stepped out of the car when fans surrounded her.**

Never before had a song **reached the top of the charts so quickly.**

Rarely do you **meet a celebrity with such talent and style.**

44.7 REWRITE THE SENTENCES TO SHIFT THE EMPHASIS USING THE PROMPTS

They don't go to the movies together often. [rarely]
Rarely do they go to the movies together.

❶ He only felt safe at home. [only when]

❷ Fans chanted his name as soon as he walked on stage. [hardly]

❸ They became the number one band and then split up immediately. [no sooner]

❹ It was the first time anyone had seen so many fans in one place. [never before]

44.8 LISTEN TO THE AUDIO AND ANSWER THE QUESTIONS

Two friends, Marta and Jeremy, are discussing celebrities and their children.

	True	False
Marta has just seen Don and Sara Moran on a television show.	☐	✓
1 Don has always encouraged people to photograph his children.	☐	☐
2 Jeremy thinks the parents may have made a deal with the photographers.	☐	☐
3 Marta dislikes photos of celebrities' children in the papers.	☐	☐
4 Marta suspects that Don and Sara want their children to be famous.	☐	☐

44.9 REWRITE THE SENTENCES PUTTING THE WORDS IN THE CORRECT ORDER

alarm | lunch | had | went | off. | I | finished | the | Hardly | when

Hardly had I finished lunch when the alarm went off.

1 rain | stopped | sooner | No | than | it | the | had | snow. | to | began

2 did | she | Only | she | when | heard | recognize | him. | his | voice

3 this | car | is | Not | affordable! | but | only | also | it's | fast,

4 if | you | will | help | me | Only | I | finish | on | time.

44 ✓ CHECKLIST

⚙ Inversion after adverbials ☐   **Aa** Media and celebrity ☐   🧩 Adding emphasis to statements ☐

45 Shifting focus

You can add emphasis to part of a sentence in English by splitting it into two clauses. This allows you to focus attention on the the new or important information.

⚙ **New language** Focusing with clauses
Aa Vocabulary Phrases for emphasis
🧩 **New skill** Shifting focus

45.1 KEY LANGUAGE FOCUSING WITH "WHAT" CLAUSES

You can add "what" with the verb "be" to a simple statement to make it more emphatic. This structure is often used with verbs expressing emotions, such as "love," "hate," "like," and "want."

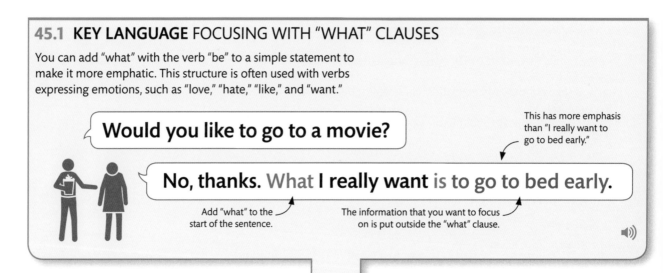

Would you like to go to a movie?

No, thanks. What I really want is to go to bed early.

This has more emphasis than "I really want to go to bed early."

Add "what" to the start of the sentence.

The information that you want to focus on is put outside the "what" clause.

45.2 FURTHER EXAMPLES FOCUSING WITH "WHAT" CLAUSES

What we hated was the bad service.   **What I like here is the weather.**

What they loved the most were the museums.

45.3 MATCH THE BEGINNINGS OF THE SENTENCES TO THE CORRECT ENDINGS

What annoyed him the most was — the lack of communication.

1 What I would really appreciate is

2 What we really need are

3 What I love about this city is

4 What businesses really hate is

some legal advice.

when people leave bad reviews online.

more volunteers to help during the week.

the lack of communication.

the nightlife and the culture.

45.4 KEY LANGUAGE FOCUSING WITH A NOUN

If the subject of the sentence cannot be replaced with "what" (for example, people, places, or times) you can use a general noun that has a similar meaning.

I've been to many countries.
The place **I most enjoyed visiting** was Nepal.

I've read about some great people.
The woman **I respect the most** is Marie Curie.

I don't know why the show was canceled.
The reason **they gave** was not good enough.

I have lots of fun memories.
The evening **I most remember** is my first concert.

🔊

45.5 FILL IN THE GAPS USING THE NOUNS IN THE PANEL

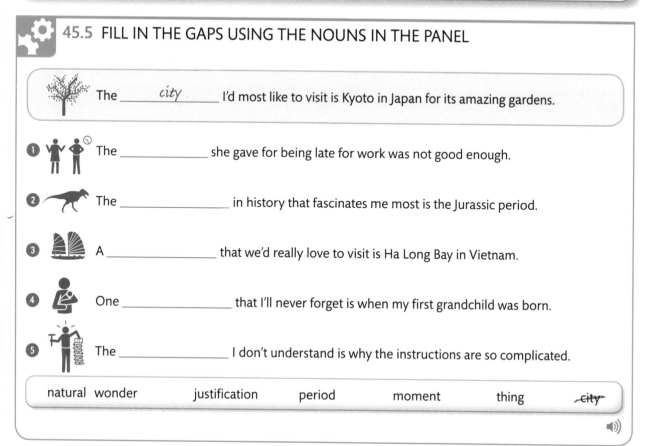

The _____*city*_____ I'd most like to visit is Kyoto in Japan for its amazing gardens.

❶ The _____ she gave for being late for work was not good enough.

❷ The _____ in history that fascinates me most is the Jurassic period.

❸ A _____ that we'd really love to visit is Ha Long Bay in Vietnam.

❹ One _____ that I'll never forget is when my first grandchild was born.

❺ The _____ I don't understand is why the instructions are so complicated.

| natural wonder | justification | period | moment | thing | ~~city~~ |

🔊

45.6 KEY LANGUAGE FOCUSING WITH "IT" CLAUSES

You can also emphasize part of a sentence by adding "it is" or "it was" and "that."

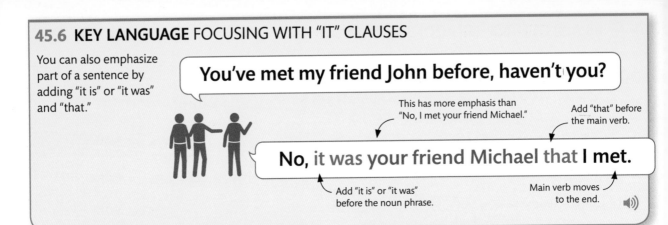

You've met my friend John before, haven't you?

No, it was your friend Michael that I met.

This has more emphasis than "No, I met your friend Michael."

Add "that" before the main verb.

Add "it is" or "it was" before the noun phrase.

Main verb moves to the end.

45.7 FURTHER EXAMPLES FOCUSING WITH "IT" CLAUSES

The second clause is most commonly introduced by "that," but "which" or "who" (and, less formally, "when" and "where") can also be used.

It is the engine that I need to replace.

It was the doctor who I needed to call.

It was 1998 when I last saw my cousins.

45.8 RESPOND TO THE AUDIO OUT LOUD, USING FOCUSING CLAUSES

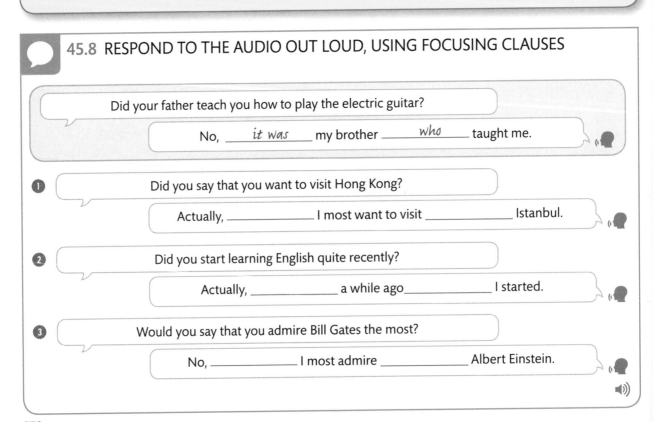

Did your father teach you how to play the electric guitar?

No, _____it was_____ my brother _____who_____ taught me.

❶ Did you say that you want to visit Hong Kong?

Actually, _____ I most want to visit _____ Istanbul.

❷ Did you start learning English quite recently?

Actually, _____ a while ago_____ I started.

❸ Would you say that you admire Bill Gates the most?

No, _____ I most admire _____ Albert Einstein.

45.9 LISTEN TO THE AUDIO AND ANSWER THE QUESTIONS

A parenting expert is giving a radio interview about social networks and digital parenting skills.

The expert says it's easy to keep up-to-date with digital trends.	**True** ☐	**False** ☑

1 She says that there is a lot of online help for parents.   **True** ☐   **False** ☐

2 She encourages parents to set up their own social networking accounts.   **True** ☐   **False** ☐

3 She says young people should only think carefully about what they post publicly.   **True** ☐   **False** ☐

4 It is quite easy to change or delete your digital footprint.   **True** ☐   **False** ☐

5 The CEO said people might have to change their names in the future.   **True** ☐   **False** ☐

---

45 ✓ CHECKLIST

⚙ Focusing with clauses ☐   **Aa** Phrases for emphasis ☐   🧩 Shifting focus ☐

↻ REVIEW THE ENGLISH YOU HAVE LEARNED IN UNITS 42–45

NEW LANGUAGE	SAMPLE SENTENCE	☑	UNIT
REPORTING WITH PASSIVES	It has been reported that **three sailors have disappeared.**	☐	42.1
MODALS IN THE PASSIVE	**Barbara** should be told **the exciting news.**	☐	42.3
HEDGING	**It is** arguably **the strangest statue around.** **The prisoners** seem to have **vanished.**	☐	43.1, 43.3
INVERSION AFTER NEGATIVE ADVERBIALS	Not only is she **a famous singer, but she's also a very good actor.**	☐	44.1
INVERSION AFTER TIME ADVERBIALS	No sooner had Tina **released an album than she starred in her first movie.**	☐	44.5
FOCUSING WITH "WHAT" CLAUSES AND NOUNS	What **I really want** is to go to bed early. The place **I most enjoyed visiting** was Nepal.	☐	45.1, 45.4
FOCUSING WITH "IT" CLAUSES	**No,** it was your friend Michael that **I met.**	☐	45.6

46 Vocabulary

46.1 CRIME AND THE LAW

He refused to admit he had committed a crime.

commit a crime
[break the law]

I got away with cheating in my last exam.

get away with something
[do a bad thing without being caught]

She denied all knowledge of the gang and their activities.

deny all knowledge
[say that you know nothing about something or somebody]

The jury was chosen from a random group of people.

jury
[the people who decide whether a person is guilty of a crime]

It took the jury several hours to reach a verdict.

reach a verdict
[come to a decision about somebody's guilt or innocence]

In the end the jury found him guilty of the robbery.

find somebody (not) guilty
[officially decide that someone has (not) broken the law]

They were sure beyond reasonable doubt that she did it.

(beyond) reasonable doubt
[(without) uncertainty about somebody's guilt]

The jury convicted the criminal and the judge sent him to prison.

convict a criminal
[find somebody guilty of a crime]

She was sentenced to 80 hours of community service.

sentence somebody to something
[decide on a punishment in accordance with the law]

This morning the judge passed sentence on the attacker.

pass sentence
[say what punishment a criminal will have]

He was released from prison after serving a sentence of five years.

serve a sentence
[spend time in prison]

The police help enforce the law.

enforce
[make people obey a rule or a law]

After he left prison, he never offended again.

offend
[break a law or a rule]

They arrested the woman for damaging cars.

arrest
[use the power of the law to take and question somebody]

In most countries it is the law that all cars must be insured.

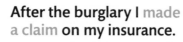

be insured
[be covered by insurance]

After the burglary I made a claim on my insurance.

make a claim
[request that an insurance company pays you money]

It can be difficult to get a job with a criminal record.

criminal record
[a list of crimes that a person has committed]

Fewer police officers on the street may lead to a crime wave.

crime wave
[a lot of crimes happening suddenly in the same area]

The rate of street crime, such as mugging, has risen.

street crime
[crime committed in a public place]

Police are training more experts to deal with white-collar crime.

white-collar crime
[financial, nonviolent crime]

47 Relative clauses

Relative clauses are sections of a sentence that provide more information about a noun in the main statement. They can be defining or non-defining.

⚙ **New language** Relative clauses
Aa Vocabulary Crime and criminals
New skill Specifying and elaborating

47.1 KEY LANGUAGE DEFINING RELATIVE CLAUSES

Relative clauses are made up of a subject, a verb, and usually an object. They usually start with a relative pronoun, which can be the subject or the object of the relative clause. Defining relative clauses specify which person or thing you're talking about in the main clause.

Here the relative pronoun "who" is the subject of the relative clause.

MAIN CLAUSE
SUBJECT + VERB + OBJECT

RELATIVE CLAUSE
SUBJECT + VERB + OBJECT

I'm writing about people who are in prison.

"Who" is the subject of "are."

Here the relative pronoun "which" is the object of the relative clause.

MAIN CLAUSE
SUBJECT + VERB + OBJECT

RELATIVE CLAUSE
OBJECT + SUBJECT + VERB

This is the car which the criminal stole.

"Which" is the object of "stole."

"The criminal" is the subject of "stole."

47.2 MARK WHETHER THE RELATIVE PRONOUN IS THE SUBJECT OR THE OBJECT OF THE RELATIVE CLAUSE

This is the criminal **that** I saw.
Subject ☐ **Object** ☑

① The man **who** went to prison was innocent.
Subject ☐ **Object** ☐

② This is the man **who** called the police.
Subject ☐ **Object** ☐

③ That's the bank **that** she robbed last week.
Subject ☐ **Object** ☐

④ Did you believe the story **that** he told you?
Subject ☐ **Object** ☐

⑤ Some police wear jackets **that** protect them.
Subject ☐ **Object** ☐

⑥ Did you see the man **who** was driving the car?
Subject ☐ **Object** ☐

⑦ That's the security alarm **that** I told you about.
Subject ☐ **Object** ☐

47.3 KEY LANGUAGE RELATIVE PRONOUNS

English uses different relative pronouns to talk about people and things.

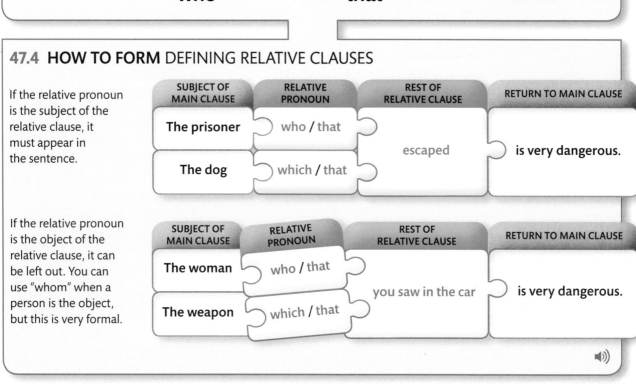

47.4 HOW TO FORM DEFINING RELATIVE CLAUSES

If the relative pronoun is the subject of the relative clause, it must appear in the sentence.

SUBJECT OF MAIN CLAUSE	RELATIVE PRONOUN	REST OF RELATIVE CLAUSE	RETURN TO MAIN CLAUSE
The prisoner	who / that	escaped	is very dangerous.
The dog	which / that		

If the relative pronoun is the object of the relative clause, it can be left out. You can use "whom" when a person is the object, but this is very formal.

SUBJECT OF MAIN CLAUSE	RELATIVE PRONOUN	REST OF RELATIVE CLAUSE	RETURN TO MAIN CLAUSE
The woman	who / that	you saw in the car	is very dangerous.
The weapon	which / that		

47.5 MATCH UP THE PARTS OF THE SENTENCES

The dogs	is a person	are very well trained.
① Those children	is the one	who want to be detectives.
② That computer	that work with the police	the criminal.
③ This is the officer	that I use	to make video calls.
④ A cybercriminal	who arrested	that was stolen.
⑤ That is the phone	are the ones	who acts illegally online.

47.6 KEY LANGUAGE NON-DEFINING RELATIVE CLAUSES

Non-defining relative clauses say more about a noun in the main clause. The main clause would still make sense without it.

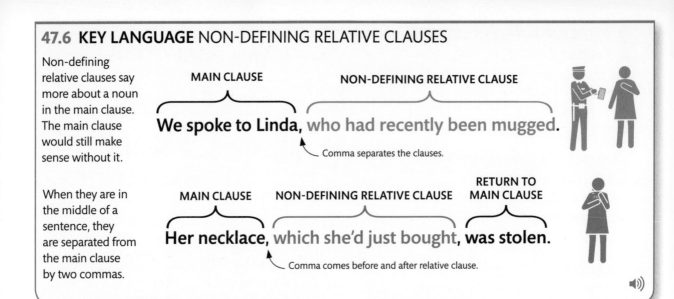

MAIN CLAUSE

NON-DEFINING RELATIVE CLAUSE

We spoke to Linda, who had recently been mugged.

Comma separates the clauses.

When they are in the middle of a sentence, they are separated from the main clause by two commas.

MAIN CLAUSE   NON-DEFINING RELATIVE CLAUSE   RETURN TO MAIN CLAUSE

Her necklace, which she'd just bought, was stolen.

Comma comes before and after relative clause.

47.7 FURTHER EXAMPLES NON-DEFINING RELATIVE CLAUSES

The suspect, whom we had been following, was arrested.

"Whom" is only used in very formal situations.

All the burglars were arrested, which was a great relief.

The relative pronoun can refer to the entire previous clause

47.8 REWRITE THE SENTENCES, ADDING COMMAS WHERE NECESSARY

The burglars who were arrested last night will be in court today.
The burglars, who were arrested last night, will be in court today.

❶ The violent criminals were not sent to jail which surprised the victim.

_____

❷ Detective Smith who arrested the fraudster works in a special department.

_____

❸ Vivian Jones who had worked for the bank for 10 years was arrested yesterday.

_____

47.9 LISTEN TO THE AUDIO AND ANSWER THE QUESTIONS

Five people are being asked how they would cut crime in the city.

When does Joan think young people should be banned from the city center?

On Saturdays	☐
Before 10pm	☐
After 10pm	☑

1 Where does Derrick think there should be more surveillance cameras?

On every street corner	☐
On a few street corners	☐
In bars and restaurants	☐

2 What should bars and restaurants do, according to Maxine?

Help to clear up the trash	☐
Stop serving takeout food	☐
Charge more money for takeout food	☐

3 What does Javier think should happen to troublemakers?

They ought to spend a night in a police cell.	☐
They ought to be banned from the city.	☐
They ought to be fined.	☐

4 What does Tamal think should happen to the young people?

Other places should be built for them.	☐
They should be banned from city centers.	☐
They should annoy other people instead.	☐

47.10 READ THE ARTICLE AND ANSWER THE QUESTIONS

PIZZA POLICE!

Police deliver two years for a pizza craving.

Burglar Dan Weatley let his need for a pizza get him into big trouble last month. One afternoon, he broke into a house and stole jewelry, a laptop, and a credit card. As soon as the owner returned home, she called the police and then her bank to report the stolen credit card. Meanwhile Dan, who felt hungry after his busy day, ordered a pizza using the victim's card. The bank alerted the police about the use of the credit card. The police officers, who went with the pizza delivery man to Weatley's home address, found all the day's stolen goods and more from previous burglaries. Mr. Weatley, who admitted committing the burglaries, was yesterday sent to prison for two years.

Weatley carried out the crime in the daytime.
True ☑ **False** ☐ **Not given** ☐

1 The victim called the police and her bank.
True ☐ **False** ☐ **Not given** ☐

2 The pizza company told the police that the stolen credit card had been used.
True ☐ **False** ☐ **Not given** ☐

3 Weatley ordered a pizza to the house he had broken into.
True ☐ **False** ☐ **Not given** ☐

4 Weatley had previously been to jail for burglary.
True ☐ **False** ☐ **Not given** ☐

---

47 ✔ CHECKLIST

⚙ Relative clauses ☐   **Aa** Crime and criminals ☐   🧩 Specifying and elaborating ☐

48 More relative clauses

Relative words define or describe a noun in the main part of the sentence. Different relative words are used depending on the nouns that they relate to.

⚙ **New language** Where, when, whereby, whose
Aa Vocabulary Courtroom phrases
🧩 **New skill** Using relative words

48.1 KEY LANGUAGE "WHERE," "WHEN," AND "WHEREBY"

"Where" is the relative word used to refer to a place.

That is the place where the judge sits.
[The judge sits there.]

"When" is the relative word used to refer to a time.

He is looking forward to the day when he'll be released from prison.
[He's looking forward to the day of his release.]

"Whereby" is the relative word used to refer to a process.

A trial is the process whereby a person is found guilty or innocent of a crime.
[To be found guilty, you must go through a trial process.]

48.2 CROSS OUT THE INCORRECT WORDS IN EACH SENTENCE

That is the restaurant where / ~~when~~ / ~~whereby~~ we first met.

1. Courtrooms are places where / when / whereby lawyers argue their cases in front of a judge.

2. Thursday is the night where / when / whereby we usually go to the movies.

3. Sentencing is the legal process where / when / whereby a judge decides the punishment.

4. Morning coffee break is the time where / when / whereby we gossip most.

5. A police station is the place where / when / whereby most criminals are taken at first.

48.3 FILL IN THE GAPS USING THE PHRASES IN THE PANEL AND "WHERE," "WHEN," OR "WHEREBY"

Prison is the place _____ *where most criminals* _____ serve their sentences.

❶ The camera's timer let the police know the exact time _____ .

❷ They have developed a system _____ for life outside jail.

❸ Do you know the date _____ goes to court?

❹ This is the café _____ great food for the public.

❺ Conveyancing is a process _____ to another.

❻ I remember the day _____ to become a lawyer.

❼ This cell is the place _____ are held until a verdict is reached.

one person sells property   ~~most criminals~~   prisoners can prepare   the suspect

the robbery took place   the suspects   the prisoners cook   my sister decided

🔊

48.4 LISTEN TO THE AUDIO AND ANSWER THE QUESTIONS

Two members of a jury are talking about a burglary trial.

The man is unsure if the defendant is guilty.
True ☐ **False** ☐ **Not given** ☑

❶ The woman suggests that they take a vote.
True ☐ **False** ☐ **Not given** ☐

❷ Most of the people think that he's guilty.
True ☐ **False** ☐ **Not given** ☐

❸ The defendant had been to jail before.
True ☐ **False** ☐ **Not given** ☐

❹ The woman says the defendant was well dressed.
True ☐ **False** ☐ **Not given** ☐

❺ The defendant appeared on security video footage.
True ☐ **False** ☐ **Not given** ☐

❻ Several computers were stolen in the burglary.
True ☐ **False** ☐ **Not given** ☐

❼ The defendant said that he was unable to drive.
True ☐ **False** ☐ **Not given** ☐

48.5 KEY LANGUAGE "WHOSE"

"Whose" is the relative word used to show possession or belonging.

This is the lawyer whose client lied in court.

[This lawyer's client lied in court.]

48.6 FURTHER EXAMPLES "WHOSE"

"Whose" can also be used to refer to things that belong to countries, organizations, towns, and so on.

The UK is an example of a country whose traffic laws are very strict.

[This UK has very strict traffic laws.]

Smith & Smith, whose success rate is very high, is a very well-respected law firm.

[Smith & Smith has a very high success rate.]

48.7 REWRITE THE SENTENCES USING "WHOSE"

Judge Wright hand writes all her letters. Her computer skills are not very good.

Judge Wright, whose computer skills are not very good, hand writes all her letters.

① Rodrigo deserves to be successful. His training regime is rigorous.

_____

② My sister has become very famous. Her first book was a huge success.

_____

③ My neighbor Sara loves training dogs. Her dogs always win competitions.

_____

④ That company has excellent trading figures. Its employees work very hard.

_____

⑤ That school is very well respected. Their students always do well in exams.

_____

JURY FINDS HOCKLY GUILTY

Burglar sentenced to 18 months for theft

Burglar Gavin Hockly was jailed for 18 months yesterday. The jury, who had taken two days to reach a decision, finally found Hockly guilty last week. He was accused of stealing a computers from a small technology firm. Hockly, had pleaded not guilty, but the jury did not believe his evidence.

Police originally arrested Hockly when they checked security video footage of the street in front of the burgled premises. He was seen walking around the area each of the six days leading up to the burglary. Hockly said that he was visiting a friend in the area, but when the police asked for more details, he could not remember the full name of his friend or where he lived.

The stolen computers were taken by car to a garage where they were later discovered by police. Despite saying that he

could not drive, the jury was shown videos found on social media of Hockly driving a car.

The most important evidence against Hockly was that his fingerprints were found on the stolen computers. Hockly said that someone had asked him to help carry the computers from the back of a van into the garage. The jury clearly did not believe his account of events.

How long did the jury take to find Gavin Hockly guilty?
The jury took two days to find him guilty.

1 What made the police arrest Hockly in the first place?

_____

2 Why couldn't the police interview the friend Hockly was visiting?

_____

3 Why did the jurors not believe that Hockly could not drive?

_____

4 Why did Hockly say his fingerprints were on the computers?

_____

---

48 ⊘ CHECKLIST

⚙ Where, when, whereby, whose ☐   **Aa** Courtroom phrases ☐   🧩 Using relative words ☐

Modal verbs in the future

Some modal verbs change form when used to talk about the future. Others cannot be used in the future at all, and have to be replaced with other modal verbs or phrases.

⚙ **New language** "Will be able to," "will have to"
Aa Vocabulary Legal terms
✹ **New skill** Expressing future ability and obligation

49.1 KEY LANGUAGE "CAN" IN THE FUTURE

It is not grammatically possible to talk about the future using "can." "Will be able to" is used instead.

At the moment, I can play the trombone quite well.

⬇

If I work harder, I will be able to play at concerts.

"Will can" is incorrect.

The negative is formed with "not able to" or "unable to."

Unfortunately, I can't read music very well.

⬇

If I don't learn, I won't be able to join the orchestra.

You can also use "will be unable to," but it's less common.

49.2 REWRITE THE SENTENCES TO REFER TO THE FUTURE

Can the police find a way to stop people from littering?
Will the police be able to find a way to stop people from littering?

❶ Unfortunately, he can't pay his parking fines.

_____

❷ Can you install a security camera in the store?

_____

❸ I can't understand all these legal regulations.

_____

❹ Hopefully, my sister can explain it all to me. She's a lawyer.

_____

49.3 KEY LANGUAGE "MUST" AND "HAVE TO" IN THE FUTURE

There is no future form of "must." The future of "have to" is formed with the auxiliary verb "will."

In some countries, people { must / have to } recycle. It's the law.

In the future, I think everyone **will have to** recycle.

"Will must" is incorrect.

The negative is formed by adding "not" between "will" and "have."

One day, I hope I **will not have to** work so hard.

49.4 REWRITE THE SENTENCES PUTTING THE WORDS IN THE CORRECT ORDER

| I | parking | fine? | have | Will | pay | to | a |

Will I have to pay a parking fine?

① have | You | will | to | longer | work | soon. | hours

_____

② able | you | be | won't | here. | to | park | Tomorrow

_____

③ able | them? | Will | police | arrest | to | be | the

_____

④ police. | will | I | have | the | to | call

_____

⑤ law? | Will | enforce | they | to | new | be | able | the

_____

191

WORLD

GET OUT OF MY LANE!

Two-speed walking lanes are becoming increasingly common in shopping malls.

More and more shopping malls around the world are planning to introduce two-speed walking lanes for shoppers, consisting of a fast lane and a slow lane. The fast lanes are for shoppers who are in a hurry, but anyone who wants to browse slowly or use their phone as they walk has to use the slow lane.

Shopping malls in cities such as Chongqing, Antwerp, and Liverpool have already introduced this system. The idea is that faster people will be able to overtake slower shoppers. Researchers have found that younger shoppers in particular are really frustrated by people walking slowly. Mall owners worry that this frustration might encourage people to stay away and shop online instead.

However, the plans are not without their downsides. Some people argue that officials will not be able to enforce the new rules effectively. And in Chongqing, it has been reported that many shoppers were too busy looking at their phones to notice that they were straying into the wrong lane!

Who are the two different walking lanes for?

One is for fast walkers and one is for those who want to walk slowly.

① Where have these lanes already been introduced?

_____

② Who are particularly frustrated by slower shoppers?

_____

③ Why are shopping malls concerned about these frustrated shoppers?

_____

④ What difficulty might officials face with the two-speed lanes system?

_____

⑤ What was one of the problems with the scheme when it was introduced in Chongqing?

_____

49.6 LISTEN TO THE AUDIO AND FILL IN THE GAPS USING THE WORDS IN THE PANEL

 A radio show is reporting on a new law concerning farmers' land.

A new law has just been _____*passed*_____ by the government. This new law _____ members of the public to walk on farmers' land. Walkers will have to _____ reasonable rules set by the landowners. If they _____ these rules, they could be _____ from walking in the area or they could even be _____. Some farmers, however, think that the police will not be able to _____ the law.

permits   banned   break   observe   enforce   ~~passed~~   arrested

49.7 READ THE CLUES AND WRITE THE ANSWERS IN THE CORRECT PLACES ON THE GRID

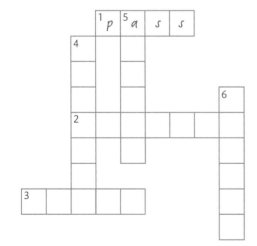

1. To make a new law or rule official
2. To follow a rule or law
3. To not follow a rule or law
4. To make sure a rule or law is obeyed
5. To stop someone and take them to a police station
6. To allow something to happen

enforce   ~~pass~~   permit
break   arrest   observe

50 Modal verbs overview

Modal verbs are used to talk about likelihood, ability, permission, and obligation, among other things. They often refer to hypothetical situations.

⚙ **New language** Using modal verbs
Aa Vocabulary Modal verbs
🧩 **New skill** Asking, offering, and predicting

50.1 KEY LANGUAGE MODAL VERBS

Modal verbs share certain characteristics. They don't change form depending on the subject, they are always followed by an infinitive, and their question and negative forms are made without "do."

| Logical deductions | It can't be Jane because she's on vacation.
It could / might / may be Dave. I don't know.
It should be my dad. He said he'd call me.
It must be Tom, since nobody else ever calls. |

| Obligation | You must arrive on time for work. |

| Permission | You can have more cake if you want.
You may take as much as you like. |

| Ability | I can speak three languages.
I can't read Latin because it's too difficult.
I couldn't study it when I was at school. |

| Requests | Can / Could you give me a ride home later?
Would you email James for me, please?
Will you lock up the office tonight? |

| Advice and suggestions | You should / ought to go to the doctor.
You could try the new medicine. |

| Offers | Can I help you with those?
Shall I carry some of your bags? |

50.2 FILL IN THE GAPS USING THE MODAL VERBS IN THE PANEL

The rules say that you _____*must*_____ finish before 5pm.

1 I appreciate that it's difficult, but I think you _____ talk to him about it.

2 Finally, after months of studying, I _____ read music.

3 I'm sorry, but I'm terribly busy at the moment, Mr. Jones. _____ tomorrow be okay?

4 I followed the recipe, so it _____ to taste great, but sometimes it doesn't.

5 I've tried really hard, but I just _____ make these figures add up.

6 I'm feeling very unwell. _____ I be excused?

| can't | can | ~~must~~ | should | May | would | ought |

50.3 CROSS OUT THE INCORRECT WORDS IN EACH SENTENCE

  Before you drive a car on your own, you ~~will~~ / ~~could~~ / must pass a test.

1   It's very hot in here. Would / Should / Shall you open a window, please?

2   This coffee has sugar in it! It will / must / ought to be yours.

3   I don't know when the movie will finish. It can / shall / might not be until after 10pm.

4   Shall / Would / Will I help you carry those dishes to the kitchen?

5   My lawnmower has broken. Could / Should / Would I borrow yours, please?

6   I can't / should / ought to swim very well at all, but my sister is an excellent swimmer.

50.4 REWRITE THE SENTENCES CORRECTING THE ERRORS

You should have took your shoes off when you enter the building.
You should have taken your shoes off when you entered the building.

1 She was was the lead singer in the band because she did could sing very well.

_____

2 Do you would pick me up from work this evening, please?

_____

3 The tree looks like it may to fall down soon.

_____

4 If she doesn't study hard enough, she doesn't might get into medical school.

_____

🔊

50.5 READ THE TEXT AND ANSWER THE QUESTIONS

Little cultural differences often shock students the most.
True ✓ **False** ☐

1 Some students are surprised that British houses have shutters.
True ☐ **False** ☐

2 Some students think British people eat a lot of potatoes.
True ☐ **False** ☐

3 One student said that he ate mashed potatoes every night with his host family.
True ☐ **False** ☐

4 In the UK, most animals must stay outside at night.
True ☐ **False** ☐

Student surprises!

What surprises exchange students when they stay with British families?

More often than not, it's the small cultural differences that shock students the most when they stay with British families. Some students, for example, are surprised that houses have curtains, rather than shutters. Other students say they are shocked by the amount of potatoes that British people eat. One student once said to me, "Tonight, it could be mashed, it might be fried or it may even be boiled but, whatever it is, it will be potatoes!"

The British love of pets can also surprise students, and the fact that pets can sleep inside the house or even in bedrooms can be shocking for some. In many cultures, animals must stay outside.

Simon is telling his friend about his recent trip to the United States.

What does Simon say about the internal flights?

They cost too much ☐
They were easy to book ☐
They were fairly cheap ☑

❷ According to Simon, what should you **not** do with chopsticks?

Leave them standing in rice ☐
Eat rice with them ☐
Use the same pair more than once ☐

❶ What type of accommodation did Simon stay in?

Hotels ☐
B&Bs ☐
Family homes ☐

❸ What did Simon think about spending time with a Native-American family?

It was really interesting ☐
It was fairly interesting ☐
It was really boring ☐

---

50 ⊘ CHECKLIST

⚙ Using modal verbs ☐   **Aa** Modal verbs ☐   🧩 Asking, offering, and predicting ☐

♺ REVIEW THE ENGLISH YOU HAVE LEARNED IN UNITS 47–50

NEW LANGUAGE	SAMPLE SENTENCE	☑	UNIT
DEFINING RELATIVE CLAUSES	I'm writing about people who are in prison. This is the car which the criminal stole.	☐	47.1
NON-DEFINING RELATIVE CLAUSES	We spoke to a Linda, who had been mugged. Her necklace, which she'd just bought, was stolen.	☐	47.6
"WHERE," "WHEN," "WHEREBY"	That is the place where the judge sits.	☐	48.1
"WHOSE"	This is the lawyer whose client lied in court.	☐	48.5
"CAN" IN THE FUTURE	If I work harder, I will be able to play at concerts.	☐	49.1
"MUST" AND "HAVE TO" IN THE FUTURE	In the future, I think everyone will have to recycle.	☐	49.3
MODAL VERBS	You must arrive on time for work. You should go to the doctor if you feel sick.	☐	50.1

51 Vocabulary

51.1 CUSTOMS AND CULTURES

My father believes that family values are very important.

values
[the principles and beliefs that somebody holds]

We taught our children to follow the same practices as us.

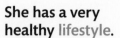

practices
[ways of doing things, often traditional]

We lead a quiet way of life in the country.

way of life
[a typical routine or pattern of behavior]

She has a very healthy lifestyle.

lifestyle
[the way a person leads their life]

They loved being in the stadium soaking up the atmosphere.

soak up
[take time to absorb and enjoy experiences as much as possible]

I try to blend in on vacation and not look like a tourist.

blend in
[look or seem similar to the surrounding place or people]

I'm so sorry! I didn't mean to cause offense.

cause offense
[do something that upsets others]

It took me a while to acclimate to the weather.

acclimate (US) / acclimatize (UK)
[get used an environment, surroundings, or culture]

I like to try traditional dishes when I travel.

traditional
[part of old customs or beliefs]

There are some interesting local customs and dances.

local custom
[something that is done locally as part of tradition]

**My friend speaks
a southern dialect.**

dialect
[the way that a language
is spoken in a certain area]

**Many religions have rituals that
haven't changed for centuries.**

ritual
[an action that is always performed
in the same way]

**Countries often have a great deal
of cultural diversity
within them.**

diversity
[range or variety]

**Many different nationalities
were at the conference.**

nationality
[people from a nation with a
shared culture and language]

**Some people believe globalization
is bad for local customs.**

globalization
[the increasing similarity between
different cultures across the world]

A lot of stereotypes are false.

stereotype
[a fixed, often incorrect, idea about
what a person or thing is like]

**My parents like children
who have good manners.**

manners
[polite or accepted social behavior]

**She picked up lots of bad
habits from her brother.**

bad habit
[something wrong that you
do regularly]

The city is steeped in history.

steeped in something
[be completely involved in
or surrounded by something]

**I don't usually eat with chopsticks,
but when in Rome.**

**when in Rome
(do as the Romans do)**
[when you travel, act as
the local people do]

52 Talking about groups

Sometimes you may want to talk generally about groups of people or different nationalities. It is important that you know the correct way to do this.

⚙️ **New language** Using adjectives as nouns
Aa Vocabulary Countries and nationalities
🧩 **New skill** Generalizing politely

52.1 KEY LANGUAGE NATIONALITY ADJECTIVES AS NOUNS

To make generalizations about people from a particular country, modify the nationality adjective. If the adjective ends in "–ch," "-sh," "-ese," or "-ss," you generally add "the." Most other nationalities take an "s," but not "the."

-CH / -SH / -ESE / -SS

Chinese design history is really fascinating.

⬇️

The Chinese have invented many great things.

MOST OTHER NATIONALITIES

Australian rugby is very competitive.

⬇️

Australians love to watch their team play.

🔊

52.2 FURTHER EXAMPLES NATIONALITY ADJECTIVES AS NOUNS

 The Spanish   The Japanese   The British   Americans   Greeks   Russians

🔊

⚙️ 52.3 WRITE THE CORRECT NAMES FOR THE DIFFERENT GROUPS OF PEOPLE

German = *Germans*

1 ➕ Swiss = _____

2 🔵 Brazilian = _____

3 Swedish = _____

4 Indian = _____

5 French = _____

6 Korean = _____

7 Kenyan = _____

🔊

52.4 KEY LANGUAGE "THE" WITH ADJECTIVES FOR CERTAIN GROUPS

Some groups or classes of people are also referred to using nouns that have been formed from adjectives.

Rich people have bought most of the new houses in this town.

Almost all the houses here are owned by the rich.

52.5 FURTHER EXAMPLES "THE" WITH ADJECTIVES FOR CERTAIN GROUPS

 Emergency treatment for the injured is essential.

 The media sometimes portrays the young as lazy.

 Many charities try to protect the poor.

 The elderly often need the support of their families.

52.6 FILL IN THE GAPS USING THE WORDS IN THE PANEL

Not every country's government gives financial help to the ____*unemployed*____ .

1 The _____ are often without a house as a result of some very bad luck.

2 Often, the _____ are described as being addicted to gadgets and phones.

3 The _____ often give lots of money to charity, but we don't know about it.

4 Many countries have laws to ensure that the _____ can access public transportation.

5 After the accident, the _____ were all taken to a nearby hospital.

6 The _____ have often cared for others all their lives and deserve care in return.

~~unemployed~~   elderly   homeless   rich   young   injured   disabled

52.7 READ THE FORUM AND ANSWER THE QUESTIONS

THE SOCIAL CONTRACT

HOME | FORUM | NEWS | CONTACT

POSTED BY JEN AT 10:38AM

Who is responsible?

Sometimes I feel very sad for those people in my country who are unable to provide for themselves. Everything is about money, not about caring. How do you think your country treats vulnerable people in society?

Mi (Hanoi): The Vietnamese have many public and private hospitals to help the sick. We respect the elderly and do whatever we can to take care of them. Often, public transportation isn't easily accessible for the disabled, but usually people will offer help.

Pepe (Milan): Italians are very proud of how they care for the elderly. It would be very wrong for me to leave my mother or father in a difficult situation. They looked after me as I was growing up, and now it's my responsibility to look after them.

Simon (Oxford): As the young have to spend more and more time working to earn money for their own family's needs, it becomes harder to have time to spend with parents. But we still respect the elderly and often help pay for their care.

Jen thinks her country's citizens care more about money than people.   **True** ☑ **False** ☐

① Jen only wants to know how different people treat the sick.   **True** ☐ **False** ☐

② Pepe believes that Italians have no time to look after the elderly.   **True** ☐ **False** ☐

③ Pepe thinks his parents should be able to look after themselves.   **True** ☐ **False** ☐

④ Mi says that Vietnam has both public and private hospitals.   **True** ☐ **False** ☐

⑤ Mi says that all public transportation in Vietnam has disabled access.   **True** ☐ **False** ☐

⑥ Simon says that the English spend a lot of their time at work.   **True** ☐ **False** ☐

⑦ According to Simon, the English do respect the elderly.   **True** ☐ **False** ☐

52.8 LISTEN TO THE AUDIO, THEN NUMBER THE STATEMENTS IN THE ORDER THAT THEY ARE DESCRIBED

A teacher from an urban multicultural school is talking about research into stereotypes that she carried out with her students.

A "I might come from a cold country, but I still get cold over here. Nobody believes me!" ☐

B "It's annoying. People think I should cook all the time, but I don't like it." [1]

C "People thought I wasn't allowed to get my hair cut whenever I wanted." ☐

D "I know that my country is rich, but it doesn't mean everyone from there is." ☐

E "Lots of times people are shocked or surprised that I'm not a vegetarian." ☐

F "Not everyone from my country can run long distances. I'm a terrible runner!" ☐

52.9 RESPOND TO THE AUDIO, SPEAKING OUT LOUD

In professional sports, what happens when people hurt themselves?

The injured   *leave the field and are treated by medical staff.*

1 What happens if someone loses their job in your country?

The unemployed _____

2 How do young people in your country treat old people?

The elderly _____

3 Do you think young people are represented fairly by the media?

The young _____

52 ✓ CHECKLIST

⚙ Using adjectives as nouns ☐   **Aa** Countries and nationalities ☐   Generalizing politely ☐

53 Old and new situations

New situations may seem unusual, but over time they become familiar. You can use phrases that contain "be used to" and "get used to" to talk about this.

🔧 **New language** "Be used to" and "get used to"
Aa Vocabulary Moving and living abroad
🧩 **New skill** Talking about old and new situations

53.1 KEY LANGUAGE "BE USED TO" AND "GET USED TO"

To "get used to (doing) something" means that you adapt to new or different circumstances so that they become familiar.

Waking up early for my new job was difficult at first, but eventually I got used to it.

To "be used to (doing) something" means that you have done it long enough that it is normal and familiar.

I've lived in the city for years, so I am used to the bad pollution.

🔊

53.2 FURTHER EXAMPLES "BE USED TO" AND "GET USED TO"

When I travel, I get used to different customs very quickly.
[I find it easy to adapt to different customs when I travel.]

I got used to the cold weather within a couple of weeks.
[I adapted to the cold weather within two weeks.]

I am used to spicy food as I've always eaten it.
[I am accustomed to eating spicy food.]

We were used to the old teacher, so it was a shame when she left.
[We were accustomed to our previous teacher, but then she left.]

🔊

> **TIP**
> Do not confuse these phrases with "used to" (without "be" or "get"), which is used when talking about a regular past action.

53.3 CROSS OUT THE INCORRECT WORDS IN EACH SENTENCE

> When I visit the UK, it takes me a while to get / ~~be~~ used to driving on the left side of the road.

1. My parents are / get used to living in an old building, but the creaking floorboards scare me!

2. They were / get used to eating with chopsticks, but it was new to me. I found it hard!

3. My friend said I'd am / get used to eating my dinner later at night after a few weeks.

4. It took a while, but now I get / am used to recycling all my paper and plastic each week.

5. His friends found it strange, but he was / get used to doing things without using the computer.

6. It was difficult at first, but I was / got used to the new routine after a few months.

7. We were / get used to the old system at work, but then it changed completely.

8. Eventually I got / am used to answering the phone in English. It almost feels natural now!

53.4 REWRITE THE SENTENCES CORRECTING THE ERRORS

> It has taken me a long time to get use to cycling in the city.
> _It has taken me a long time to get used to cycling in the city._

1. I don't think I will ever got used to the noise in my street at night.

2. I'm so used drinking coffee every morning that I can't function without it.

3. They said that they could not be used to the icy weather.

4. Don't worry. After a while you'll got used to the cold water.

5. Do you think that you'll used to the long hours in your new job?

53.5 REVIEW "USED TO"

You can use "used to" (without "be" or "get") with an infinitive to talk about past habits. You can also use it to talk about fixed states in the past, but only in an undetermined timeframe.

Refers to a past habit.

We used to play tennis every day, but now we prefer golf.

Refers to a past state.

We used to live in London before we moved to Sydney.

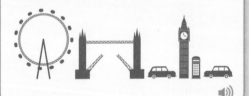

53.6 FILL IN THE GAPS WITH THE CORRECT FORMS OF THE WORDS IN THE PANEL

When I was living abroad, I used to ___go out___ a lot so that I could meet people and make friends. Even though I was nervous, I used to _____ to any offer people made to try something new. Also, I didn't _____ things to fit around my old routines, but got used to _____ things in line with local customs instead. These were quite unusual at first, but I _____ used to them now. The staff in my local café are used to me _____ mistakes when I talk, but they always appreciate the effort and help me.

| be | agree | make | force | ~~go out~~ | do |

53.7 MATCH THE BEGINNINGS OF THE SENTENCES TO THE CORRECT ENDINGS

You may have to get used to days —————→ you're used to. That's the adventure!

1. Be sure to experiment and try not — they got used to the different culture.

2. Visit the country before you move — to start getting used to the culture.

3. Ask other people from abroad how ——→ when you are homesick. It's not unusual.

4. Don't worry if things aren't what — is a great way to get to know new people.

5. Trying activities in your new country — to only do things you used to do at home.

53.8 LISTEN TO THE AUDIO AND ANSWER THE QUESTIONS

International news journalist Julie Holmes was asked to describe her greatest culture shocks.

How does Julie feel now when people ask her personal questions?

She feels surprised and offended ☐
She is surprised but not upset ☐
She is no longer surprised by it ☑

1 What examples of personal information has Julie been asked for?

Her age and whether she is married ☐
Her salary and when she will have children ☐
Her age and when she will have children ☐

2 What was a pleasant culture shock for Julie when she was in Spain?

Friends inviting her to family lunches ☐
Lunches lasting a long time ☐
Lunches being quick and efficient ☐

3 What happened after Julie missed her train?

She got a taxi to her home town ☐
She stayed overnight with a friend ☐
She got the last bus home that night ☐

4 What happened in a busy road in Hanoi?

Julie helped an old lady cross the road ☐
Julie crossed the road on her own ☐
An old lady helped Julie cross the road ☐

53.9 RESPOND TO THE AUDIO, SPEAKING OUT LOUD

These festivals are so noisy. Do you think it'll bother you?

Yes, but we'll have to ___get___ ___used to___ the noise.

1 You always stay up so late! Don't you feel tired the next day?

Not anymore. I _____ _____ it now.

2 Why does everyone in the village paint that pattern on their doors?

It's tradition! We _____ _____ doing it.

3 Is it still strange for you to see people dressed in these costumes?

It was at first, but now I _____ them.

4 Were you able to cope with the hot weather when you first moved here?

No, it took me many years to _____ it.

---

53 ✓ CHECKLIST

⚙ "Be used to" and "get used to" ☐ **Aa** Moving and living abroad ☐ 🧩 Talking about old and new situations ☐

54 Articles

Articles are some of the shortest and most common words in the English language. There are several rules stating which article, if any, should be used.

⚙ **New language** Articles
Aa Vocabulary Commonly misspelled words
🧩 **New skill** Saying words with silent letters

54.1 KEY LANGUAGE THE DEFINITE ARTICLE

Use the definite article "the" when the person or thing you are referring to is easily identifiable.

We went on a tour and the guide was excellent.

It is clear from the context that this means the tour guide.

This includes situations where a person or thing has already been mentioned.

There's a bus trip or a lecture. I'd prefer the bus trip.

The bus trip has already been mentioned.

Use the definite article before superlatives.

The Colosseum is probably the most famous site in Rome.

The definite article is used before superlatives such as "most famous."

The definite article is also used with unique objects.

I'm going to the Trevi Fountain before I check out.

The Trevi Fountain is a unique object.

It is also used for people with unique titles.

"Pope" is a title.

The Pope is visiting another country this week.

54.2 KEY LANGUAGE THE INDEFINITE ARTICLE

Use the indefinite articles "a" and "an" when the exact person or thing you are referring to is unknown.

We are trying to choose a vacation.

The vacation is a new thing that is being introduced.

Also use the indefinite article to talk about an entire class of people or things generally.

India is a fascinating country to visit.

54.3 CROSS OUT THE INCORRECT WORDS IN EACH SENTENCE

Many of ~~a / an~~ / the largest cities in the world are in China.

1. I want to visit a / an / the really modern city like Tokyo.

2. I've always wanted to go up a / an / the Empire State Building.

3. Should we go to a / an / the restaurant we ate at on Friday?

4. Did you ride on a / an / the gondola in Venice?

54.4 KEY LANGUAGE THE ZERO ARTICLE

You do not need an article with uncountable and plural nouns when you want to talk generally rather than specifically. This is also called the zero article.

"Sand" is an uncountable noun.

I don't like the beach. I get sand everywhere.

You can see famous sights all over New York City.

The number of sights is indefinite.

54.5 REWRITE THE SENTENCES CORRECTING THE ERRORS

The Maracanã stadium in Rio de Janeiro is in a north of the city.
The Maracanã stadium in Rio de Janeiro is in the north of the city.

1. Have you ever been on guided tour of Rio de Janeiro?

2. The Christ the Redeemer statue in Rio de Janeiro is a largest statue of its type.

3. A soccer is a hugely popular sport in Rio and Brazil in general.

4. There is famous lagoon in central Rio called Lagoa Rodrigo de Freitas.

54.6 FILL IN THE GAPS USING THE CORRECT ARTICLES, LEAVING A GAP FOR ZERO ARTICLE

The Republic of Costa Rica in Central America has _____ estimated population of just under 5 million people and one of _____ highest life expectancy levels in the West. Its incredible beauty and the diverse nature of the flora and fauna in its rainforests make _____ Costa Rica a top destination for tourists. Indeed, tourism is _____ country's number one source of foreign exchange. As well as famous cash crops like bananas and coffee, Costa Rica boasts 1,000 species of orchids and _____ huge number of bird species. In fairly recent years, Costa Rica has tried to cut down its reliance on the income produced by the export of coffee beans, bananas, and beef by becoming _____ producer of _____ microchips. Unfortunately, _____ microchip market has turned out to be as unstable as that for cash crops.

54.7 LISTEN TO THE AUDIO AND ANSWER THE QUESTIONS

Three people are talking about the geography of countries that they know well.

	True	False
The ocean is on the eastern border of Chile.	☐	☑
① Chile contains extremely dry deserts and also lakes made from glaciers.	☐	☐
② Most of South Korea's islands are to the east of the country.	☐	☐
③ The weather in South Korea can be quite dramatic.	☐	☐
④ Morocco is in the south of Europe, near North Africa.	☐	☐
⑤ Morocco is generally drier in the south than the north.	☐	☐

Aa 54.8 READ THE CLUES AND WRITE THE ANSWERS IN THE CORRECT PLACES ON THE GRID

TIP
The answers are all words that are commonly misspelled in English.

1 occasionally

❶ Sometimes, but not very often

❷ Different from one moment to the next

❸ Strange and unusual

❹ Person from a country other than your own

❺ To divide or keep things apart

❻ How tall something is

weird   occasionally   height

foreigner   separate   changeable

54.9 PRONOUNCIATION SILENT LETTERS

Some words contain letters that are written, but not spoken (also called silent letters). The letters **b**, **k**, **t**, and **h** can all be silent in some words.

plum**b**er

knee

lis**t**en

honest

54.10 MARK THE SILENT LETTERS AND SAY THE SENTENCES OUT LOUD

You never lis**t**en to me!

❶ I doubt we will ever see them again.

❷ To be honest, the plumbing here is unusual.

❸ Can you knock on my door in an hour?

❹ I know you want to watch the final performance.

54 ✅ CHECKLIST

⚙ Articles ☐   **Aa** Commonly misspelled words ☐   🧩 Saying words with silent letters ☐

211

55 Abstract ideas

Most abstract nouns are uncountable. Some, however, can be either countable or uncountable, and the two forms often mean slightly different things.

🔧 **New language** Concrete and abstract nouns
Aa Vocabulary Education systems
🧩 **New skill** Talking about abstract ideas

55.1 KEY LANGUAGE CONCRETE AND ABSTRACT NOUNS

Abstract nouns refer to ideas, events, concepts, feelings, and qualities that do not have a physical existence. Concrete nouns, however, are things that you can experience through your senses.

He has a lot of books, but not much knowledge.

"Books" is a countable, concrete noun.

"Knowledge" is an uncountable, abstract noun.

55.2 FURTHER EXAMPLES CONCRETE AND ABSTRACT NOUNS

teacher   classroom

CONCRETE NOUNS

paper   chair   exam

progress   freedom

ABSTRACT NOUNS

truth   sadness   health

55.3 WRITE THE NOUNS FROM THE PANEL IN THE CORRECT GROUPS

CONCRETE NOUNS		ABSTRACT NOUNS	
computer		*relaxation*	

building   ~~relaxation~~   professor   pride   misery   hate   sun   clock

beauty   artist   anger   library   photograph   heat   trouble   ~~computer~~

212

55.4 KEY LANGUAGE COUNTABLE AND UNCOUNTABLE ABSTRACT NOUNS

Some abstract nouns have both countable and uncountable forms.
The forms have a slight difference in meaning, with the countable
form being specific and the uncountable form being more general.

COUNTABLE		UNCOUNTABLE

I've been there a few times.

Each "time" is a
specific occasion.

There's plenty of time left.

"Time" refers to the
concept in general.

He has had many successes.

"Successes" are the
specific achievements.

Hard work leads to success.

"Success" refers to
achievement in general.

She has some great qualities.

"Qualities" refers to features
of her character.

It has a reputation for quality.

"Quality" refers to a
high standard.

We learned several new skills.

These are the particular
abilities learned.

It takes skill to do that job.

"Skill" is the general ability
to do something.

55.5 CROSS OUT THE INCORRECT WORD IN EACH SENTENCE

> The top four racing drivers have very similar average speed / speeds.

1. She was deep in thought / thoughts so we did not disturb her.

2. In college, you can meet people from many different culture / cultures.

3. My father formed many lasting friendship / friendships in college.

4. This house is amazing. There are so many interesting space / spaces.

5. My brother does a lot of work for several local charity / charities.

6. Apparently, this is the worst weather in living memory / memories.

7. In these difficult times it's so important not to give up hope / hopes.

55.6 FILL IN THE GAPS USING THE ABSTRACT NOUNS IN THE PANEL

Australians have a lot of _____pride_____ in their system of _____ .
The system in Australia is quite hard to describe because it is largely controlled
by the states or territories, rather than the federal _____ .
Depending on where they live, students must go to school from five years old
until 16 or 17 _____ old. There is also nursery level education, but
this is not compulsory. After secondary school, students have a number of
options to develop their _____ . They can choose to undertake
vocational education and training (VET) by taking a _____ in a
subject such as computer programming, engineering, or tourism, where they
also learn key workplace _____ . Alternatively, young people can
apply to go into higher education or, of course, look for work. Generally, the
system in Australia is recognized as being a _____ .

skills   ~~pride~~   education   success   course   abilities   years   government

55.7 LISTEN TO THE REPORT AND ANSWER THE QUESTIONS

Two people are discussing education
systems in different parts of the world.

The female speaker comes from England.	True ☑	False ☐	Not given ☐

① The English system is similar to the Australian system.   **True** ☐ **False** ☐ **Not given** ☐

② In the UK, education is compulsory until the age of 19.   **True** ☐ **False** ☐ **Not given** ☐

③ The male speaker comes from Finland.   **True** ☐ **False** ☐ **Not given** ☐

④ Students in Finland take lots of exams.   **True** ☐ **False** ☐ **Not given** ☐

⑤ Finnish schools are inspected every year.   **True** ☐ **False** ☐ **Not given** ☐

55.8 REWRITE THE SENTENCES CORRECTING THE ERRORS

There's really no need to rush. We have plenty of times left.
There's really no need to rush. We have plenty of time left.

① We had a training day to help us develop our customer service skill.

_____

② These products don't have any redeeming quality. They are so cheaply built!

_____

③ Your plan is not very sensible. It needs a bit more thoughts.

_____

④ There are time when I wonder if I should have become a teacher.

_____

⑤ Some of the applicants don't have enough experiences for the job.

_____

---

55 ✓ CHECKLIST

⚙ Concrete and abstract nouns ☐   **Aa** Education systems ☐   🧩 Talking about abstract ideas ☐

↻ REVIEW THE ENGLISH YOU HAVE LEARNED IN UNITS 53–55

NEW LANGUAGE	SAMPLE SENTENCE	☑	UNIT
USING ADJECTIVES AS NOUNS	The Chinese **have invented many things.** All the houses here are owned by **the rich.**	☐	52.1, 52.4
"BE USED TO" AND "GET USED TO"	It took me weeks to get used to **getting up** early. Now, I am used to **it.**	☐	53.1
ARTICLES	The Pope **is visiting another country.** We are trying to choose **a vacation.**	☐	54.1, 54.2, 54.4
CONCRETE AND ABSTRACT NOUNS	He has a lot of **books,** but not much knowledge.	☐	55.1
COUNTABLE AND UNCOUNTABLE ABSTRACT NOUNS	I've been there a few **times.** There's plenty of **time** left.	☐	55.4

215

56.1 TECHNOLOGY AND THE FUTURE

We must make arrangements for childcare this weekend.

make arrangements
[plan ahead so that something can happen]

Every December I make a prediction about what will happen next year.

make predictions
[say what you think might happen in the future]

There's no point having good intentions if you don't do anything.

have good intentions
[have good or positive plans]

He worked hard to realize his dream of being a tennis player.

realize a dream
[make a dream or hope real]

I didn't study for the exam, but I'll hope for the best!

hope for the best
[hope for a successful or positive outcome]

My parents had a big influence on the type of food I enjoy.

have an influence on something
[change or affect something]

The internet has had an impact on how we communicate globally.

have an impact on something
[affect something powerfully]

Being able to meet my favorite singer was a dream come true.

a dream come true
[something that has been wished for and has now happened]

It's only a matter of time before someone buys one of my paintings.

only a matter of time
[something that will happen, but it is not possible to say when]

We will have to wait and see what the future holds for us.

what the future holds
[what will happen in the future]

This electric car will save us money in the long run.

in the long run
[eventually, after a long time]

Having an internet connection is vital in this digital age.

digital age
[an era based on digital information, when technology is dominant]

Her design won an award for technical innovation.

innovation
[a new invention or idea]

The internet has seen a revolution in communication.

revolution
[a huge change in ideas or methods]

That company is famous for its cutting-edge design.

cutting-edge
[extremely modern and innovative]

I really hope this isn't the shape of things to come.

the shape of things to come
[the way things are likely to develop in the future]

Have you seen the latest model of their smartphone? It's amazing!

the latest model
[the most recent version of a product]

The team made an important medical breakthrough.

breakthrough
[an important discovery or achievement]

She has a new kitchen filled with state-of-the-art appliances.

state-of-the-art
[the most modern and up-to-date]

We need to future-proof the design, not just look at today's market.

future-proof
[design something to work in the future, even if technology changes]

57 Future hopes

To talk about wishes for the future, usually when you want something to change, you use the past tense modals "would" and "could."

🔧 **New language** "Wish" with "would" or "could"
Aa Vocabulary Hopes for the future
🧩 **New skill** Talking about future hopes and wishes

57.1 KEY LANGUAGE "WISH" FOR FUTURE HOPES

Use "wish" with "could" to talk about hopes for yourself.

I wish I could move somewhere warm.
[I would like to be able to move somewhere warmer.]

Use "wish" with "would" when someone else is doing something you don't like and you want them to change.

She wishes her teacher would give her less work.
[She wants her teacher to give out less homework in future.]

57.2 FURTHER EXAMPLES "WISH" FOR FUTURE HOPES

I wish I could **get a new job in a different department.**

I wish I could **go to the concert with my friends this evening.**

Colin is always talking about cars. I wish **he would stop.**

I wish **they wouldn't make it so hard to buy tickets online.**

57.3 REWRITE THE SENTENCES CORRECTING THE ERRORS

> This homework is so boring! I wish I would do something else.
> _This homework is so boring! I wish I could do something else._

1 That college seems really great. I could wish I go there.

_____

2 We can't change their development plans, but we wish we can.

_____

3 Sarah wishes her husband would to buy her flowers more often.

_____

4 My favorite band is coming to our city. I wish can go!

_____

57.4 FILL IN THE GAPS USING "COULD," "WOULD," OR "WOULDN'T"

The safari I want to go on lasts four weeks. I wish I ___could___ get more time off work.

1 I wish you _____ criticize my clothes. I think I look fabulous!

2 My neighbor plays the trumpet all the time. I wish he _____ be a little quieter.

3 Mike's car always breaks down. He wishes he _____ afford a new one.

4 We work far too hard. I wish we _____ do this more often!

---

57 ✓ CHECKLIST

⚙ "Wish" with "would" or "could" ☐   **Aa** Hopes for the future ☐   👥 Talking about future hopes and wishes ☐

58 The future continuous

You can use the future continuous with "will" to make predictions about the future, and also to speculate about what might be happening at the current moment.

⚙ **New language** The future continuous with "will"
Aa Vocabulary Polite requests
🧩 **New skill** Planning your career

58.1 KEY LANGUAGE THE FUTURE CONTINUOUS WITH "WILL"

The future continuous describes an event that will be in progress at a given time in the future. The event will start before the stated time and may continue after it.

PRESENT CONTINUOUS

FUTURE CONTINUOUS

Right now I'm working in a café. In 10 years' time, I hope I will be running a restaurant.

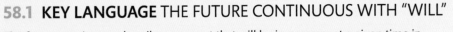

NOW   10 YEARS' TIME

58.2 FURTHER EXAMPLES THE FUTURE CONTINUOUS WITH "WILL"

This time next week,
I'll be relaxing **on a beach.**

This time tomorrow,
she'll be taking **her last exam.**

58.3 HOW TO FORM THE FUTURE CONTINUOUS WITH "WILL"

SUBJECT	"WILL"	"BE"	PRESENT PARTICIPLE	OBJECT
I	will	be	running	a restaurant.

58.4 FILL IN THE GAPS BY PUTTING THE VERBS IN THE FUTURE CONTINUOUS WITH "WILL"

By this time next year, I think I _____*will be living*_____ (live) in a different country.

1 In a few years' time, I think you _____ (run) this place.

2 I suppose you _____ (feel) too tired to go out after work this evening.

3 Tomorrow evening, Jorge's band _____ (perform) at a concert.

4 I guess she _____ (not come) to the office party if she doesn't like the boss.

5 Jane bought two tickets so I think she _____ (bring) a friend to the exhibition.

6 Meilin has already told me that she _____ (not check) her emails today.

58.5 USE THE FUTURE CONTINUOUS WITH "WILL" TO DESCRIBE THE EVENTS ON THE TIMELINE, SPEAKING OUT LOUD

WORKING IN THE SAME OFFICE	WORKING IN A NEW DEPARTMENT	WORKING AT HEADQUARTERS	MANAGING HEAD OFFICE	ENJOYING MY RETIREMENT
NEXT WEEK	1 YEAR'S TIME	5 YEARS' TIME	10 YEARS' TIME	20 YEARS' TIME

This time next week, _*I will still be working in the same office.*_

1 In a year's time, _____.

2 In 5 years' time, _____.

3 In 10 years' time, _____.

4 In 20 years' time, _____.

58.6 KEY LANGUAGE THE FUTURE CONTINUOUS WITH "ANYWAY"

The future continuous can also be used to talk about events that are going to happen as a matter of course or "anyway."

Oh no, I've run out of milk.

I can get some for you later.

No, please don't worry!

It's okay, I'll be driving **past the store anyway.**

58.7 KEY LANGUAGE NEUTRAL QUESTIONS

The future continuous is also used to ask neutral questions. These are questions asked for information, not to make a request.

NEUTRAL QUESTION

Future continuous.

Will you be coming into work tomorrow?

Yes, I will.

OK, let's talk about the report then.

REQUEST

Future with "will."

Will you come into work tomorrow, please?

Sure, no problem.

 58.8 REWRITE THE QUESTIONS USING THE FUTURE CONTINUOUS WITH "WILL"

Are all of your family coming?
Will all of your family be coming?

❶ Are you leaving soon?
_____

❷ Are you going to watch all of those DVDs?
_____

❸ Are the children coming too?
_____

❹ Will you eat all of those cakes?
_____

❺ Are you going to the store?
_____

58.9 SAY THE QUESTIONS OUT LOUD, PUTTING THE VERBS IN THE FUTURE CONTINUOUS WITH "WILL"

Will you be driving (drive) to work tomorrow?

3 _____ (take) the kids to school tomorrow?

1 _____ (eat) all that popcorn on your own?

4 _____ (return) your books to the library?

2 _____ (get) your hair cut any time soon?

5 _____ (cook) some food later on?

58.10 LISTEN TO THE AUDIO AND ANSWER THE QUESTIONS

Brian and Jeanette are talking about their plans after work.

Jeanette offers to give Brian a ride after work.
True ✓ **False** ☐

1 Brian asks Jeanette to drive him to his house because his car has broken down.
True ☐ **False** ☐

2 Brian's car is a valuable antique and worth a lot of money.
True ☐ **False** ☐

3 Brian's wife does not want him to get a motorcycle.
True ☐ **False** ☐

4 Brian likes being spontaneous.
True ☐ **False** ☐

5 Jeanette thinks Brian should be more careful with his money.
True ☐ **False** ☐

6 They are going to meet in Brian's office at 5 o'clock.
True ☐ **False** ☐

58.11 KEY LANGUAGE THE FUTURE CONTINUOUS TO TALK ABOUT THE PRESENT

You can also use the future continuous to speculate about
something that might be happening at the present moment.

 Have you noticed that Andrew isn't at work today?

 He'll be working on his presentation at home.

 It's more likely that he'll be watching the golf on TV!

58.12 LISTEN TO THE AUDIO AND MARK WHO SAID EACH SENTENCE

Darren and Kate are talking
about why Jonas might not
be at work today.

He'll be playing basketball with his nephew.
Darren ☐ **Kate** ☑ **Nobody** ☐

① His nephew will be studying for his big exam.
Darren ☐ **Kate** ☐ **Nobody** ☐

② He'll be playing football with his brother.
Darren ☐ **Kate** ☐ **Nobody** ☐

③ I imagine he'll be doing something fun though.
Darren ☐ **Kate** ☐ **Nobody** ☐

④ He'll be preparing for tomorrow's big meeting.
Darren ☐ **Kate** ☐ **Nobody** ☐

⑤ He'll be practicing his presentation.
Darren ☐ **Kate** ☐ **Nobody** ☐

⑥ He'll be panicking about the annual accounts.
Darren ☐ **Kate** ☐ **Nobody** ☐

58.13 USE THE IMAGES TO SAY SENTENCES USING THE FUTURE CONTINUOUS WITH "WILL"

She'll be doing the gardening.

① _____ a book at home.

② _____ with her friend.

③ _____ on the treadmill.

What will you be doing in five years' time?

HOME | ENTRIES | ABOUT | CONTACT

POSTED FRIDAY, 28 AUGUST

 Melissa: In five years' time? I think I'll be working for a different company. Hopefully I'll have a more important role and be earning more money. One thing's for sure, I'll be going on a lot more vacations abroad!

 Boris: If I look back five years, nothing much has changed. So, in five years' time, I predict I'll be working in the same job. I hope I'll be working with the same colleagues but they've got more ambition than me.

 Jeremy: Hopefully I'll be living in a different country by then. I want to study abroad and have lots of exciting experiences. I won't be getting married or anything like that because I want to put my studies first.

 Erika: I'm getting married next month and I hope that in five years' time, we'll be looking after two children. Who knows? Maybe by that point we'll be taking our oldest child to school for the very first time.

Is Melissa optimistic about her career?
Yes, she thinks she'll end up with a more important role, earning more money.

1 Apart from work, what else does Melissa think will change?

_____

2 Is Boris optimistic about his future career?

_____

3 What does Jeremy hope he will be doing in five years' time?

_____

4 What is Erika doing in her short-term future?

_____

5 What might Erika be doing at school in five years' time?

_____

---

58 ⊘ CHECKLIST

⚙ The future continuous with "will" ☐ **Aa** Polite requests ☐ 🧩 Planning your career ☐

59 The future perfect

You can use the future perfect to talk about events that will overlap with, or finish before, another event in the future.

⚙ **New language** The future perfect
Aa Vocabulary Life plans
🧩 **New skill** Making plans and predictions

59.1 KEY LANGUAGE THE FUTURE PERFECT

You can use the future perfect to say that an action or event will be finished before a certain future time.

They will have built the skyscraper by next year.

NOW   NEXT YEAR

59.2 FURTHER EXAMPLES THE FUTURE PERFECT

Cai will have read all his course books by next week.

Sam will have finished the laundry by this afternoon.

59.3 HOW TO FORM THE FUTURE PERFECT

SUBJECT	"WILL"	"HAVE"	PAST PARTICIPLE	OBJECT	TIME REFERENCE
They	will	have	built	the skyscraper	by next year.

59.4 FILL IN THE GAPS BY PUTTING THE VERBS IN THE FUTURE PERFECT

By next March, I _____*will have bought*_____ (buy) my own house.

❶ By the end of the night, I _____ (watch) all the films in the series.

❷ You _____ (experience) so many different things by the time you return.

❸ Dimitri _____ (cycle) around the world by this time next year.

❹ By next year, she _____ (see) all of her favorite bands live.

❺ I hope he _____ (clean) the car by the time he goes to the wedding.

❻ Before I leave tonight, I _____ (finish) all my work.

59.5 USE THE FUTURE PERFECT TO WRITE SENTENCES ABOUT THE EVENTS ON THE TIMELINE

GRADUATE

MOVE ABROAD

START A BUSINESS

MARRY SOMEONE

RETIRE

| 23 YEARS OLD | 25 YEARS OLD | 30 YEARS OLD | 35 YEARS OLD | 60 YEARS OLD |

By the time I'm 23, _*I will have graduated from college.*_

❶ By the time I'm 25, _____

❷ By the time I'm 30, _____

❸ By the time I'm 35, _____

❹ By the time I'm 60, _____

227

59.6 KEY LANGUAGE THE FUTURE PERFECT CONTINUOUS

You can use the future perfect continuous to predict the length of an activity. This tense looks back from that imagined time in the future.

By July, I will have been working here for a year.

LAST JULY   NOW   JULY

59.7 FURTHER EXAMPLES THE FUTURE PERFECT CONTINUOUS

By the time this is all ready, I will have been cooking all day!

By the time I arrive home, I will have been driving for 6 hours.

By this time next month, I will have been learning English for a year!

59.8 HOW TO FORM THE FUTURE PERFECT CONTINUOUS

TIME REFERENCE	SUBJECT	"WILL"	"HAVE"	"BEEN"	PRESENT PARTICIPLE	REST OF SENTENCE
By July,	I	will	have	been	working	here for a year.

59.9 READ THE PARAGRAPH AND CROSS OUT THE INCORRECT OPTIONS

Dear Graham,

By now you will have returned / been returning from your honeymoon. I hope you had a great time! Don't forget that we're having a party for Jane on Saturday. She will have been working / worked here for 20 years on Friday! I hope Frank will have sent / been sending you an email with all the details by the time you get this. I'll see you at the party. I hope you'll have caught / been catching up with all your work by then!

Sian

59.10 LISTEN TO THE AUDIO AND ANSWER THE QUESTIONS

It's Jon and Eva's last day of high school. They're talking about their future plans.

Jon and Eva took the same exams at school.
True ☐   False ☐   Not given ☑

1 Jon will finish his college course before Eva.
True ☐   False ☐   Not given ☐

2 Jon wants to work for a big marketing agency.
True ☐   False ☐   Not given ☐

3 Eva hopes to work in a big accountancy firm.
True ☐   False ☐   Not given ☐

4 Jon says that they could do work for each other.
True ☐   False ☐   Not given ☐

59.11 LISTEN AGAIN AND MARK THE CORRECT SUMMARY

1 Jon is taking a course in accountancy while Eva is going to study marketing. He wants to run his own business, but she does not. ☐

2 Jon is going to start working now while Eva is going to study accountancy. He wants to run his own business, but she does not. ☐

3 Jon is taking a course in marketing while Eva is going to study accountancy. He wants to run his own business, but she does not. ☐

4 Jon is taking a course in marketing while Eva is going to study accountancy. She wants to run her own business, but he does not. ☐

59 ✓ CHECKLIST

⚙ The future perfect ☐   **Aa** Life plans ☐   🧩 Making plans and predictions ☐

60 The future in the past

There are a number of constructions in English that you can use to describe thoughts about the future that someone had at some point in the past.

New language "Would" and "was going to"

Aa Vocabulary Changing plans

New skill Saying what you thought

60.1 KEY LANGUAGE THE FUTURE IN THE PAST USING "WOULD"

Where you would use "will" to talk about a future event from the present, you use "would" to talk about your past view of it.

EARLIER   NOW

I think I will finish the gardening today. It shouldn't take too long.

I thought I would finish today, but there is still a lot left to do.

 ## 60.2 CROSS OUT THE INCORRECT WORDS IN EACH SENTENCE

I thought I ~~will~~ / would go to France last summer, but I didn't. I will / ~~would~~ go next year instead.

1. David said that he will / would try to get me a ticket to the game, but he doesn't / didn't manage to.

2. I would / will buy the movie on DVD. I thought I will / would see it at the movie theater, but I didn't.

3. Last year she thought she will / would be promoted, but she wasn't. Maybe next year she would / will be.

4. I bring / brought all the food for the picnic because I knew that Tom won't / wouldn't remember.

5. We knew that the concert will / would be amazing, so we buy / bought really good tickets.

6. My brother promised that he won't / wouldn't show anyone pictures of me from when I was / were little.

60.3 KEY LANGUAGE THE FUTURE IN THE PAST USING "WAS GOING TO"

Where you would use "going to" to talk about a future event from the present, you use "was / were going to" to talk about your past view of it.

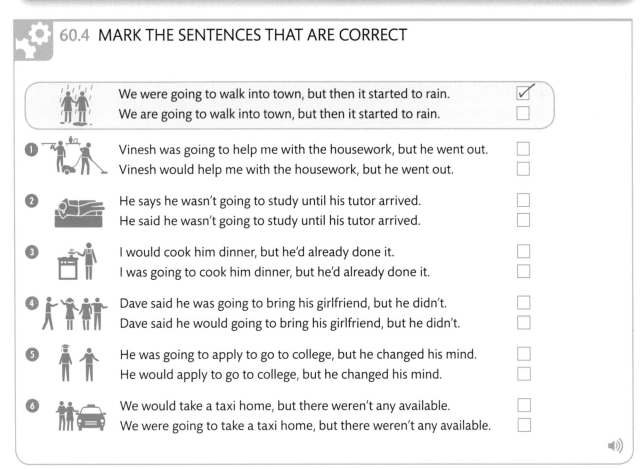

EARLIER

NOW

This traffic is awful! I think I'm going to be late for work.

I thought I was going to be late, but I'm right on time.

60.4 MARK THE SENTENCES THAT ARE CORRECT

We were going to walk into town, but then it started to rain. ☑
We are going to walk into town, but then it started to rain. ☐

1. Vinesh was going to help me with the housework, but he went out. ☐
   Vinesh would help me with the housework, but he went out. ☐

2. He says he wasn't going to study until his tutor arrived. ☐
   He said he wasn't going to study until his tutor arrived. ☐

3. I would cook him dinner, but he'd already done it. ☐
   I was going to cook him dinner, but he'd already done it. ☐

4. Dave said he was going to bring his girlfriend, but he didn't. ☐
   Dave said he would going to bring his girlfriend, but he didn't. ☐

5. He was going to apply to go to college, but he changed his mind. ☐
   He would apply to go to college, but he changed his mind. ☐

6. We would take a taxi home, but there weren't any available. ☐
   We were going to take a taxi home, but there weren't any available. ☐

231

60.5 KEY LANGUAGE THE FUTURE IN THE PAST USING THE PAST CONTINUOUS

You can also use the past continuous to talk about an arranged future event from a time in the past.

LAST MONDAY MORNING   LAST MONDAY AFTERNOON   NOW

**Jenny was extremely nervous on Monday morning.
She was taking her driving test that afternoon.**

60.6 SAY EACH SENTENCE OUT LOUD IN THE PAST TENSE

They are thinking of telling him the good news about his job.

They were thinking of telling him the good news about his job.

1. Sarah is planning to take her children to the park on Tuesday.

2. Peter's nervous because he's meeting his girlfriend's parents.

3. I am planning to go out that evening because my parents are having guests over.

4. We can't make it to the party on Friday because we're visiting some friends that day.

5. I'm planning to book a vacation just after the New Year.

60.7 LISTEN TO THE AUDIO AND DECIDE WHICH THINGS ACTUALLY HAPPENED

---

60 ✅ CHECKLIST

⚙️ "Would" and "was going to" ☐ **Aa** Changing plans ☐ 🧩 Saying what you thought ☐

♻️ REVIEW THE ENGLISH YOU HAVE LEARNED IN UNITS 57–60

NEW LANGUAGE	SAMPLE SENTENCE	☑	UNIT
"WISH" FOR FUTURE HOPES	I wish I could move somewhere warm. She wishes her teacher would give her less work.	☐	57.1
THE FUTURE CONTINUOUS WITH "WILL"	In five years' time I will be working in a restaurant.	☐	58.1
THE FUTURE CONTINUOUS AS A MATTER OF COURSE	I'll be driving past the store anyway. Will you be coming into work tomorrow?	☐	58.6 58.7
THE FUTURE CONTINUOUS TO TALK ABOUT THE PRESENT	He'll be working on his presentation by now.	☐	58.11
THE FUTURE PERFECT	Cai will have read all his course books by next week.	☐	59.1
THE FUTURE PERFECT CONTINUOUS	In September, I will have been working here for a year.	☐	59.6
THE FUTURE IN THE PAST	I thought I would finish the gardening today. I thought I was going to be late.	☐	60.1, 60.3, 60.5

61.1 ART AND CULTURE

Reviews can have a big influence on a film's success.

influence
[the effect someone or something has]

The documentary inspired me to start painting.

inspire
[give somebody the enthusiasm to do something they may not have done otherwise]

Mary was strongly influenced by his speech.

strongly influenced by something
[greatly affected by something or somebody]

I can highly recommend the new restaurant.

highly recommend
[say that something is very good and tell others about it]

The reviewers always heap praise on him.

heap praise / criticism on something
[say that something is extremely good / bad]

I was so engrossed in the book that I didn't hear the phone.

be engrossed in something
[be extremely absorbed in something]

Make up your mind, do you prefer the red or black one?

make up your mind
[finally make a decision]

I chose the red one, but then I changed my mind.

change your mind
[alter or change a decision or feeling about something]

I know you're a vegetarian and will bear it in mind when I cook.

bear something in mind
[hold something in consideration when doing or thinking about something else]

Don't be afraid to speak your mind.

speak your mind
[say what you feel, even if it is controversial]

We have candles to help create a romantic atmosphere.

create an atmosphere
[to set a particular mood or tone]

This opera is a bit too highbrow for me. I prefer movies.

highbrow / lowbrow
[complicated / simple artistic or cultural ideas]

The movie's plot was too complicated to understand.

plot
[the series of events that makes up the story in a book, film, or play]

My favorite character was the funny best friend.

characters
[the fictional people in a book, film, or play]

I really enjoyed the opening scene of the play.

opening / closing scenes
[the first / last moments of a book, film, or play]

The dramatic chain of events was almost unbelievable.

chain of events
[a sequence of causes and effects]

Have you seen the latest TV drama about firefighters?

drama
[a play, movie, television show, or radio show about a serious subject]

I like to relax by reading romance novels.

novels
[long, written stories that are fictional]

The book left a lasting impression on me. It was incredible.

lasting impression
[a feeling or effect that lasts a long time]

The new film has had glowing reviews from all the critics.

glowing reviews
[very positive reviews]

62 Leaving words out

When you want to communicate clearly, it can be helpful to avoid repetition. One way to do this is to drop any unnecessary words.

⚙ **New language** Ellipsis
Aa Vocabulary Entertainment
🧩 **New skill** Leaving out unnecessary words

62.1 KEY LANGUAGE ELLIPSIS

If the meaning of a sentence is clear from the surrounding text, you can use ellipsis (leaving out certain words) to avoid repetition. This is most common after "and," "but," and "or." Sometimes you can drop a repeated verb in a different form.

He bought tickets, but [he] didn't go.

Often a repeated subject is dropped after "and," "but," and "or."

She loved the original and [she loved] the sequel.

If the meaning remains clear, a repeated subject and verb can be dropped.

I'm happy to go out or [I'm happy to] stay home.

Generally, you can omit words that have already been mentioned and do not require repetition.

62.2 FILL IN THE GAPS WITH THE REPEATED WORDS THAT HAVE BEEN DROPPED

I told him I would book the tickets, but I haven't [_booked the tickets_] yet.

① They wanted to see the band perform live, but now they can't [_____].

② He was fantastic in the television series and [_____] the movie adaptation.

③ If you want to see a movie we could go to the multiplex or [_____] the art house.

④ The reviews said that the acting was bad and [_____] the soundtrack was terrible.

⑤ The two lead actors did all the stunts and [_____] sang all the songs themselves.

⑥ I am quitting my job this week. I will call you later to explain why [_____].

62.3 READ THE ARTICLE AND ANSWER THE QUESTIONS

> *Marine Blue* was directed by Fay Little.
> **True** ☐ **False** ☑

1. The reviewer thinks the film will be a success.
   True ☐ **False** ☐

2. The plot in the film was unusual and exciting to follow.
   True ☐ **False** ☐

3. The special effects in *Marine Blue* were not very good.
   True ☐ **False** ☐

4. The plot of *Death Reviewed* was not very exciting.
   True ☐ **False** ☐

5. *Death Reviewed* was emotional and extremely moving.
   True ☐ **False** ☐

THIS WEEK'S NEW OPENINGS

Find out what to see (and what to avoid) this week.

The new film starring Fay Little will surely be another box office hit for director Lee Jones. Thriller *Marine Blue* is released on Thursday and brings back characters Max and Alice. The plot was original and surprising, although some elements may prove highly controversial. *Marine Blue* was heavily subsidised, but the money was incredibly well spent as the visual effects and soundtrack are stunning. A must see!

The new play *Death Reviewed* is supposed to be a tragedy. It is just tragic. Terrible acting, painfully slow dialogue, and a completely predictable plot make it a disaster. The play did leave me deeply moved, but only because the ticket prices were so astronomically high! Bitterly disappointed.

62.4 FILL IN THE GAPS USING THE WORDS IN THE PANEL TO COMPLETE THE COLLOCATIONS FROM 62.3

The film was very dull and the plot was [painfully *slow*].

1. I knew that the family would turn out to be aliens. It was [completely   ].

2. I was so [deeply   ] by the sad scenes that I cried for hours!

3. We loved the last film, but were [bitterly   ] by this one.

4. We waited too long! The ticket prices are now [astronomically   ].

5. The plot is shocking and the theme is [controversial].

6. The government helped pay for the film. It was [subsidized].

| predictable | moved | ~~slow~~ | heavily | highly | high | disappointed |

237

62.5 CROSS OUT THE WORDS THAT CAN BE LEFT OUT OF EACH SENTENCE

He might have been in the original film or ~~he might have been in~~ the remake.

1 I was planning to buy tickets for the show, but now I can't buy tickets for the show.

2 The film had great special effects and the film had a wonderful soundtrack.

3 He was chosen for the orchestra and he played brilliantly.

4 This evening I'm going to have dinner and then I'm going to watch a play.

5 They said that they would come to the launch party, but they haven't come to the launch party.

6 They should join in or they should not bother coming.

62.6 MATCH THE BEGINNINGS OF THE SENTENCES TO THE CORRECT ENDINGS

He has always made thrillers and

1 The actors were good, but

2 The performance starts at 8 and

3 You could buy a season ticket or

4 The building is beautiful, but

5 The cast are all exhausted, but

6 The audience was very loud and

doesn't have very good acoustics.

ends just after midnight.

full of young children!

he always will.

very satisfied with the performance.

sign up for membership.

seemed uncomfortable on screen.

62.7 KEY LANGUAGE CONVERSATIONAL ELLIPSIS

You can also leave words out of sentences that don't include "and," "but," and "or" if the meaning can be understood from the context. This kind of ellipsis does not have strict rules, and is very common in informal everyday speech, particularly when giving replies.

What time does the movie start?

Eight.

[It starts at eight o'clock.]

What kind of popcorn would you like?

Salted, please.

[I would like salted popcorn, please.]

What did you think of the film?

Complete nonsense.

[I thought the film was complete nonsense.]

62.8 LISTEN TO THE AUDIO, THEN NUMBER THE FULL STATEMENTS IN THE ORDER THAT YOU HEAR THEIR SHORT FORMS

A "Good evening." ☐

B "No, it's a horror film." ☐

C "I think that it's better than the book version." ☐

D "I'd like two seats, please." ☐

E "Is this film a drama?" 1

F "So, what did you think of the film?" ☐

G "Are you sure about that?" ☐

62 ✓ CHECKLIST

⚙ Ellipsis ☐   **Aa** Entertainment ☐   🧩 Leaving out unnecessary words ☐

63 Substituting words

As well as ellipsis (leaving words out), you can also avoid repeating yourself by replacing some phrases with shorter ones. This is called substitution.

⚙ **New language** Substitution
Aa Vocabulary Books and reading
🧩 **New skill** Replacing phrases

63.1 KEY LANGUAGE SUBSTITUTING WITH "ONE / ONES" AND "SOME"

"One" and "ones" can be used to replace singular and plural countable nouns. To use "ones," you must be referring to a specific group of things. Use "some" when the group is not defined.

SINGLE COUNTABLE NOUNS

Does anyone have a copy of the book?

Yes, I have one.

"One" replaces "a copy of the book."

PLURAL COUNTABLE NOUNS

Are there any bookstores near here?

Yes, there are some on Main Street.

There are a few great ones across town.

"Ones" can only be used if you modify it to define the specific things that you mean.

🔊

63.2 CROSS OUT THE INCORRECT WORDS IN EACH SENTENCE

He's such a great writer. I think his best novels are the later ~~one~~ / ones / ~~some~~.

① The book with the long title is the one / ~~ones~~ / ~~some~~ I wanted.

② The buildings in New York were taller than the ~~one~~ / ones / ~~some~~ in Paris.

③ If you still want a copy of that book, there are ~~one~~ / ~~ones~~ / some over here.

④ If you need an umbrella, I can lend you one / ~~ones~~ / ~~some~~.

⑤ Have you seen her new sunglasses? The ~~one~~ / ones / ~~some~~ with the silver frames?

🔊

63.3 MATCH THE BEGINNINGS OF THE SENTENCES TO THE CORRECT ENDINGS

I have a few recommendations → if you want some.

1. They bought me a signed copy,

2. I think the most engrossing novels

3. If you want to join a book club,

4. I know you want to buy a new car,

5. If you need a plastic bag,

are the ones about spies.

there are some in the box over there.

make sure it's one with regular meetings.

if you want some.

but the one we have is only a year old.

but I already had one.

 63.4 FILL IN THE GAPS USING "ONE," "ONES," OR "SOME"

BookCon review notes

Black Glasses is Martin Owens' fourth book in this series. Like the third book, this ___one___ is all about the brilliant detective Amanda Brook. Unlike the other _____ in the series though, this time her personal life starts falling apart. Excellent plot as usual.

I have read some boring books in my time, but Sara Umborne's Pink Tree is the dullest _____ ever. Sadly, I can't tell you much about the book as I gave up after 20 pages.

Little Water Princess is a fabulous book for little children, or even older _____ ! There are few words, but the illustrations are beautiful. Lots of the pictures pop up, but _____ are 2D. A lovely gift idea.

There are endless books about cooking pasta, but How to Cook Pasta by Daniela Capril is the best _____ on the market today.

63.5 KEY LANGUAGE SUBSTITUTING WITH "DO"

You can also replace verbs and their complements with substitute words to avoid repetition. "Do" and "did" are often used to replace present and past simple tense verbs, for example.

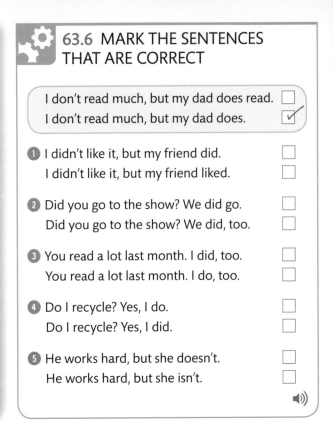

Different forms of "do" replace "think."

I think this homework is really difficult.

I did too, so I asked for help.

I don't. It's easy.

63.6 MARK THE SENTENCES THAT ARE CORRECT

I don't read much, but my dad does read. ☐
I don't read much, but my dad does. ☑

1. I didn't like it, but my friend did. ☐
   I didn't like it, but my friend liked. ☐

2. Did you go to the show? We did go. ☐
   Did you go to the show? We did, too. ☐

3. You read a lot last month. I did, too. ☐
   You read a lot last month. I do, too. ☐

4. Do I recycle? Yes, I do. ☐
   Do I recycle? Yes, I did. ☐

5. He works hard, but she doesn't. ☐
   He works hard, but she isn't. ☐

63.7 LISTEN TO THE AUDIO AND ANSWER THE QUESTIONS

Two friends, Deborah and Clive, are in a bookstore.
Listen to them discussing the different titles available.

Deborah has Nadine Hussein's new cookbook. **True** ☐ **False** ☑

1. Clive thinks more cookbooks should be written. **True** ☐ **False** ☐

2. Clive thinks Deborah does not bake at home. **True** ☐ **False** ☐

3. Clive is going to Rome the following weekend. **True** ☐ **False** ☐

4. Clive prefers guidebooks with lots of pictures. **True** ☐ **False** ☐

5. Deborah is going to help Clive choose some novels. **True** ☐ **False** ☐

6. Clive believes that Deborah is going to bake later. **True** ☐ **False** ☐

63.8 KEY LANGUAGE SUBSTITUTING WITH "SO" AND "NOT"

In positive clauses after verbs of thinking, you can use "so" to avoid repetition. Use "not" or "not... so" in negative sentences.

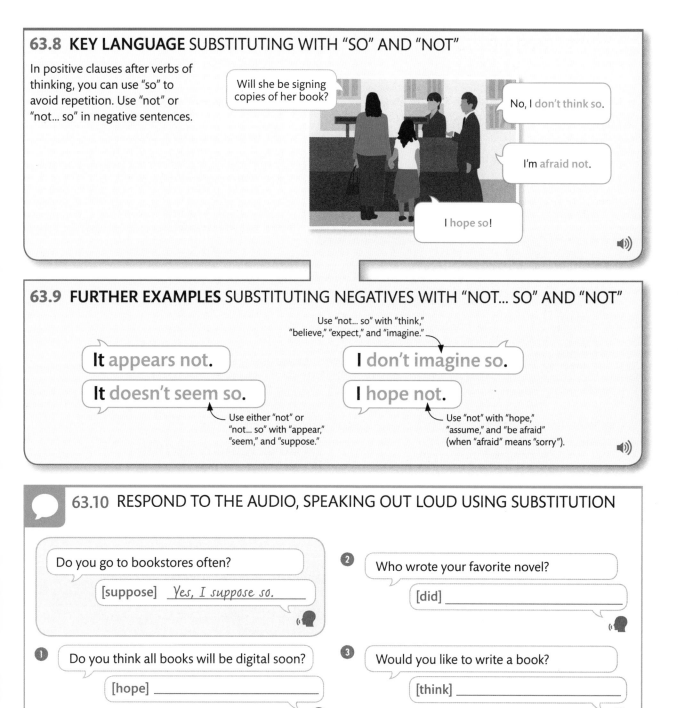

Will she be signing copies of her book?

No, I don't think so.

I'm afraid not.

I hope so!

63.9 FURTHER EXAMPLES SUBSTITUTING NEGATIVES WITH "NOT... SO" AND "NOT"

Use "not... so" with "think," "believe," "expect," and "imagine."

It appears not.

It doesn't seem so.

Use either "not" or "not... so" with "appear," "seem," and "suppose."

I don't imagine so.

I hope not.

Use "not" with "hope," "assume," and "be afraid" (when "afraid" means "sorry").

63.10 RESPOND TO THE AUDIO, SPEAKING OUT LOUD USING SUBSTITUTION

Do you go to bookstores often?

[suppose] _Yes, I suppose so._

❶ Do you think all books will be digital soon?

[hope] _____

❷ Who wrote your favorite novel?

[did] _____

❸ Would you like to write a book?

[think] _____

---

63 ✓ CHECKLIST

⚙ Substitution ☐   **Aa** Books and reading ☐   🧩 Replacing phrases ☐

64 Shortening infinitives

As well as ellipsis and substitution, you can also shorten (or "reduce") infinitives to prevent repetition. This will help you to sound more natural when speaking.

⚙ **New language** Reduced infinitives
Aa Vocabulary Music and performance
New skill Avoiding repetition

64.1 KEY LANGUAGE REDUCED INFINITIVES

You can use "to" on its own rather than repeat the entire infinitive verb. You can only do this if the meaning remains clear.

Let's go to see that new DJ tonight.

I don't really want to [go to see the new DJ].

If the previous sentence or clause contains the verb "be," then you must use to "be" in the next clause or sentence.

She was really critical of the new album.

It's difficult not to be [critical of it].
The singing is awful!

64.2 CROSS OUT ALL OF THE WORDS THAT YOU CAN LEAVE OUT

I want to get the best tickets for the show, but can't afford to ~~get them~~.

① I tried to contact Max about the concert tickets, but wasn't able to contact him.

② My brother often forgets our dad's birthday, but this year he's promised not to forget.

③ Georgia was enjoying the performance. At least, she seemed to be enjoying it.

④ Ian is going to the new nightclub, but I don't really want to go to there.

⑤ The festival tickets cost a lot more than they used to cost.

⑥ I want to come with you, but I won't be able to come with you.

64.3 KEY LANGUAGE DROPPING THE ENTIRE INFINITIVE CLAUSE

You can leave out the entire infinitive clause, or just keep "to" after some verbs, such as: "agree," "ask," "forget," "promise," "start," and "try."

Chris is going to come to the show. He $\begin{Bmatrix} \text{promised [to come]} \\ \text{promised to [come]} \end{Bmatrix}$.

You can also leave out the entire infinitive or use "to" after some nouns, such as: "chance," "plans," "promise," "idea," and "opportunity."

I haven't seen this band before. I'd love the $\begin{Bmatrix} \text{chance [to see them]} \\ \text{chance to [see them]} \end{Bmatrix}$.

It is also possible to do this after certain adjectives, such as: "delighted," "afraid," "willing," and "determined."

I want to perform on stage, but I'm $\begin{Bmatrix} \text{afraid [to perform on stage]} \\ \text{afraid to [perform on stage]} \end{Bmatrix}$.

64.4 LISTEN TO THE AUDIO AND ANSWER THE QUESTIONS

 Two students are talking about learning to play musical instruments.

Luca has a double bass in his case.
True ☐ **False** ☑

1 Luca says the cello is harder to play than the guitar.
True ☐ **False** ☐

2 Tanya plays the trumpet now.
True ☐ **False** ☐

3 Luca will be joining a new orchestra next week.
True ☐ **False** ☐

4 Luca was confident about his orchestra audition.
True ☐ **False** ☐

5 Tanya is a member of the college orchestra.
True ☐ **False** ☐

6 Tanya cannot audition again.
True ☐ **False** ☐

7 Tanya and Luca have played together before.
True ☐ **False** ☐

64.5 KEY LANGUAGE VERBS WITH COMPLEMENTS

You cannot leave out the entire infinitive after verbs that need complements (phrases that complete their meaning), such as: "advise," "afford," "be able," "choose," "decide," "expect," "hate," "hope," "love," "need," and "prefer." After these, you must keep the "to."

We want to see a band tonight, but we really can't afford to.

64.6 FURTHER EXAMPLES VERBS WITH COMPLEMENTS

 I tried to get to the front of the crowd, but I wasn't able to.

 You could bring some snacks along, but you don't need to.

 I had piano lessons as a child, but I didn't choose to.

 I have never been to the opera, but I would love to.

64.7 FILL IN THE GAPS USING THE WORDS IN THE PANEL

I asked my sister to sing with me and she said she'd be ___*delighted*___ .

1. I would like to read music, but it will be a long time until I'm _____ to.

2. Don't forget that it's suppose to rain tonight. Try to leave before it _____ .

3. Some people aren't nervous about performing, but I'm too _____ to.

4. Some artists don't like to have family in the audience on the first night, but I _____ to.

5. It's such a shame. I would absolutely love to see him sing, but cannot _____ to.

6. I've seen other artists who love talking to the audience, but I _____ to.

7. You don't need to worry. I will come along to all of your recitals. I _____ .

| afford | starts | ~~delighted~~ | promise | afraid | prefer | hate | able |

64.8 KEY LANGUAGE "WANT" AND "WOULD LIKE"

You normally keep the "to" rather than drop the entire infinitive after "want" or "would like."

He asked if I wanted to go, and I said I would like to.

In "if" clauses, however, you can often use "to" on its own or drop the whole infinitive after "want" or "would like."

You can come with us if you { want / want to } **.**

You must keep the "to" if the clause is negative.

Don't go to the concert if you don't want to.

🔊

64.9 MARK THE SENTENCES THAT ARE CORRECT

Thanks for the offer! I would really like to. ☑
Thanks for the offer! I would really like. ☐

1. I asked him to come, but he didn't want. ☐
   I asked him to come, but he didn't want to. ☐

2. You can have one if you want. ☐
   You can have one if you do. ☐

3. You can stay, but I don't really want to. ☐
   You can stay, but I don't really want. ☐

4. If you're free to meet, I would still like to. ☐
   If you're free to meet, I would still like. ☐

5. You can call me "Sam" if you want to call. ☐
   You can call me "Sam" if you want. ☐

🔊

64.10 RESPOND TO THE AUDIO, SPEAKING OUT LOUD

Will you record my performance tonight?

[promise] Yes, _I promise._ 🗣

1. Are you going to sell your CD collection?

   [decide] No, _____ 🗣

2. Will you practice every day?

   [try] Yes, _____ 🗣

3. Would you like to come to the concert?

   [afford] Yes, but _____ 🗣

🔊

---

64 ✓ CHECKLIST

⚙ Reduced infinitives ☐   **Aa** Music and performing ☐   🧩 Avoiding repetition ☐

65 Expressing reactions

Although discourse markers often don't add content in themselves, they can ease the flow of a conversation and add information about the speaker's opinion.

⚙ **New language** Informal discourse markers
Aa Vocabulary Advanced prefixes
New skill Structuring conversation

65.1 KEY LANGUAGE COMMON INFORMAL DISCOURSE MARKERS

Use "actually" to correct a listener's misunderstanding or incorrect expectation.

TIP
Be aware of how body language conveys extra meaning when talking face-to-face.

I don't think this painting is worth that much.

Actually, it sold at auction for $2 million.

Wow! Do you like it?

I don't, actually. It's not very impressive.

Use "by the way" to show a change of subject.

I think this one is fantastic, too. Oh, by the way, did you read the article about the painter in *The Times*?

Use "as I was saying" to return to a previous subject after a change of subject or interruption.

As I was saying, this is a fantastic painting. I really like the way the sea is painted.

Use "anyway" to return to a subject after interruption, change subject, or end a topic or conversation.

Anyway, I should say goodbye. I want to visit the gallery shop before it closes.

🔊

65.2 CROSS OUT THE LEAST APPROPRIATE WORDS IN EACH SENTENCE

 I know you say he's talentless, but actually / ~~by the way~~ this is a very impressive sculpture.

1 These gardens are fabulous. Did you bring your camera, as I was saying / by the way ?

2 Yes, but by the way / as I was saying before, I really think I could paint that myself.

3 No, I don't hate all modern art. I actually / as I was saying really like some street art.

4 Anyway / Actually, to get back to my question, would you pay two million dollars for that?

5 These paintings aren't the reason I come here. I anyway / actually prefer the architecture.

🔊

65.3 RESPOND TO THE AUDIO, SPEAKING OUT LOUD AND USING THE MOST APPROPRIATE DISCOURSE MARKERS

You like Manet's paintings, don't you?

Yes, but _____actually_____ this painting is by Monet.

1 The brushstrokes in the sky are amazing.

Aren't they? _____ , where are we going for dinner?

2 It's too early to eat! Do you like this painting?

Yes, but _____ , I'm getting really hungry.

3 I think we've seen everything.

We haven't, _____ . There's another floor!

4 Are you tired of paintings yet?

_____ , I'm really inspired. I love this landscape.

5 I agree. This is the best painting here.

_____ , we should head back to the car soon.

🔊

65.4 READ THE ARTICLE AND ANSWER THE QUESTIONS

The show is by well-known established artists.
True ☐ **False** ☑

① The first room in the show contained paintings.
True ☐ **False** ☐

② There is a small room before the second room.
True ☐ **False** ☐

③ There were many artists in the second room.
True ☐ **False** ☐

④ The young performer will make you happy.
True ☐ **False** ☐

⑤ The final room makes you feel very relaxed.
True ☐ **False** ☐

⑥ The reviewer recommends the exhibition.
True ☐ **False** ☐

ART SCENE

Dean Hill Art School Exhibition

The opening of the Dean Hill Art Exhibition highlighted the mix of influences on these creative final-year students. The paintings in the first room were clearly inspired by classical artists and the more modern neoclassical movement.

From this more traditional first room, you are led to a small anteroom to wait for the next "performance." You are then taken to a dark room with lots of

ropes hanging from the ceiling. Without giving too much away for future visitors to the show, you will see a young boy dressed in blue and red and you will laugh and probably be reminded of a certain superhero.

The next room was another complete change. This time an angry antisocial woman made us all feel very uncomfortable with the idea of progress in a modern world. It was a typical postmodern performance.

A hugely varied exhibition by talented, proactive artists. Well worth a visit.

Aa 65.5 MATCH THE BEGINNINGS OF THE SENTENCES TO THE CORRECT ENDINGS

"Ante-" and "pre-" as in "anteroom" and "preschool"   means "beyond."

① "Super-" as in "superhero" and "supernatural"   means "for."

② "Anti-" as in "antisocial" and "antibiotics"   means "after."

③ "Pro-" as in "proactive" and "proceed"   mean "before."

④ "Neo-" as in "neoclassical" and "neoliberal"   means "against."

⑤ "Post-" as in "postmodern" and "postwar"   means "new."

🔊

65.6 FILL IN THE GAPS USING THE PREFIXES IN THE PANEL

To find a career in your field, you need to be very ___*pro*___active.

1 Many children go to _____school before they are five years old.

2 My husband is 40 years old, but he still enjoys _____hero comics and films.

3 A lot of the architecture here is _____classical and looks Roman.

4 I think that dropping litter in public is extremely _____social.

5 Before the ceremony began, we were told to wait in a small _____room.

6 Many 20th-century art movements have been called _____modern.

| post | pre | anti | neo | super | ante | ~~pro~~ |

---

65 ✓ CHECKLIST

⚙ Informal discourse markers ☐   **Aa** Advanced prefixes ☐   🧩 Structuring conversation ☐

↻ REVIEW THE ENGLISH YOU HAVE LEARNED IN UNITS 62–65

NEW LANGUAGE	SAMPLE SENTENCE	☑	UNIT
ELLIPSIS	She went to see the play and loved it. Seen the film?	☐	62.1, 62.5
SUBSTITUTION WITH "ONE / ONES" AND "SOME"	Do you need a pencil? I have one. Would you like a cookie? There are some left.	☐	63.1, 63.3
SUBSTITUTION WITH "DO" AND "SO"	You read a lot last month. I did, too. Is Mary going to come? I hope so.	☐	63.5, 63.7
REDUCED INFINITIVES AND DROPPED INFINITIVE CLAUSES	I don't really want to. I asked her to buy me tickets and she agreed.	☐	64.1, 64.3
REDUCED VERBS WITH COMPLEMENTS	We want to see our friend's band play, but can't afford to.	☐	64.5
INFORMAL DISCOURSE MARKERS	Actually, it sold at auction for $2 million.	☐	65.1

66 Getting things done

Sometimes you might want to talk about other people doing things for you, rather than doing things yourself. To do this, you need to use different grammar.

⚙ **New language** "Have / get something done"
Aa Vocabulary Services and repairs
🧩 **New skill** Describing things people do for you

66.1 KEY LANGUAGE "HAVE / GET SOMETHING DONE"

Use "have" or "get" with a noun and the past participle to talk about something someone else does for you or to you. "Get" is less formal than "have."

Did you get your computer updated?

[Did somebody update your computer for you?]

Yes, the company has the computers updated **regularly.**

[Yes, somebody regularly updates them for the company.]

🔊

66.2 FURTHER EXAMPLES "HAVE / GET SOMETHING DONE"

Use the structure with "should" to give advice.

You should get your connection checked.

[I think you should arrange for someone to check your connection.]

Will you get the oven fixed **soon?**

[Will somebody fix the oven for you soon?]

They haven't had the locks changed **yet.**

[They haven't arranged for somebody to change the locks for them.]

The store has its produce checked **daily.**

[Somebody checks the store's produce each day.]

🔊

66.3 HOW TO FORM "HAVE / GET SOMETHING DONE"

You change the form of "have" or "get" to use different tenses in the simple and continuous forms.

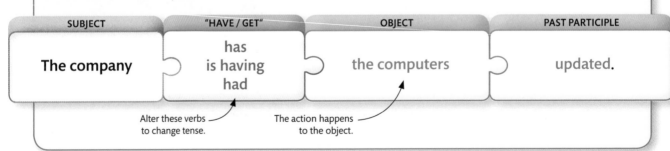

SUBJECT	"HAVE / GET"	OBJECT	PAST PARTICIPLE
The company	has is having had	the computers	updated.

Alter these verbs to change tense.

The action happens to the object.

66.4 MARK THE SENTENCES THAT DESCRIBE THE PICTURES

Jane is repairing her car. ✓
Jane is getting her car repaired. ☐

Ahmed has been fixing his oven. ☐
Ahmed is getting his oven fixed. ☐

Sally's having her nails painted. ☐
Sally's painting her own nails. ☐

Natasha got her photograph taken. ☐
Natasha took a photograph. ☐

Gavin is getting his hair cut. ☐
Gavin is cutting his hair. ☐

Joe did the ironing at home. ☐
Joe had the ironing done at the mall. ☐

Annie is delivering some flowers. ☐
Annie had some flowers delivered. ☐

They're having their house painted. ☐
They're painting their own house. ☐

66.5 MATCH THE BEGINNINGS OF THE SENTENCES TO THE CORRECT ENDINGS

We're getting our furniture — replaced at the moment.

1. I'm taking the car to — and have your hair cut.

2. You should go to a salon — to get her teeth checked.

3. I don't want to cook. Should we — trained to deal with malware.

4. They've just had their staff — checked for malware. It's so slow.

5. I'm going to have my computer — the garage to get it fixed.

6. I took my daughter to the dentist — a deluxe kennel built for him.

7. They bought a dog and had — get a pizza delivered?

66.6 REWRITE THE SENTENCES CORRECTING THE ERRORS

When are we going to get repaired the TV?
When are we going to get the TV repaired?

1. Remember, today we're have the bedroom carpets fitted.

2. Your coat is really filthy. It should get you dry-cleaned.

3. My eyes hurt when I read. I should had them tested soon.

4. My friend has his wallet stolen when he was in Barcelona.

5. I get to have my birth certificate translated into Spanish for my application.

66.7 RESPOND TO THE AUDIO, SPEAKING OUT LOUD USING "HAVE / GET"

Is that Maria over there in the salon?

Yes, _she's getting her hair cut_ (she / her hair / cut).

1 Does Jacob clean the house himself?

No, _____ (he / it / clean) by someone else.

2 Why is Anneke putting on make-up?

The photographer's here. _____ (she / her picture / take).

3 Is your oven still broken?

Yes, but _____ (I / it / fix) on Monday.

4 Why is all your furniture covered?

The painter's coming. _____ (we / the house / paint).

5 Are you going to make dinner tonight?

No, _____ (I / a pizza / deliver).

6 Do you go to the dentist regularly?

Yes, _____ (I / my teeth / check) twice a year.

7 Do you go to the store for your newspaper?

No, _____ (we / it / deliver) to the house.

---

66 ✓ CHECKLIST

⚙️ "Have / get something done" ☐   **Aa** Service and repairs ☐   🧩 Describing things people do for you ☐

Complex agreement

One of the basic principles of English is that subjects and verbs must agree. Some subjects, however, can behave as singular or plural nouns depending on their context.

⚙ **New language** Complex agreement

Aa Vocabulary Collective nouns

New skill Using the correct agreement

67.1 KEY LANGUAGE COLLECTIVE NOUNS

Collective nouns have a singular form, but refer to a number of people or objects as a group. In US English they generally take a singular verb. In UK English they can often be used with either singular or plural verbs.

If the subject describes a singular body then the verb form must be singular.

The team is getting a new manager next year.

[The team as a whole is getting a new manager.]

The team are feeling excited about the news.

[Each individual member of the team is feeling excited.]

If the subject describes a collection of individuals, then the verb form can be plural in UK English.

🔊

67.2 FILL IN THE GAPS USING THE COLLECTIVE NOUNS IN THE PANEL

Some of my wife's _____ *family* _____ are coming to visit.

1. The legal _____ in my office is the largest in the company.

2. Members of the _____ are rehearsing in different rooms in the building.

3. The _____ is having an emergency meeting in New York.

4. The soccer _____ is arriving later this evening.

5. The entire _____ was delighted by the guest performer last night.

| ~~family~~ | team | orchestra | government | department | audience |

🔊

67.3 KEY LANGUAGE UNCOUNTABLE NOUNS WITH SINGULAR AGREEMENT

Names or titles of books and other works of art that end in a plural noun are treated as singular in terms of agreement.

Though "tales" is plural, *The Canterbury Tales* is a singular work of literature.

The Canterbury Tales **was first published in the 1400s.**

Other uncountable nouns appear to be plural because they end in an "-s," but have singular agreement. These include many place names and academic subjects.

Mathematics is becoming a more popular subject.

67.4 FURTHER EXAMPLES UNCOUNTABLE NOUNS WITH SINGULAR AGREEMENT

 Little Women **is a novel by Louisa May Alcott.**

 Athletics was an important part of the ancient Olympic Games.

 The Netherlands is known for its tulip industry.

 Politics has long been a topic for academic debate.

67.5 MARK THE SENTENCES THAT ARE CORRECT

The news starts at 10 tonight. ☑
The news start at 10 tonight. ☐

1. I want to study economic. ☐
   I want to study economics. ☐

2. Is athletics popular in your country? ☐
   Are athletics popular in your country? ☐

3. *Cats* are a successful musical. ☐
   Cats is a successful musical. ☐

4. The Philippines are an island country. ☐
   The Philippines is an island country. ☐

5. Physics are my favorite subjects. ☐
   Physics is my favorite subject. ☐

6. *Hard Times* was written by Dickens. ☐
   Hard Times were written by Dickens. ☐

7. The United States has nine time zones. ☐
   The United States have nine time zones. ☐

67.6 KEY LANGUAGE AGREEMENT AFTER "EITHER... OR" AND "NEITHER...NOR"

When you use "either... or" or "neither...nor" to join two nouns, the verb agrees with the second noun. However, if the last noun is singular and the first is plural, you can use either a singular verb or a plural verb.

 Either a tablet or a laptop is needed for the course.

The verb agrees with the second, singular noun.

 Neither the teacher nor the children were happy.

The verb agrees with the second, plural noun.

 Neither the classrooms nor the office $\begin{Bmatrix} \text{has} \\ \text{have} \end{Bmatrix}$ **internet access.**

The verb can have singular or plural agreement.

 67.7 MATCH THE BEGINNINGS OF THE SENTENCES TO THE CORRECT ENDINGS

I think either an email or a letter	is a great pet for a family.
1 Neither her mother nor her father	is safe to drive anymore.
2 Either a cat or a dog	are happy with the announcement.
3 Either the diner or the coffee shop	is fine for sending this kind of news.
4 Neither the boss nor the workers	has worked hard enough at school.
5 We think that neither Tom nor Katya	was there to pick her up from school.
6 Either the giraffes or the elephant	are the most popular animals in the park.
7 Neither my car nor my motorbike	is fine for our meeting.

67.8 LISTEN TO THE AUDIO AND ANSWER THE QUESTIONS

Two friends, Gavin and Nadiya, are talking about new gadgets.

> Gavin's new watch is six months old.
> True ☐ False ☐ Not given ☑

1 The new watch is available in different colors.
True ☐ False ☐ Not given ☐

2 Nadiya is impressed by the watch's battery life.
True ☐ False ☐ Not given ☐

3 Gavin thinks all his old gadgets look great.
True ☐ False ☐ Not given ☐

4 Nadiya was initially impressed by smartphones.
True ☐ False ☐ Not given ☐

5 "R&D" stands for "Research and Development."
True ☐ False ☐ Not given ☐

6 Gavin sells his old gadgets on the internet.
True ☐ False ☐ Not given ☐

7 Gavin will give Nadiya his "old" watch.
True ☐ False ☐ Not given ☐

67.9 SAY THE SENTENCES OUT LOUD, CHOOSING THE CORRECT WORDS

> Neither writing nor speaking to people in English is / ~~are~~ difficult any more.

1 The school is / are getting new equipment for its technology department.

2 Computer studies is / are my favorite subject at college at the moment.

3 Neither the cable nor the batteries is / are included with the new digital radio.

4 The Bahamas has / have many beaches, including some with pink sand.

5 I don't know what's wrong with it! Either the engine or the fan is / are broken.

67 ✓ CHECKLIST

⚙ Complex agreement ☐   **Aa** Collective nouns ☐   🧩 Using the correct agreement ☐

68 "So" and "such"

You can use "so" and "such" with certain words to add emphasis. They are similar in meaning, but they are used in different structures.

☼ **New language** "So" and "such" for emphasis
Aa Vocabulary Medical science
☀ **New skill** Emphasizing descriptions

68.1 KEY LANGUAGE "SO" AND "SUCH"

"Such" can be added before a noun to add emphasis. It can also be added before an adjective and noun combination. The "such" goes before "a / an."

"SUCH" + "A / AN" + NOUN

The trial was such a success.

"SUCH" + "A / AN" + ADJECTIVE + NOUN

It was such an important experiment.

TIP
"Such" + "a / an" + noun is more common with fairly extreme nouns rather than neutral ones.

"So" can be added before an adjective or an adverb to add emphasis.

"SO" + ADJECTIVE

The reaction is so dangerous.

"SO" + ADVERB

The surgery went so well!

68.2 CROSS OUT THE INCORRECT WORDS IN EACH SENTENCE

The disease spread so / ~~such~~ slowly that he didn't notice it for many years.

1. Even at the start of her career, she was so / such a well-respected scientist.

2. My brother fell off his bike this morning. The injury was so / such bad that we called a doctor.

3. Colds spread so / such fast between children, particularly in large groups.

4. I was hoping to get some positive news, but the test results were so / such a disappointment.

5. I'm pleased that he's so / such an experienced surgeon. It's very reassuring!

68.3 KEY LANGUAGE "SO" AND "SUCH" WITH "THAT"

You can use "that" with "so" and "such" to introduce a particular result caused by the fact you are emphasizing.

"SUCH" + "A / AN" + NOUN + "THAT"

The disease is such a mystery that it doesn't even have a name yet.

"SUCH" + "A / AN" + ADJECTIVE + NOUN + "THAT"

This is such a strange injury that it is hard to diagnose.

"SO" + ADJECTIVE + "THAT"

Medical research is so expensive that drugs are often costly.

"SO" + ADVERB + "THAT"

He recovered so quickly that he was able to go home the next day.

 68.4 MATCH THE BEGINNINGS OF THE SENTENCES TO THE CORRECT ENDINGS

The doctor was so tired that —————————→ he nearly fell asleep!

1. Dentistry is such a difficult job that — you have to train for many years.

2. He recovered so rapidly that — he was soon able to walk again.

3. She had such steady hands that — she could perform delicate operations.

4. The medicine tasted so bad that — I nearly spat it all out!

5. It is such a new treatment that — only a few patients have had it.

68.5 KEY LANGUAGE "SO" WITH QUANTIFIERS

"So" is also used before quantifiers like "few," "little," "many," and "much."

TIP
Don't use "so" or "such" on their own before comparative adjectives.

She had so little experience that I was really nervous.

Use "so much" before comparatives.

These treatments are so much better than the old ones.

68.6 FURTHER EXAMPLES "SO" WITH QUANTIFIERS

So many lives have been saved by advances in science.

This hospital is so much cleaner than the other one.

So few people have survived this illness. I'm very lucky.

Diseases can spread so much faster as a result of air travel.

68.7 REWRITE THE SENTENCES CORRECTING THE ERRORS

So much young doctors have to work very long hours.
So many young doctors have to work very long hours.

1 Surgeons train hard, which is why they make such few mistakes.

_____

2 I think these tablets work such much better than the others.

_____

3 Doctors have to pass so much exams during their training.

_____

4 Thank you, doctor. I feel such better than I did last week.

_____

68 MEDICINE TODAY

RATS TRAINED TO DETECT DISEASE

An incredible breakthrough

People from all over the world fear and dislike rats, believing them to be dirty, diseased, and generally dangerous. But a little-known fact is that rats are so intelligent that they can be trained to do many things for humans that we cannot do ourselves. In Mozambique, rats are even being used to sniff out tuberculosis (TB).

Rats have a sense of smell that is ___*so*___ well developed that they can _____ traces of TB in test _____ given by humans. They signify when they smell TB by rubbing their legs together and are then given a treat through a syringe. There are a number of reasons why this is _____ an important breakthrough. First, the rats are able spot the _____ in its early stages, which is so much better than testing later because then treatment can be started right away on any patients who have tested positive. TB is _____ if it is detected in its early stages. If left undetected, it can be _____ . Second, rats only take 30 minutes to test nearly 100 samples. This is so _____ more efficient than human laboratory _____ , which can take up to four days to do the same number. Finally, using rats is so much cheaper than buying expensive devices and paying a lot of money per test. This is important because TB is still a global concern. The situation in Mozambique was so bad _____ TB was declared a national emergency in 2006. By 2014, 60,000 people were said, by the ministry of health, to be _____ .

testing	~~so~~	that	detect	treatable	disease
deadly		much	such	samples	infected

---

68 ✓ **CHECKLIST**

⚙ "So" and "such" for emphasis ☐   **Aa** Medical science ☐   🧩 Emphasizing descriptions ☐

69 Using articles to generalize

"The" is the most commonly used word in the English language. It can be used in many different situations, as can the indefinite article "a," and the zero article.

🔧 **New language** Generic "the"
Aa Vocabulary Exploration and invention
🧩 **New skill** Using advanced articles

69.1 KEY LANGUAGE GENERIC "THE"

You can use "the" with a single countable noun to talk about a class of things in general. Inventions, musical instruments, and species of animal are often referred to in this way.

The telescope **changed the way we see the night sky.**

Referring to an invention, not an individual telescope.

The violin **is often the key instrument in an orchestra.**

Referring to a type of musical instrument, not an individual instrument.

The cheetah **can run faster than any other land animal.**

Referring to a species of animal, not an individual animal.

69.2 CROSS OUT THE INCORRECT WORDS IN EACH SENTENCE

Look over there! There's a / ~~an~~ / ~~the~~ lion and her cub.

① Apparently, a / an / **the** French horn is the most difficult instrument to play.

② Alexander Graham Bell is often credited with inventing a / an / **the** telephone.

③ My sister has a / an / the saxophone that she plays in her school orchestra.

④ A / An / **The** blue whale is the largest animal that has ever lived on Earth.

69.3 **ANOTHER WAY TO** TALK ABOUT A CLASS OF THINGS

You can also use a plural countable noun
without an article to talk about a class of things.

Telescopes **changed the way we see the night sky.**

Referring to the invention, not
a particular group of telescopes.

Violins **are often the key instruments in an orchestra.**

Referring to the type of musical instrument,
not a particular group of violins.

Cheetahs **can run faster than any other land animal.**

Referring to the species of animal,
not a particular group of cheetahs.

69.4 REWRITE THE SENTENCES CORRECTING THE ERRORS

Thomas Edison is widely acknowledged as the inventor of a moving picture.
Thomas Edison is widely acknowledged as the inventor of the moving picture.

1 I enjoy playing a piano, but I hated having lessons as a child.

_____

2 Mountain gorilla are one of the most endangered species on Earth.

_____

3 In 2007, a Russian lawyer paid nearly $4 million for the violin.

_____

4 Sloth is a slow animal, but the Galápagos tortoise is even slower.

_____

5 Steve Wozniak designed and built a 1976 Apple I computer.

_____

6 This concert is incredible. I love the sound of trumpet.

_____

69.5 KEY LANGUAGE DEFINITE AND INDEFINITE ARTICLES WITH NAMES

You normally use the zero article with the name of a person.

This is my uncle, Neil Armstrong.

In this case, "the" is pronounced "thee."

You can use the definite article before a person's name to differentiate them from another person with the same name.

He's not the Neil Armstrong, is he?

[He isn't the famous person with that name, is he?]

You can use the indefinite article when the focus is on a particular name, rather than the person.

I'm afraid there isn't a "Joseph Bloggs" on the list.

[The particular name given is not on the list.]

 69.6 FILL IN THE GAPS USING THE CORRECT ARTICLES, LEAVING A GAP FOR THE ZERO ARTICLE

The Space Race produced two truly iconic moments in _the_ history of humankind. The first happened on April 12, 1961, when Yuri Gagarin became _____ first human in space. The entire Vostok 1 mission, including one orbit around Earth, lasted only 1 hour 29 minutes. Gagarin's voyage changed how people all over _____ world thought about _____ space.

Just over eight years later in July 1969, _____ Neil Armstrong, "Buzz" Aldrin, and Michael Collins traveled to space in _____ Apollo 11 space craft. On July 20, 1969, Armstrong stepped onto _____ Moon's dusty surface. What he actually said next is _____ interesting story in itself. For many years he argued that he had said, "That's one small step for a man, one giant leap for mankind." After listening to repeated transmission recordings, however, he admitted that he may have dropped the indefinite article "_____ ." Either way, it was _____ huge step for mankind.

266

69.7 LISTEN TO THE AUDIO AND ANSWER THE QUESTIONS

 A radio show is reviewing a museum exhibition about women in space.

The reviewer states that only women will like this exhibition. **True** ☐ **False** ☑

1 The exhibition is being held in the City Museum. **True** ☐ **False** ☐

2 All of the exhibits in "There's Space for Women" are replicas. **True** ☐ **False** ☐

3 Valentina Tereshkova was the first female cosmonaut in 1992. **True** ☐ **False** ☐

4 Jan Davis and Mark Lee flew in space when they were married. **True** ☐ **False** ☐

5 The first person in space from South Korea was a woman. **True** ☐ **False** ☐

6 An astronaut is definitely visiting the exhibition this month. **True** ☐ **False** ☐

7 You can book tickets for the exhibition online. **True** ☐ **False** ☐

---

69 ✅ **CHECKLIST**

⚙ Generic "the" ☐ **Aa** Exploration and invention ☐ 🧩 Using advanced articles ☐

🔄 **REVIEW** THE ENGLISH YOU HAVE LEARNED IN UNITS 67–69

NEW LANGUAGE	SAMPLE SENTENCE	☑	UNIT
"HAVE / GET SOMETHING DONE"	**Did you** get your software updated**?**	☐	66.1
COMPLEX SUBJECT-VERB AGREEMENT	The team is **getting a new manager next year.** The team are **feeling excited about the news.**	☐	67.1, 67.3, 67.6
"SO" AND "SUCH"	**The trial was** such **a success.** **The reaction is** so **dangerous.**	☐	68.1, 68.3, 68.5
GENERIC "THE"	The **telescope changed the way we see** the **night sky.**	☐	69.1
ARTICLES WITH NAMES	**He's not** the **Neil Armstrong, is he?** **I'm afraid there isn't** a **Joseph Bloggs on the list.**	☐	69.5

Answers

1.2

Hi José,
Today **is** my first day in my new job, so **I am leaving** the house early.
I'm a bit nervous, but **I'm also** very excited!
Anyway, **I'm already running** late, and **I need** to leave to catch the bus. **Don't forget** to pick up some milk on your way home from work tonight!
See you later!

1.4 ◀))

1 I **have been reading** for hours. My eyes **have started hurting**.
2 Has the mail **arrived** yet? I **have been expecting** a letter all week.
3 My leg **has been hurting** all day, but I **haven't seen** a doctor yet.
4 Have you **seen** my keys? I **have been looking** for them for ages.
5 Have you **heard** about Carl? He **has decided** to move.
6 I **have finished**! I **have been writing** this essay for ages.
7 Have you ever **visited France**? We **have been looking** at brochures.
8 I **have been trying** to reach Tao all day, but he **has not answered** yet.

1.6 ◀))

1 They aren't very welcoming, **are they**?
2 He should try harder to be friendly, **shouldn't he**?
3 She hasn't made many friends here, **has she**?
4 He doesn't like going to new places, **does he**?
5 They're so happy to be here, **aren't they**?
6 They would be here if they could, **wouldn't they**?

1.8

1 Answer required
2 Answer not required
3 Answer not required
4 Answer required
5 Answer not required
6 Answer not required

1.9 ◀))

1 People don't have their own office space here, **do they**?

2 You have been introduced to Mr. Thomas, **haven't you**?
3 You'd like to come to dinner with us all tonight, **wouldn't you**?
4 Oscar and Kate aren't here yet, **are they**?

2.3 ◀))

1 She has long, wavy hair.
2 Sorry, I don't believe you.
3 That jacket fits you very well.
4 I rarely think about the past.
5 Jess is having a great time at the party.
6 That milk smells dreadful.
7 I'm thinking about going home soon.
8 I'm slowly realizing the problem here.
9 You seem unhappy. Can I help?

2.4

Hi Sara,
I'm writing about Gavin. I **think** there's something wrong. I'm not **suggesting** that it's anything serious, but he doesn't **seem** to be his usual happy self. Maybe he's not **fitting** in well in his new job. I was going to **suggest** that the three of us go out for a drink, or perhaps you would **prefer** a meal. Let me know what you think.
Tina

3.2 ◀))

1 She doesn't have any **close** family left, only an uncle.
2 Sometimes the only solution is to **do** your best and hope.
3 All their lives they appeared to be **happily** married.
4 Unfortunately, the financial crisis ruined his **career**.
5 He first **went** into business when he was only 17.
6 Looking at old photographs can stir up **memories**.
7 I can distinctly **remember** meeting him 20 years ago.
8 Looking at them, the difference in age is **clearly** visible.

3.3

1 False   2 False   3 True   4 False
5 False   6 True   7 False

3.4 ◀))

1 poles apart   2 a popular belief
3 opinions are divided   4 firmly believe

3.5 Model Answers

1 Mariam is from northern France.
2 She studied architecture in college.
3 She met her husband on a photography field trip.
4 The turning point was when a wildlife magazine published her photos.
5 Yes, Mariam and Julian have two children.
6 They are planning to travel to Japan and Korea next year.

3.6

1 25 years ago   2 23 years ago
3 3 years ago   4 1 month ago

3.7 ◀))

1 Lisa **went** to Thailand 25 years **ago**.
2 Bill **was teaching** when Lisa arrived in Thailand.
3 Lisa and Bill **got married** 23 years ago, **in** March.
4 Lisa **had been traveling** for 25 years before she returned.
5 Barbara **graduated** from college **last** month.

3.8 ◀))

1 I got married **while I was living in China.**
2 I was **living in China when** I had a baby.
3 I wrote my thesis **while I was studying part-time.**
4 I was **studying part-time when** I started a small business.

4.4 ◀))

GENERAL: **awful, terrible, awesome**
SPECIFIC: **cruel, expensive, tasty**
SIZE: **enormous, huge, tiny**
SHAPE: **round, oval, square**
AGE: **elderly, modern, ancient**
COLOR: **green, red, orange**
MATERIAL: **silk, leather, metal**

4.5 ◀))

1 I don't like him at all. He's a **terrible, rude** man. Let's not invite him to the party.
2 My mother thinks he's a **nice, intelligent young** boy.
3 Dad, look at this **sweet, friendly brown** puppy! Can we take him for a walk?

4 Should we buy this **wonderful**, **comfortable** sofa for the living room? We really need a new one.

4.6
1 True 2 Not given 3 False 4 True
5 False

4.7
2

4.8 ◀))
1 His last employer said he was **un**trustworthy.
2 She doesn't realize how **in**sensitive she is.
3 He's 25 now, but he's rather **im**mature at work.
4 I'm afraid she's quite an **in**efficient worker.
5 He gossips and is **un**kind to his co-workers.
6 Her office desk and her work are **dis**organized.
7 He makes mistakes because he's **im**patient.
8 She's **dis**loyal to the company.

4.9 ◀))
POSITIVE ADJECTIVES: **helpful, excellent, popular, proactive, mature**
NEGATIVE ADJECTIVES: **disloyal, unkind, frustrating, impatient, arrogant**

05

5.3 ◀))
1 With busy work and social lives, it's **true that** most people have little time to study.
2 Languages are so useful. It is **a shame that** so few people learn a second language.
3 Learning doesn't have to be expensive. It is not **essential to** spend a lot of money.
4 Try internet study groups. It is **easy to** meet other language learners online.
5 Don't worry if you need time. It's **unlikely that** you'll be able to speak fluently quickly.

5.5 ◀))
1 Remember, it's important **to** be relaxed about making mistakes.
2 With so many options, it's no longer difficult **to** find language courses online.
3 **To** take the exam now would be a waste of time. She hasn't studied at all.
4 **It** is unlikely that he will finish the class before the end of the year.
5 Don't give up! It's true **that** the more you study, the better you will become.

5.6
1 Dave 2 Mei 3 Sam 4 Mei 5 Alice

5.7 ◀))
1 I am surprised that my son **has** an aptitude for copying accents.
2 Unfortunately, I have a **complete** inability to remember vocabulary.
3 Some people appear to have a natural **ability** to speak a number of languages.
4 My father had a remarkable **capacity** to memorize lists of words.

5.8 ◀)) Model Answers
1 It is important to be able to communicate with people across the world.
2 It's best to be patient with yourself and take things slowly.
3 It is difficult to make sure that you practice every day when you are busy.

07

7.2 ◀))
1 Be careful, it's absolutely **pouring down** with rain.
2 He's behind on his work, so he needs to **catch up**.
3 They are **taking down** the offensive posters today.
4 She'll have a backup. She always **backs up** her files.
5 They **split up** every time they have an argument.

7.4 ◀))
1 I'll **pick** your shopping **up** for you.
2 They're **putting** posters **up** outside again.
3 Have you **checked** the restaurant menu **out**?
4 He hasn't **set** the computer **up** yet.

7.5 ◀))
1 He should ask **her** out if he wants to.
2 Remember to take **it** out later.
3 You should send **it** back if it's broken.
4 Could you turn **them** off when you leave?

7.7 ◀))
1 My big brother is a CEO. I have a lot to **live up to**.
2 Slow down! I can't **keep up with** you any more, I'm tired.
3 His parents aren't very strict. He **gets away with** everything!

7.8
1 B 2 F 3 C 4 D 5 A 6 E

7.9
1 Komodo dragons 2 Tour guide
3 Blog 4 Travel guides 5 Good pay

7.10 ◀))
1 cut off
2 stop off
3 take off
4 set off

7.11 ◀))
1 Our plane was due to **take off** an hour ago.
2 We have to **set off** really early for our vacation.
3 He went with her to the train station to **see her off**.
4 They missed the ferry, so they were **cut off** from the mainland.

08

8.2 ◀))
1 I **was walking** down the road when someone **asked** me to take their photo.
2 Someone **was talking** during the tour until we **told** them to be quiet.
3 I **stopped** twice to take photos while I **was driving** through the country.
4 We **decided** to order some champagne while we **were eating** lunch.
5 We were lost and our feet **were aching** before we finally **found** a map shop.

8.3 ◀))
1 My feet really ached by the end of the day because **we had walked all around the city**.
2 The trip was perfect because **we had spent a long time planning it**.
3 We got completely lost because **we had crossed over the wrong bridge**.
4 We went to see a great show because **our tour guide had recommended it**.

8.6 ◀))
1 We **had been waiting** for at least an hour when the taxi finally arrived.
2 I eventually went to the pharmacy because I **had not been feeling** well for days.
3 We went to see the movie because they **had been promoting** it for months.
4 The streets were beautiful and white because it **had been snowing** all night.

8.7
① False ② True ③ True ④ True

8.8
③

8.9
① bright and early
② off the beaten track
③ travel light

09

9.2 🔊
① It's such a sunny day! You could go to the park later if you have time.
② You really must try the new Italian restaurant on Main Street.
③ You ought to have a big party with all your friends. It would be great!

9.3 🔊
① Everything about this hotel from the dark interior to the hard stares of the grumpy staff was unwelcoming. **They ought to hire a new receptionist!**
② The hotel's employees are wonderful. They did everything to make our honeymoon perfect. **You should tell them if it's a special occasion.**
③ Not bad although the furniture in the hotel was falling apart. The walls were very thin and it was quite noisy. **You might want to bring earplugs.**
④ I paid for a room with a view of the ski slopes, but all I could see was the wall of the building across from us. **You could ask to change rooms if this happens.**
⑤ Outstanding! I can understand the rave reviews for this great place. Our balcony overlooked the ocean. **You must ask for a room with an ocean view!**

9.4
① Like ② Like ③ Dislike ④ Like
⑤ Dislike

9.7 🔊
① That snake is poisonous. You **must** go to the doctor about that bite or it'll get worse.
② We **had better** go back to the boat. It's leaving soon and we don't want to miss it.
③ Perhaps you **could** go to France this summer. That would be nice.
④ Everyone says the castle is stunning and that we **must** see the view from the tower.

9.8
① Like ② Like ③ Disike ④ Like ⑤ Like
⑥ Dislike

9.9 Model Answer
Hi **Jake**,
I'm traveling back tonight. I can't believe my trip is over already! I really enjoyed **relaxing on the beach and swimming in the ocean.** The town was **beautiful and the restaurants were amazing. We ate out every night.** You really should **visit. You must ask if they have any vacancies at the Hotel Del Mar. The food was so fresh and the hotel's employees were wonderful.**
Lots of love,
Sara

10

10.2 🔊
① I don't have much money. **I definitely won't go on vacation this year.**
② He's worked so hard for his exams. **He'll pass them all, no problem.**
③ She's a talented young pianist. **She might be famous one day.**
④ Look at the line outside the stadium. **We probably won't get tickets.**
⑤ You don't have a very good voice. **You definitely won't ever be in an opera.**
⑥ My sister loves to travel. **She'll probably go to Australia one day.**
⑦ Joe goes running every day. **He might be running a marathon soon.**

10.3
① likely to happen
② definitely will happen
③ probably won't happen
④ unlikely to happen

10.4
① funda**men**tally ② es**sen**tially
③ sur**pri**singly ④ pre**dic**tably
⑤ **for**tunately ⑥ **in**terestingly
⑦ **luck**ily ⑧ un**for**tunately

10.5 Model Answers
① They're buying them as short-term investments or as places to live part-time.
② They can't afford to buy a house because of rising house prices.
③ There are fewer people there as it's empty most of the year.
④ They're reserving a certain percentage of new buildings for local people and they're introducing higher fees for overseas buyers.

10.6 🔊
① This is only a **short-term** solution. We'll have to fix the fence properly soon.
② OK, we'll order pizza tonight, but **in the long run** we need to sort out a meal plan.
③ I don't understand this new digital system, but I know it's **the shape of things to come.**
④ It was **only a matter of time** before the company hit its targets.

12

12.2 🔊
① All my siblings love playing football, especially my brother.
② We are all quite interested in our family history, so we've made a family tree.
③ I love talking to my aunt, because she has lots of interesting stories from her travels abroad.
④ My grandmother thinks I should get married, but I am not as traditional as she is.
⑤ We don't have family gatherings very often, since my grandparents live abroad.

12.3
① D ② A ③ C

12.5 🔊
① Elizabeth had two children, **whereas / yet** Mary had none.
② The two elderly sisters were **equally / similarly** wealthy.
③ The father left the army **due to / owing to** a serious arm injury.
④ James and Tom were identical twins. **Therefore / Hence**, they looked alike.

12.6 🔊
① You have failed to respond to our messages. **Hence**, your subscription has been canceled.
② My friends say I take after my dad, **because** we both like mountain biking.
③ After a successful book tour, the professor's lectures were **equally** well-received.
④ I love my aunts, **especially** Meera, because she's so funny.

12.7
① False ② True ③ True ④ False

13

13.5 🔊
1 My mother **used to walk** five miles to school and back.
2 I **didn't use to like** using the Internet, but now I think it's great!
3 **Did** you **use to eat** your lunch at school?
4 My grandmother's house **didn't use to have** electricity.
5 Whenever I had a toothache, my dad **would take** me to a scary dentist.

13.6
1 used to complain   2 would walk
3 used to get upset   4 didn't use to do
5 used to write   6 would

13.7
1 They go to the movies together
2 Documentaries and news archives
3 Older family members
4 It's very important to them
5 Understanding other people's values

13.8 🔊
1 acceptance   2 honesty   3 values
4 greedy   5 character   6 interrupt

13.9   Model Answers
1 They started talking because they were both researching their family history.
2 They both had a brother they hadn't seen for 50 years and they had both been teachers after leaving the army.
3 It was surprising because they lived very close to each other for 50 years.
4 Last week, the two brothers met for the first time in half a century.

14

14.3 🔊
1 The giraffe is **just as** tall **as** the house.
2 The flower is **not as / nowhere near as** large **as** the tree.
3 The phone is **not as / half as** expensive **as** the laptop.
4 The baby is **not as / nowhere near as** old **as** the man.
5 The pizza is **not as / almost as / not quite as** wide **as** the plate.

14.5
1 The old video   2 The car   3 The new house   4 Andrew   5 Less often

14.6
1 a lawyer   2 Jon   3 40 minutes   4 rainy
5 with her family   6 good

14.7 🔊
1 Thankfully, our baby is a **heavy** sleeper and only wakes once a night.
2 The commute to work takes ages, even when there is **light** traffic.
3 Feeling sick every day is a **high** price to pay for going on a cruise.
4 I only really wake up in the morning after a **strong** coffee.
5 My mother has a **low** opinion of anyone who doesn't work hard.

14.8
Alex and Sue are both chefs. She owns a café and he works in a famous restaurant. Her cooking is **just as** good **as** his, maybe even better, although her cooking is mostly savory and she has a sweet tooth. Unfortunately, just because her food costs **half as** much **as** his, some people do not have as **high** an opinion of her skills. Her café is seen as somewhere with **low** prices to grab a bite to eat, not somewhere to wine and dine. Sue says this is a small price to pay for owning her own business. Some people just like to go out of their way to pay **twice as** much **as** they should for a three-course meal in Alex's restaurant, rather than enjoy a delicious piece of cake or pastry in Sue's café.

14.9 🔊
1 sweet tooth   2 grab a bite to eat
3 wine and dine   4 savory   5 go out of your way

15

15.4 🔊
1 The longer the film went on, the more bored I became.
2 The more it rained, the quicker the vegetables grew.
3 The more she told me not to laugh, the more I laughed.
4 The more sugar a dessert contains, the worse it is for you.

15.5 🔊
1 The louder my music is, the **angrier** my mother gets.
2 The **younger** the skier is, the less frightened they are of falling.
3 The **more annoyed** my teacher gets, the more I giggle nervously.

4 **The faster** the car went, **the louder** the passengers screamed.

15.7 🔊
1 The more the merrier.
2 The bigger the better.
3 The stronger the better.

15.9
1 Not given   2 True   3 False   4 True

15.10   Model Answers
1 Older people require more financial support in their old age.
2 In the first suggested solution, people are responsible for their own care in old age.
3 In the second suggested solution, the government is responsible for people's care in old age.
4 The final suggested solution is to increase the official retirement age.

17

17.2 🔊
SEQUENCING: **first**, **second**
ADDING: **additionally**, **furthermore**
EXAMPLES: **such as**, **for example**
CONCLUDING: **overall**, **to sum up**

17.3 🔊
1 Others, **such as** Sydney University and Toronto, are renowned for their stunning historical buildings.
2 **Moreover**, there are newer universities like Moscow and Xiamen that have equally impressive buildings.
3 **For instance**, Moscow State University is incredibly impressive at night.
4 **Additionally**, a number of modern university buildings in Australia are spectacular.
5 **Overall**, there are some amazing educational buildings around the world.
6 **To sum up**, it can be worth your time to look at educational buildings, even if you are visiting as a tourist.

17.4
1 False   2 True   3 Not given   4 Not given   5 False

17.7 🔊
1 You must pay to play tennis **unless you join the club.**
2 If you are a history student, **you can join the historical society.**

3 If you join the water sports club, **you can learn how to sail.**

4 You can join today **unless you need more time to think.**

17.8 ◀))

1 If you hear **discourse** markers, use them to help organize your notes.

2 When you take notes, **use** a simple shorthand with symbols and abbreviations.

3 If your handwriting is messy, try to **make** sure it is readable.

4 Unless you record every lecture, try to **review** your notes soon after.

17.9
2

17.10 Model Answer

Active note-taking examples:
Think about expected content before lecture.
Use own words for notes (paraphrase).
Find relationships between parts of lecture.
Write down follow-up questions.

18

18.3
1 B **2** C **3** D **4** A

18.5 ◀))

1 The vast **majority** of the lecture halls have wireless internet access.

2 **Just** over a quarter of classes are recorded for students to listen to online.

3 After one week, **most** people know their way around campus.

4 Only a **tiny** minority of our students do not have smartphones.

5 Well **over** half of our students eat a hot meal on campus.

6 Just **over** two-thirds of our professors can speak two languages.

18.7
1 True **2** False **3** True **4** True **5** False

18.9 ◀)) Model Answers

1 Really? **I heard that there are 40 different clubs.**

2 Is that so? **I read that most students prefer to live on campus.**

3 Are you sure? **I was told that they have a dedicated team to help with future career decisions.**

19

19.4
2

19.5 ◀))

1 English is **spoken** by millions of people across the world.

2 Online courses **are being studied** by a variety of students.

3 The courses **are being paid for** by a number of universities.

4 Certificates **can be printed out** at home by participants.

5 Some exams can **be taken** in several different languages.

19.6 ◀))

1 Eighty percent **of the courses are written in English.**

2 Credits **are offered for MOOC courses (by some universities).**

3 Technical help **is provided for the participants (by some people).**

4 Next year, MOOCs **will be taken by millions of students.**

19.8 ◀))

1 downfall **2** crackdown **3** backup
4 login **5** input **6** leftovers **7** check-in
8 outset

19.9
1 Not given **2** True **3** Not given

19.10 ◀))

1 The things we learn are **tested** in a weekly online exam.

2 The face-to-face lessons expand on the online course **input**.

3 From the **outset**, I knew this course would be successful.

4 Lack of motivation has always been my **downfall** in online learning.

5 The course is **written** by language-learning experts.

6 They have made changes to make it easier to **log in** to your account.

7 There has also been a **crackdown** on security to prevent cheating.

20

20.3 ◀))

1 I'm going to take a water bottle **in case the exam room is hot.**

---

2 Suppose you cannot afford to study. **Maybe you could apply for funding.**

3 I am studying really hard tonight **in case we have a test tomorrow.**

4 What if I forget to bring a calculator? **Maybe they will have spares.**

20.6
1 Likely **2** Unlikely **3** Likely
4 Unlikely **5** Likely **6** Unlikely
7 Likely **8** Unlikely

20.8
1 False **2** False **3** False **4** True

20.9
1 Unlikely **2** Likely **3** Likely
4 Unlikely

20.10 ◀)) Model Answers
1 I'd like to meet Abraham Lincoln.
2 I would make fruit and vegetables free for everybody.
3 I'll apply for a place at college.

22

22.3 ◀))

1 **Before** seeing that job listing, I thought I would never find my perfect job.

2 After **qualifying** as an engineer, I volunteered in Cambodia.

3 **Instead of** working in a low-paid job, I decided to train as an accountant.

4 Without **passing** my exams, it would be difficult to have a decent career.

22.4
1 False **2** True **3** Not given **4** True
5 False **6** Not given

22.5 ◀))

1 keen **2** have an eye for detail
3 post **4** in the near future
5 take the position

22.6
1 True **2** Not given **3** False **4** True
5 False

22.7
1 Work experience and skills
2 Say what you were doing
3 Less than two sides of paper

22.8 ◀))

1 The job was quite challenging in terms of improving the consumer experience.

❷ I traveled to Vietnam where I volunteered for a number of educational projects.
❸ I am a qualified fire warden and am trained in writing risk assessments.
❹ I have an in-depth knowledge of real estate due to having eight years' experience.

23

23.2 🔊
❶ I was wondering **when you are available**.
❷ I'd like to know **why you have applied for this job**.
❸ Do you have any idea **what our best-selling product is**?
❹ I'm curious to know **who your last manager was**.

23.4 🔊
❶ We were wondering **if / whether you like working with animals**?
❷ Would you mind telling us **if / whether you've applied for any other jobs**?
❸ Could you tell me **if / whether you have any computer skills**?
❹ We'd like to know **if / whether you have relevant experience**.

23.5 🔊
❶ We were wondering why you left your last job.
❷ Could you tell us about your future career ambitions?
❸ I'd like to know whether you like taking risks.

23.6
❶ False ❷ True ❸ False ❹ True

23.8
❶ He has learned new techniques and skills
❷ She had already read about them
❸ He used to be very critical of himself
❹ It was part of his second-year project

23.9 🔊 Model Answers
❶ Well, my last role required a lot of teamwork.
❷ Actually, quite a lot. I have researched your company online.
❸ Let's see, I hope to be directing a large company.
❹ Good question. I think I have exactly what you're looking for.

24

24.2 🔊
❶ The new product launch caused **the profits to rise**, which was excellent news.
❷ I recently lost my job, but I **managed** to find a new one quite quickly.
❸ The employees were furious, so they **threatened** to not work yesterday.
❹ I always get scared when my boss **invites me to** her office. It's never good news.
❺ Sometimes it can be good to **volunteer** to do extra work. It'll impress your boss.
❻ On Fridays, my manager sometimes **allows me** to leave early to enjoy the weekend.

24.4 🔊
❶ Over the years we have enjoyed **leading** the market when it comes to the environment.
❷ An auditor has advised us **to change** some of our policies in order to improve further.
❸ One change we would like **to make** is to no longer supply disposable cups.
❹ We're sure that you will approve of us **trying** to become more environmentally friendly.
❺ The change will prevent our company **throwing away** up to 25,000 cups each year.
❻ Bringing your own mug will enable us **to stick** to this new initiative.
❼ We hope that you approve of the company **making** a change like this. It's for a great cause.
❽ I'll send another quick memo on Friday **to remind** you to bring your own mug to work.

24.7 🔊
❶ He appealed **to** the audience, asking them to stop booing the actors in the play.
❷ She always shouts **at** him when he doesn't take the dog for a walk.
❸ You should wait **for** Jane to arrive before talking to Max about this important issue.
❹ I'm sure that I can count **on** you to support your boss at this difficult time.
❺ I've arranged **for** the doctor to see you tomorrow morning at 10am.
❻ My children never listen **to** me when I tell them what to do.

24.8 Model Answers
❶ They used to design the business cards, but they don't anymore.
❷ They focused on providing the quality materials and printing.

❸ YouToPrint passed on the savings to the customers by lowering their prices.
❹ You can tap them on a smartphone and they take you straight to a website.

25

25.3 🔊
❶ Barbara gave it **to** me.
❷ We gave **them** some candy. / We gave some candy to them.
❸ James passed **me** the documents. / James passed the documents to me.

25.5 🔊
❶ The teacher gave homework **to** the students.
❷ He made a speech **for** the business.
❸ He gave advice **to** them.
❹ He's collecting money **for** the charity.

25.6
❶ Not given ❷ True ❸ False

25.7 Model Answers
❶ The business will start trading next month.
❷ Starting a business is expensive, and Colin doesn't have much money.
❸ Not many companies have made walking map apps.
❹ If it fails, he will be happy that he tried.

25.8
I've been planning to start my own map shop for years, and finally I've done all the paperwork and all the **red tape** is out of the way. We don't formally open until next month, but I'm getting everything ready now so we can really **hit the ground running**. It hasn't been cheap though. Starting a business is very expensive and I don't have a **blank check** to buy thousands of maps. The walking map app is the **ace up my sleeve** though. Not many people do those yet and I hope to have **cornered the market** by the end of next year. Of course, it might all go horribly wrong, but **nothing ventured, nothing gained**, eh?

25.9
❶ For all **your** map needs.
❷ We **have** 20 years' experience.
❸ we are **ahead** of the times.
❹ will be **launching**
❺ will be **available**
❻ once **you've** returned
❼ **an** enormous stock

27.3 🔊
① We had to run the meeting **ourselves**.
② Do you ever send meeting reminders to **yourself**?
③ I taught **myself** how to play the guitar.
④ Do you and Priya see **yourselves** as team players?
⑤ He put **himself** forward for a big promotion.
⑥ The company promotes **itself** online.

27.5 🔊
① I'm very impressed that they planned this conference **themselves**!
② I spent all evening doing research for this presentation **myself**.
③ The area is traditional, but the city **itself** is full of modern offices.
④ Nobody helped us. We won this contract **ourselves**.
⑤ I couldn't believe it! The Queen **herself** presented the award.
⑥ Marta writes summaries for her boss. He can't write them **himself**.
⑦ It's very important that you fix these problems **yourself**, Jacob.
⑧ The company founders **themselves** will be making the final decision.

27.8
Steven Strange, CEO of AngloEuroCorp, left the company in unusual circumstances last week. Acting CEO Don Black was called into the CEO's office by Strange, who said, "You should **familiarize yourself** with this office and **make yourself** at home." Another employee commented on Strange's odd behavior: "He usually **absented himself** from our meetings because he didn't **concern himself** with day-to-day matters. Last Friday was different. Mr. Strange **tore himself** away from his office and attended the weekly meeting. He even thanked us for our hard work!" As he left, Strange supposedly announced: "Go home early and **enjoy yourselves**!"

27.9
① catch up ② take on ③ sort out
④ knock off ⑤ stay behind

27.10 🔊
① If you have caught up with your work, you can knock **off** early today.
② We should be proud of our sales results and congratulate **ourselves**.

③ These two women have worked **themselves** into positions for promotions.
④ I can't leave early today. I'm snowed **under** with work at the moment.

28.2 🔊
① He was fired because he continued **to ignore his duties.**
② How would you propose **to raise the money?**
③ I was so late that I began **to run for the bus.**
④ Let's go inside. I really can't stand **being cold and wet.**
⑤ I have to say that I prefer **writing to people by hand.**

28.5 🔊
① I hope you remembered **to put** the advertisement for the grand reopening in the newspaper?
② Unfortunately, when the hotel reopened, they had forgotten **to advertise**, so it was empty.
③ I'll never forget **seeing** the manager's face when there were no guests at the party.
④ Do you remember **planning** the grand opening party with Ceri last year?
⑤ Do you regret **asking** Tim to promote the reopening?
⑥ After the initial failure, the refurbished hotel went on **to be** a huge success.
⑦ Now it's famous and successful, the hotel will probably go on **being** popular for many years.

28.6 🔊
① I need to **stop** spending so much money on food at work.
② My dad says he could never **forget** meeting Elvis, even though it was a long time ago.
③ If I'm not busy tonight, I'd absolutely **love** to go to dinner with you.
④ My boss **prefers** talking on the phone to video calls.
⑤ Thanks for the offer. If you don't mind, I'd like to **continue** to do my work instead.
⑥ After the book was published, he **went on** to write an award-winning screenplay.
⑦ I **regret** to inform you that the meeting has been postponed.
⑧ It looks like it will be expensive to get catering. I **propose** making the food ourselves.

28.7
① Yes ② No ③ Yes ④ No ⑤ No
⑥ No ⑦ Yes

29.2 🔊
EXTREME: **awful, enormous, superb, tiny, disgusting**
ABSOLUTE: **unique, unknown, dead, right, wrong**
CLASSIFYING: **organic, digital, chemical, industrial, electronic**

29.3 🔊
① Have you seen this amazing designer watch?
② This new software is so slow. It's awful.
③ Because it runs on solar power, it's extremely cheap.
④ The instructions for the product are impossible.
⑤ The numbers on the watch are tiny!
⑥ I need to replace my computer. It's broken.

29.6 🔊
① It is **incredibly** important to know a lot about the product you are trying to sell.
② Did you see that **completely** digital presentation by the marketing team?
③ Don't you think that this kind of product is extremely **useful** for teenagers?
④ To copy and then sell someone else's invention as your own is **utterly** wrong.
⑤ From the initial product design to marketing is a **rather** long process.
⑥ The new designer in my department is **absolutely** fantastic.
⑦ I think the food at the conference was bad. I felt extremely **sick** this morning.
⑧ I have to say that I think it was an absolutely **superb** presentation.

29.8
① Liked it a lot ② Not very good
③ Liked it a lot ④ Didn't like it very much
⑤ Hated it

29.10
① False ② False ③ True ④ True ⑤ False

29.11 🔊
① The coffee capsules are **wholly recyclable**.
② The Blingtech3000 is an **utterly stylish** timepiece.

3 The Blingtech3000's software is **absolutely state-of-the-art**.
4 Most air freshener refills are **extremely expensive**.
5 Coz-E-Slip slippers have a **totally automatic** thermostat.
6 The slippers are supposed to be **incredibly comfortable**.

30

30.3 🔊
1 She searched for the company online **so as to find its email address.**
2 They gave her a refund **so as to keep her business.**
3 The goods were packed carefully **to protect them.**
4 They paid for express delivery **in order to get the goods on time.**
5 I booked an expensive hotel **so as to be able to relax on my trip.**

30.6
1 False **2** True **3** True **4** False
5 True **6** Not given **7** False

30.7 🔊
1 Last year we had to complain in order to get a bigger room.
2 I usually go to the same resort so that I can stay in the same hotel.
3 He bought the latest model to impress his friends.
4 I pack very carefully so as not to forget anything.
5 I went to the top of the highest mountain so that I could race down.
6 I went to a hospital in order to get an X-ray of my leg.

30.9 🔊
1 Special "outlet" stores are known **for** selling excess goods at reduced prices.
2 This process is for customers who want **to** complain about the products they have received.
3 People are employed **to** check the quality of the goods before they are sent to stores.
4 These notes are here **to** help you complete the form and submit your complaint.
5 There is a telephone number **for** unhappy customers who wish to make further complaints.
6 I think a large number of people only complain **to** get refunds.
7 This new product is **for** busy people who want to make their lives simpler.

32

32.4 🔊
1 If I **had chosen** the trip, we **would have gone** to Spain.
2 If we **had arrived** earlier, we **would not have missed** the show.
3 I **could have helped** them if they **had called** me earlier.
4 If we **had stopped** eating earlier, we **might not have felt** so sick.
5 She **would have passed** her exam if she **had worked** a bit harder.
6 If you **had shut** the door, we **might not have been** so cold.

32.6
1 B **2** A **3** A **4** A **5** B

32.8 🔊
1 I might've worked harder if I'd been paid more.
2 If more people had voted for him, he would've won.
3 If you'd left earlier, we would've arrived on time.
4 She might've finished on time if she'd started sooner.

32.9 🔊
1 If **you'd** kept the fire alight, we wouldn't have been so cold.
2 You **might have** slept better if you had brought a sleeping bag!
3 If she'd **worn** her boots, she wouldn't have had such wet feet.
4 If they'd **kept** the river clean, the fish might not have died.

32.10
1 False **2** True **3** True **4** False
5 False **6** False

32.11
2

32.14 🔊
1 I wish we **weren't** outdoors right now.
2 I think about the trip a lot. I wish I **had taken** more photos.
3 I feel sick. If only I **had eaten** fewer of those berries.
4 The bus has broken down! If only the driver **knew** how to fix it.
5 I'm so exhausted! If only I**'d slept** a little more.

32.15 🔊
1 I missed the bus again. I wish **I'd set an alarm.**
2 I caught a huge fish yesterday. If only **I'd taken a photo.**
3 I can't afford those boots. If only **I hadn't spent all my money.**
4 I was so cold this winter. I wish **I had bought a coat**.

32.16 🔊
1 He wished he'd **stopped** the fisherman from killing the seal.
2 He thought if only he'd **done** something to protect the seals
3 If I hadn't helped, I know I would've **felt** guilty forever.
4 If he'd seen me become a campaigner, he'd have **been** very proud.

33

33.3 🔊
1 People **shouldn't have** thrown things in the river. The fish population has declined dramatically.
2 Factories **should have** reduced pollution in accordance with environmental agreements.
3 Companies **should have** used fewer vehicles in order to lower their carbon footprint.
4 Factories **shouldn't have** released pollution into the water. It has poisoned the ecosystem.

33.4 🔊
1 I **ought to** have gone to bed earlier last night. I'm feeling really exhausted now.
2 We really **shouldn't have** eaten so much at lunchtime. I'm feeling sleepy now.
3 You **should have driven** more carefully on the wet road. You could have had an accident.
4 **Should I have** bought this desktop computer, or would the laptop have been better?

33.5
1 False **2** True **3** True **4** True **5** False

33.7
1 B **2** A **3** C **4** E **5** D

33.8 🔊

1 **Following** the rise of a new civilization, the islanders built statues to honor their ancestors.

2 **Throughout** this time, the islanders were cutting down lots of trees.

3 **During** his visit, the first European explorer noticed that there weren't many trees.

4 The ship HMS Blossom visited in 1825, and **by that time**, the statues had been toppled over.

5 An airport was built in 1987 and **since then**, lots of tourists have visited Easter Island.

33.9

1 Not given **2** False **3** True **4** True

34

34.2 🔊

1 Please make sure you **ask for** help if you need it.

2 Who is giving the lecture? I have never **heard of** him.

3 My brother and I are always **arguing about** current affairs.

4 The global **decline in** natural resources is worrying.

5 Thank you so much! I am so **grateful for** all you have done.

6 When you're stressed, it is good to **talk about** problems.

7 The **effect of** the economic crisis is enormous.

8 Most of the population **knows about** climate change.

9 All of the scientific evidence **points in** one direction.

34.3 🔊

1 Why do they always argue **about** everything?

2 There was a decline **in** the number of birds.

3 There's a lot to be grateful **for**.

4 This demonstrates a real lack **of** talent.

5 How do I ask **for** directions in Greek?

6 I don't think we'll ever agree **about** this.

7 I really don't want to be late **for** work.

8 My mother is very afraid **of** heights.

9 What is the long-term effect **of** this?

34.5 🔊

1 I'm so **bored with** their constant fighting about policies.

2 They've **made** a new app **for** children to learn about the Earth.

3 Do you have any **objection to** this environmental policy?

4 I often **worry about** the future of our planet.

5 You need to **apologize to** them **for** the things you said.

6 Do you think a policy like this is **suitable for** a country like ours?

34.7 🔊

1 What do **you** think of the new statistics in this report?

2 These carbon emissions **are** extremely harmful to the environment.

3 It's is very important that we think of our children's **futures**.

4 We **need** to find solutions sooner rather than later.

34.8

What are the environmental **consequences** of urbanization on such a massive scale? One major effect of urbanization is the creation of "urban heat islands." Rural areas can remain cooler **due to** the sun evaporating the moisture from the vegetation and the soil. However, in the cities there is much less soil and vegetation. **Consequently**, the sun beating on the buildings and roads **leads** to an increase in temperatures. Additional heat from vehicles, factories, and cooling units also increases temperatures. This heat then **causes** changes in local weather patterns.

Not only is there increased air pollution, but also higher levels of rainfall, **resulting** in flooding within the cities themselves and also downstream. Another **consequence** of urbanization is the increased consumption of food, energy, and durable goods. This has a far-reaching **impact** on levels of natural resources.

35

35.4 🔊

1 I'm afraid we have **little** time to catch the train. We must hurry.

2 That cake is delicious. I'll have **a little** bit more.

3 Sadly, there are **few** examples of this quality craftmanship left.

4 Great! We have **a little** spare money. Should we go out for dinner?

5 Wow! Look at all these monkeys! I think there are **a few** different species here.

6 Unfortunately, I have **few** friends. It's quite lonely here.

35.5 🔊

1 Great! There are **a few** magazines to choose from.

2 Sadly, there are **few** fish in my aquarium.

3 There is very **little** cake left, I'm afraid.

4 It should be OK. We have **a little** time left.

5 The café is closing soon. There are so **few** customers.

35.7

Ninety-year-old Ken Wilson has finally decided to have **a little** time off after volunteering at his local wildlife park for 30 years. Ken started volunteering **a few** years after he retired from teaching. He says, "I started making coffee for people in the little visitor center, but I've had quite **a few** different roles since then."

Ken has been a guide, he's surveyed butterflies, and he even managed to get his hands dirty quite **a few** times clearing litter. What does he like so much about the park? "Well, there are **few** green places left like this in big cities. For **little** or no money, a family can explore all day and learn **a little** about local wildlife. It's **a little** bit of calm in a busy world."

What will he do now? "I'd like quite **a few** days sitting in the park doing nothing." After three decades looking after the wildlife, it's time for Ken to take **a little** break.

35.10 🔊

1 Protesters have demanded fewer **harmful emissions by 2025**.

2 The charity has fewer **volunteers than last year**.

3 The new light bulbs use far less **electricity than the old ones**.

4 Unsurprisingly, there is much less **wildlife near big factory sites**.

5 Since the new traffic laws, there is a lot less **pollution in the capital city**.

35.13

1 False **2** True **3** False **4** False
5 True **6** False

35.14 🔊

1 Rachel also had the help of **a few** friends during her campaign.

2 Rachel knew that **quite a few** people held the same opinion as her.

3 The area is home to **more than** 500 plant and animal species.

4 The photography exhibition raised $25,000 in **less than** a week.

5 **Quite a few** people sent messages of support via social media sites.

6 Making Lake Lucid a popular tourist site will only take **a few** years.

37.2 🔊
1 It was raining, so I **could not** have gone sunbathing even if I had wanted to.
2 Look at him! Do you think he **might have** won the lottery?
3 If I had left the house a little earlier, I **might not** have missed the bus.
4 I don't know where she is. She **could have** gone for a run. She loves exercise.

37.3 Model Answers
1 At first she believed it, but now she thinks it couldn't have happened.
2 They were celebrating because they had just won a tournament.
3 They dressed it up in one of their golf jackets.
4 The kangaroo hit one of the golfers on the nose.
5 They couldn't continue driving home because the car keys were in the jacket the kangaroo was wearing.

37.5 🔊
1 Amal mentioned **that she was reading a scary story.**
2 Amal told me **that she had finished the book.**
3 I asked her **if / whether she was going to the movies.**
4 I asked her **what kind of movie she was going to see.**
5 I asked her **if / whether she enjoyed it.**

37.6
1 True 2 False 3 True 4 Not given
5 False

37.7 🔊
1 I was so angry that I just **saw red** and shouted.
2 The poor dog had been left in the cold and was a very **sorry sight**.
3 The watch looked genuine **at first sight**, but it wasn't.
4 I'll just have to **wait and see** about my English test results.

38.2 🔊
1 He's walking with crutches. **He must have hurt his legs.**
2 Those teenagers look very tired today. **They may have had a party last night.**
3 The plants are all dry and dead. **It can't have rained all week.**
4 Someone's left the gate open again. **It could have been the delivery man.**
5 The girl next door looks really happy. **She might have passed her exam.**

38.3 🔊
1 The ground is dry so it **can't have** rained last night.
2 She ate two more slices of cake, so it **must have** tasted nice.
3 A police car just drove past. There **might have been** a robbery.
4 He doesn't have any money. He **can't have** bought that car himself.
5 They were in the same store as us. They **might have bought** the same coat.

38.4 🔊
1 I missed a call. It **may** have been Diego, he said he might call.
2 I haven't checked my emails yet, so she **might** have replied already, I'm not sure.
3 After the run, he drank a whole bottle of water. He **must** have been really thirsty.
4 She loved both dresses, but she **can't** have bought both, as they were too expensive.
5 She hadn't slept for two days. She **must** have been exhausted.

38.5 🔊
1 She must have **passed her driving test.**
2 He must have **slept through his alarm.**
3 They must have **failed their exams.**
4 She must have **eaten too much candy.**
5 He must have **won the lottery.**

38.6
3

38.7 🔊
1 Every month my company **sends out** a newsletter to all its customers.
2 Every time my sister sees a spider, she **freaks out** and starts screaming.
3 Should we go to the movie theater and **check out** what's showing?
4 He isn't like anyone else. He really **stands out** from the crowd.

5 I can't **work out** what this guy's written. His handwriting is awful.

38.8
1 False 2 False 3 True 4 True

39.3 🔊
1 You wouldn't be such a success today **if you hadn't worked so hard at school.**
2 If my alarm had gone off, **I wouldn't be in trouble for being late.**
3 She might not be such a celebrity **if she hadn't had famous parents.**
4 He would be playing today **if he hadn't broken his leg yesterday.**
5 If you had spent less money, **you wouldn't have such great tickets.**
6 If I had given up trying, **I wouldn't be managing the business today.**
7 If we had eaten breakfast, **we might not be so hungry now.**

39.4 🔊
1 If Clara **had not stayed** up so late, she might not be so tired now.
2 She might not be a famous actress if she **had not gone** to that first audition.
3 If he **had kept playing** the guitar, he would be in a famous band by now.
4 If Juan **had listened** to all his critics, he would not be a world-famous chef today.
5 He would not be playing for a premier team if he **had not trained** every day.
6 If she **had said** "yes" to your proposal, you could be married by now.
7 They would not be so confident if they **had seen** their team training yesterday.

39.5
1 False 2 True 3 True 4 False 5 False

39.6 🔊
1 You need **reliable** staff who turn up on time and do their work.
2 He's so **courageous**. He just jumped into the fire to save the kitten.
3 My husband is really **sensitive**. He even cries during romantic films.
4 If he hadn't been so violent and **quick-tempered**, he would not be in jail today.
5 If she hadn't been so **determined**, she might not be such a successful singer.
6 Jane is very **practical**. She can fix the car and put up shelves.

39.7 Model Answers

❶ Diane would definitely change her plans because of her horoscope's advice.

❷ Diane thinks she's a typical Scorpio because she's quite passionate about things.

❸ Richard thinks that the things a horoscope says will happen to most people on most days.

❹ He says it's not surprising that people who believe in horoscopes often think they're correct.

40

40.2 ◄))

❶ Buy red or green peppers, **whichever** is the cheapest.

❷ She moves every few years to **wherever** her company asks her to go.

❸ I love going to concerts and watching live music, **whoever** is playing.

❹ My mother never likes my brother's girlfriends, **however** nice they are.

❺ The company director visits our office **whenever** she's in town.

❻ The competition winner deserves praise, **whoever** they are.

❼ The company is in a difficult situation, **whichever** way you look at it.

40.3 ◄))

❶ She's an excellent cook. I'm sure **whichever** cake I choose will be delicious.

❷ Sometimes I just can't start my car **whatever** I do. It's really frustrating.

❸ I don't think I'll ever be a good long-distance runner, **however** hard I try.

❹ During the winter months, we can visit the castle for free **whenever** we want.

❺ I will give my full support to the next head chef, **whoever** it is.

40.4 Model Answers

❶ It was a surprise because Matt had forgotten he'd even entered the competition.

❷ His sister wasn't happy because she's always trying to steal Matt's thunder.

❸ She said that she couldn't do it because she had the flu.

❹ He did the bungee jump off a canal bridge.

❺ He's planning to do a sky dive next year.

40.5 ◄))

❶ She seems to be on cloud nine this morning.

❷ Go on. Throw caution to the wind.

❸ Perhaps you should take a rain check.

❹ You're constantly trying to steal my thunder.

❺ Wow! That's a bolt from the blue.

❻ The party's happening come rain or shine.

42

42.2 ◄))

❶ There are thought to be more than **6000 languages in the world.**

❷ Maria Callas is believed by many **to have been the most talented singer ever.**

❸ The escaped criminal is not thought **to be a dangerous threat to society.**

❹ It is hoped **that many new jobs will be created.**

❺ The damage is expected **to cost more than $50,000 to repair.**

42.5 ◄))

❶ I'm so sorry! You should **have been** introduced to each other earlier this evening.

❷ Thirty people are expected to **be** awarded top prizes at the ceremony later.

❸ It would help if the school children could **be given** different instruments to try.

❹ It's been a strange tournament, and there **are** thought to be more surprises to come.

42.6 ◄))

❶ The hosts **should have been thanked (by somebody) before we left.**

❷ It has **been reported that 20 people were injured in the stampede.**

❸ Pelé is **thought to be the best soccer player ever (by many people).**

42.7 ◄))

❶ It has been announced that the Cup **has been won by the youth team.**

❷ Many homes are said **to have been destroyed by the tornado.**

❸ This celebrity couple are reported **to have married in Paris.**

42.8

Bank robber Mark Thomas is **spending** the night in jail before going to court to be **sentenced** tomorrow.

Last June, Mr. Thomas, dressed in a mask and hat and armed with a knife, demanded $10,000 from the cashier of a local bank. He was **given** the money, but at this point Mr. Thomas' planning skills must be **questioned**. Instead of escaping the area, Mr. Thomas took off his hat and mask and walked into the bank next door. He tried to deposit the money and gave the cashiers his full name, address, and bank details. Fortunately, the police had been **called** by the original bank and Mr. Thomas was quickly **arrested**. He is understood to have been **planning** the robbery for many months. He stated that he had been **saving** for a vacation, but it was taking too long to raise enough money. It is **predicted** that he will given a lengthy sentence, so he will have to wait even longer for his trip abroad.

43

43.2 ◄))

❶ There are **approximately** five hundred employees in this factory.

❷ These new figures **indicate** a downward trend in sales.

❸ The director **allegedly** took all of the money from the company.

❹ This kind of market behavior **suggests** an underlying problem.

❺ **It has been said** by some that her opinions are controversial.

❻ **It looks like** they are not enjoying the film very much.

❼ Academics **tend** to use hedging language if something is not proven.

43.4 ◄))

❶ It **appears** that two prisoners have escaped from the police station.

❷ I don't trust her. I think it **looks like** she is guilty of both crimes.

❸ They **seem** to have found more important evidence to support their case.

❹ I **believe** that the police have made a mistake and arrested the wrong man.

❺ I don't know, but it would **appear** that he stole the car when the owner was inside.

❻ With a huge number of hit records, the Beatles are **arguably** the best band ever.

❼ After a difficult year, all our figures **indicate** that sales are finally improving.

❽ It's too soon to judge. He **probably** committed the crime, but we're not sure.

❾ We used to go to Spain a lot. Sometimes we drove there, but we **often** flew.

43.5 ◄))

ADVERBS: **arguably, apparently, approximately, often, probably**

VERBS: **suggest, tend, assume, believe, indicate**

PHRASES: **it looks like, it seems that, it could be said that, to some extent, it would appear that**

43.6

1 False **2** True **3** True **4** True
5 False

43.7 🔊

1 An online video **apparently** shows her cat, Mini, protecting her.
2 **It would appear** that the snake was frightened away by Mini.
3 Interviews with neighbors **indicate** that the snake had been seen on other properties.
4 A local animal charity **suggested** that it would be unusual for such a snake to attack.
5 The charity said that these snakes **tend** to be extremely shy.
6 They also stated that **often** these kinds of snakes are pets that have escaped.

44

44.3 🔊

1 Little **did he** know that someone had already invented the same thing.
2 Only after living there for two weeks **did they** notice the smell.
3 Not **until** we spoke to the manager did the company admit their mistake.
4 Not since the children were little **had we** been on such a fun day out.
5 Only **when** she won the award did people start taking her writing seriously.

44.4 🔊

1 **Only** if the company invests more money can the project be completed.
2 **Not** until the wedding day did the groom see the bride's dress.
3 Little did they **realize** that the weather would be absolutely terrible for the festival.
4 Not **until** the final encore did the audience begin to leave their seats at the concert.
5 Only **when** she was paying for the album did she realize she already owned it.
6 Not **only** will you be famous, but you will also be rich beyond your wildest dreams.
7 Only **after** she got home from the party did she notice how late it was.

44.7 🔊

1 Only when he was at home did he feel safe.
2 Hardly had he walked on stage when the fans chanted his name.
3 No sooner had they become the number one band than they split up.
4 Never before had anyone seen so many fans in one place.

44.8

1 False **2** True **3** True **4** True

44.9 🔊

1 No sooner had the rain stopped than it began to snow.
2 Only when she heard his voice did she recognize him.
3 Not only is this car fast, but it's also affordable!
4 Only if you help me will I finish on time.

45

45.3 🔊

1 What I would really appreciate is **some legal advice.**
2 What we really need are **more volunteers to help during the week.**
3 What I love about this city is **the nightlife and the culture.**
4 What businesses really hate is **when people leave bad reviews online.**

45.5 🔊

1 The **justification** she gave for being late for work was not good enough.
2 The **period** in history that fascinates me most is the Jurassic period.
3 A **natural wonder** that we'd really love to visit is Ha Long Bay in Vietnam.
4 One **moment** I'll never forget is when my first grandchild was born.
5 The **thing** I don't understand is why the instructions are so complicated.

45.8 🔊

1 Actually, **the place** I most want to visit **is** Istanbul.
2 Actually, **it was** a while ago **that / when** I started.
3 No, **the person** I most admire **is** Albert Einstein.

45.9

1 True **2** True **3** False **4** False
5 True

47

47.2

1 Subject **2** Subject **3** Object
4 Object **5** Subject **6** Subject
7 Object

47.5 🔊

1 Those children are the ones who want to be detectives.
2 That computer is the one that was stolen.
3 This is the officer who arrested the criminal.
4 A cybercriminal is a person who acts illegally online.
5 That is the phone that I use to make video calls.

47.8 🔊

1 The violent criminals were not sent to jail, which surprised the victim.
2 Detective Smith, who arrested the fraudster, works in a special department.
3 Vivian Jones, who had worked for the bank for 10 years, was arrested yesterday.

47.9

1 On a few street corners
2 Help to clear up the trash
3 They ought to spend a night in a police cell.
4 Other places should be built for them.

47.10

1 True **2** False **3** False **4** Not given

48

48.2 🔊

1 Courtrooms are places **where** lawyers argue their cases in front of a judge.
2 Thursday is the night **when** we usually go to the movies.
3 Sentencing is the legal process **whereby** a judge decides the punishment.
4 Morning coffee break is the time **when** we gossip most.
5 A police station is the place **where** most criminals are taken at first.

48.3 🔊

1 The camera's timer let the police know the exact time **when the robbery took place**.
2 They have developed a system **whereby prisoners can prepare** for life outside jail.
3 Do you know the date **when the suspect goes** to court?
4 This is the café **where the prisoners cook** great food for the public.
5 Conveyancing is a process **whereby one person sells property** to another.
6 I remember the day **when my sister decided** to become a lawyer.
7 This cell is the place **where the suspects** are held until a verdict is reached.

48.4

48.4
1 True **2** False **3** Not given **4** False
5 True **6** True **7** True

48.7 🔊
1 Rodrigo, **whose training regime is rigorous**, deserves to be successful.
2 My sister, **whose first book was a huge success**, has become very famous.
3 My neighbor Sara, **whose dogs always win competitions**, loves training dogs.
4 That company, **whose employees work very hard**, has excellent trading figures.
5 That school, **whose students always do well in exams**, is very well respected.

48.8 Model Answers
1 They saw him on security video footage outside the burgled premises.
2 Hockly couldn't remember his full name or where he lived.
3 They were shown videos of him driving a car.
4 He said someone asked him to help carry them.

49

49.2 🔊
1 Unfortunately, he **won't be able to** pay his parking fines.
2 **Will you be able to** install a security camera in the store?
3 I **won't be able to** understand all these legal regulations.
4 Hopefully, my sister **will be able to** explain it all to me. She's a lawyer.

49.4 🔊
1 You will have to work longer hours soon.
2 Tomorrow, you won't be able to park here.
3 Will the police be able to arrest them?
4 I will have to call the police.
5 Will they be able to enforce the new law?

49.5 Model Answers
1 They've already been introduced in shopping malls in Chongqing, Antwerp, and Liverpool.
2 Young shoppers are particularly frustrated by slower shoppers.
3 They are concerned that these shoppers might start shopping online instead.
4 They might find it difficult to enforce the new rules effectively.
5 Some people strayed into the wrong lane because they were distracted by their phones.

49.6
A new law has just been **passed** by the government. This new law **permits** members of the public to walk on farmers' land. Walkers will have to **observe** reasonable rules set by the landowners. If they **break** these rules, they could be **banned** from walking in the area or they could even be **arrested**. Some farmers, however, think that the police will not be able to **enforce** the law.

49.7 🔊
1 pass **2** observe **3** break
4 enforce **5** arrest **6** permit

50

50.2 🔊
1 I appreciate that it's difficult, but I think you **should** talk to him about it.
2 Finally, after months of studying, I **can** read music.
3 I'm sorry, but I'm terribly busy at the moment, Mr. Jones. **Would** tomorrow be okay?
4 I followed the recipe, so it **ought** to taste great, but sometimes it doesn't.
5 I've tried really hard, but I just **can't** make these figures add up.
6 I'm feeling very unwell. **May** I be excused?

50.3 🔊
1 It's very hot in here. **Would** you open a window, please?
2 This coffee has sugar in it! It **must** be yours.
3 I don't know when the movie will finish. It **might** not be until after 10pm.
4 **Shall** I help you carry those dishes to the kitchen?
5 My lawnmower has broken. **Could** I borrow yours, please?
6 I **can't** swim very well at all, but my sister is an excellent swimmer.

50.4 🔊
1 She was was the lead singer in the band because she **could** sing very well.
2 **Would you** pick me up from work this evening, please?
3 The tree looks like it **may fall** down soon.
4 If she doesn't study hard enough, she **might not** get into medical school.

50.5
1 False **2** True **3** False **4** False

50.6
1 Family homes
2 Leave them standing in rice
3 It was really interesting

52

52.3 🔊
1 The Swiss **2** Brazilians **3** The Swedish
4 Indians **5** The French
6 Koreans **7** Kenyans

52.6 🔊
1 The **homeless** are often without a house as a result of some very bad luck.
2 Often, the **young** are described as being addicted to gadgets and phones.
3 The **rich** often give lots of money to charity, but we don't know about it.
4 Many countries have laws to ensure that the **disabled** can access public transportation.
5 After the accident, the **injured** were all taken to a nearby hospital.
6 The **elderly** have often cared for others all their lives and deserve care in return.

52.7
1 False **2** False **3** False **4** True
5 False **6** True **7** True

52.8
1 B **2** F **3** C **4** D **5** A **6** E

52.9 🔊 Model Answers
1 The unemployed **are given financial support until they find a new job.**
2 The elderly **are respected and seen as an important part of society.**
3 The young **are often depicted as selfish, which I think is incorrect.**

53

53.3 🔊
1 My parents **are** used to living in an old building, but the creaking floorboards scare me!
2 They **were** used to eating with chopsticks, but it was new to me. I found it hard!

3 My friend said I'd **get** used to eating my dinner later at night after a few weeks.
4 It took a while, but now I **am** used to recycling all my paper and plastic each week.
5 His friends found it strange, but he **was** used to doing things without using the computer.
6 It was difficult at first, but I **got** used to the new routine after a few months.
7 We **were** used to the old system at work, but then it changed completely.
8 Eventually I **got** used to answering the phone in English. It almost feels natural now!

53.4 ◄))
1 I don't think I will ever **get** used to the noise in my street at night.
2 I'm so used **to** drinking coffee every morning that I can't function without it.
3 They said they they could not **get** used to the icy weather.
4 Don't worry. After a while you'll **get** used to the cold water.
5 Do you think that you'll **get** used to the long hours in your new job?

53.6
When I was living abroad, I used to **go out** a lot so that I could meet people and make friends. Even though I was nervous, I used to **agree** to any offer people made to try something new. Also, I didn't **force** things to fit around my old routines, but got used to **doing** things in line with local customs instead. These were quite unusual at first, but I **am** used to them now. The staff in my local café are used to me **making** mistakes when I talk, but they always appreciate the effort and help me.

53.7 ◄))
1 Be sure to experiment and try not **to only do things you used to do at home.**
2 Visit the country before you move **to start getting used to the culture.**
3 Ask other people from abroad how **they got used to the different culture.**
4 Don't worry if things aren't what **you're used to. That's the adventure!**
5 Trying activities in your new country **is a great way to get to know new people.**

53.8
1 Her salary and when she will have children
2 Lunches lasting a long time
3 She stayed overnight with a friend
4 An old lady helped Julie cross the road

53.9 ◄))
1 Not anymore. I**'m used to** it now.
2 It's tradition! We**'re used to** doing it.
3 It was at first, but now I**'m used to** them.
4 No, it took me many years to **get used to** it.

54

54.3 ◄))
1 I want to visit **a** really modern city like Tokyo.
2 I've always wanted to go up **the** Empire State Building.
3 Should we go to **the** restaurant we ate at on Friday?
4 Did you ride on **a** gondola in Venice?

54.5 ◄))
1 Have you ever been on **a** guided tour of Rio de Janeiro?
2 The Christ the Redeemer statue in Rio de Janeiro is **the** largest statue of its type.
3 **Soccer** is a hugely popular sport in Rio and Brazil in general.
4 There is **a** famous lagoon in central Rio called Lagoa Rodrigo de Freitas.

54.6
The Republic of Costa Rica in Central America has **an** estimated population of just under 5 million people and one of **the** highest life expectancy levels in the West. Its incredible beauty and the diverse nature of the flora and fauna in its rainforests make [-] Costa Rica a top destination for tourists. Indeed, tourism is **the** country's number one source of foreign exchange. As well as famous cash crops like bananas and coffee, Costa Rica boasts 1,000 species of orchids and **a** huge number of bird species. In fairly recent years, Costa Rica has tried to cut down its reliance on the income produced by the export of coffee beans, bananas, and beef by becoming **a** producer of [-] microchips. Unfortunately, **the** microchip market has turned out to be as unstable as that for cash crops.

54.7
1 True **2** False **3** True **4** False
5 True

54.8 ◄))
1 occasionally **2** changeable **3** weird
4 foreigner **5** separate **6** height

54.10 ◄))
1 I dou**b**t we will ever see them again.
2 To be **h**onest, the plum**b**ing here is unusual.
3 Can you **k**nock on my door in an **h**our?
4 I **k**now you want to watch the final performance.

55

55.3 ◄))
CONCRETE NOUNS: **computer**, **building**, **professor**, **sun**, **clock**, **artist**, **library**, **photograph**
ABSTRACT NOUNS: **relaxation**, **pride**, **misery**, **hate**, **beauty**, **anger**, **heat**, **trouble**

55.5 ◄))
1 She was deep in **thought** so we did not disturb her.
2 In college you can meet people from many different **cultures**.
3 My father formed many lasting **friendships** in college.
4 This house is amazing. There are so many interesting **spaces**.
5 My brother does a lot of work for several local **charities**.
6 Apparently, this is the worst weather in living **memory**.
7 In these difficult times it's so important not to give up **hope**.

55.6
Australians have a lot of **pride** in their system of **education**. The system in Australia is quite hard to describe because it is largely controlled by the states or territories, rather than the federal **government**. Depending on where they live, students must go to school from five years old until 16 or 17 **years** old. There is also nursery level education, but this is not compulsory. After secondary school, students have a number of options to develop their **abilities**. They can choose to undertake vocational education and training (VET) by taking a **course** in a subject such as computer programming, engineering, or tourism, where they also learn key workplace **skills**. Alternatively, young people can apply to go into higher education or, of course, look for work. Generally, the system in Australia is recognized as being a **success**.

55.7
1 True **2** False **3** Not given **4** False
5 False

55.8

1 We had a training day to help us develop our customer service **skills**.
2 These products don't have any redeeming **qualities**. They are so cheaply built!
3 Your plan is not very sensible. It needs a bit more **thought**.
4 There are **times** when I wonder if I should have become a teacher.
5 Some of the applicants don't have enough **experience** for the job.

57

57.3

1 That college seems really great. **I wish I could** go there.
2 We can't change their development plans, but we wish we **could**.
3 Sarah wishes her husband **would buy her** flowers more often.
4 My favorite band is coming to our city. I wish I **could go**!

57.4

1 I wish you **wouldn't** criticize my clothes. I think I look fabulous!
2 My neighbor plays the trumpet all the time. I wish he **would** be a little quieter.
3 Mike's car always breaks down. He wishes he **could** afford a new one.
4 We work far too hard. I wish we **could** do this more often!

58

58.4

Note: You can use "won't" instead of "will not" in the following answers.
1 In a few years' time, I think you **will be running** this place.
2 I suppose you **will be feeling** too tired to go out after work this evening.
3 Tomorrow evening, Jorge's band **will be performing** at a concert.
4 I guess she **will not be coming** to the office party if she doesn't like the boss.
5 Jane bought two tickets so I think she **will be bringing** a friend to the exhibition.
6 Meilin has already told me that she **will not be checking** her emails today.

58.5

1 In a year's time, **I will be working in a new department.**

2 In 5 years' time, **I will be working at headquarters.**
3 In 10 years' time, **I will be managing head office.**
4 In 20 years' time, **I will be enjoying my retirement.**

58.8

1 **Will you be leaving** soon?
2 **Will you be watching** all of those DVDs?
3 **Will the children be coming** too?
4 **Will you be eating** all of those cakes?
5 **Will you be going** to the store?

58.9

1 **Will you be eating** all that popcorn on your own?
2 **Will you be getting** your hair cut any time soon?
3 **Will you be taking** the kids to school tomorrow?
4 **Will you be returning** your books to the library?
5 **Will you be cooking** some food later on?

58.10

1 False 2 False 3 True 4 True
5 True 6 False

58.12

1 Darren 2 Nobody 3 Kate 4 Darren
5 Nobody 6 Kate

58.13

1 **She'll be reading** a book at home.
2 **She'll be shopping** with her friend.
3 **She'll be running** on the treadmill.

58.14 Model Answers

1 She thinks she'll be going on more holidays abroad.
2 No, he predicts he'll be working in the same job in the same office.
3 In five years' time, he hopes he'll be studying abroad.
4 In her short-term future, she's getting married.
5 She might be taking her oldest child there for the first time.

59

59.4

1 By the end of the night, I **will have watched** all the films in the series.
2 You **will have experienced** so many different things by the time you return.

3 Dimitri **will have cycled** around the world by this time next year.
4 By next year, she **will have seen** all of her favorite bands live.
5 I hope he **will have cleaned** the car by the time he goes to the wedding.
6 Before I leave tonight, I **will have finished** all my work.

59.5

1 By the time I'm 25, **I will have moved abroad.**
2 By the time I'm 30, **I will have started a business.**
3 By the time I'm 35, **I will have married someone.**
4 By the time I'm 60, **I will have retired.**

59.9

Dear Graham,
By now you will have **returned** from your honeymoon. I hope you had a great time! Don't forget that we're having a party for Jane on Saturday. She will have **been working** here for 20 years on Friday! I hope Frank will have **sent** you an email with all the details by the time you get this. I'll see you at the party. I hope you'll have **caught** up with all your work by then! Sian

59.10

1 True 2 False 3 Not given 4 True

59.11

3

60

60.2

1 David said that he **would** try to get me a ticket to the game, but he **didn't** manage to.
2 I **will** buy the movie on DVD. I thought I **would** see it at the movie theater, but I didn't.
3 Last year she thought she **would** be promoted, but she wasn't. Maybe next year she **will** be.
4 I **brought** all the food for the picnic because I knew that Tom **wouldn't** remember.
5 We knew that the concert **would** be amazing, so we **bought** really good tickets.
6 My brother promised that he **wouldn't** show anyone pictures of me when I **was** little.

60.4

1 Vinesh was going to help me with the housework, but he went out.
2 He said he wasn't going to study until his tutor arrived.

3 I was going to cook him dinner, but he'd already done it.

4 Dave said he was going to bring his girlfriend, but he didn't.

5 He was going to apply to go to college, but he changed his mind.

6 We were going to take a taxi home, but there weren't any available.

60.6 ◀))

1 Sarah **was planning** to take her children to the park on Tuesday.

2 Peter **was** nervous because he **was meeting** his girlfriend's parents.

3 I **was planning** to go out that evening because my parents **were having** guests over.

4 We **couldn't** make it to the party on Friday because we **were visiting** some friends that day.

5 I **was planning** to book a vacation just after the New Year.

60.7

1 B **2** A **3** B

62

62.2 ◀))

1 They wanted to see the band perform live, but now they can't [**see the band perform live**].

2 He was fantastic in the television series and [**he was fantastic in**] the movie adaptation.

3 If you want to see a movie, we could go to the multiplex or [**we could go to**] the art house.

4 The reviews said that the acting was bad and [**the reviews said that**] the soundtrack was terrible.

5 The two lead actors did all the stunts and [**the two lead actors**] sang all the songs themselves.

6 I am quitting my job this week. I will call you later to explain why [**I am quitting my job this week**].

62.3

1 True **2** True **3** False **4** True

5 False

62.4 ◀))

1 I knew that the family would turn out to be aliens. It was completely **predictable**.

2 I was so deeply **moved** by the sad scenes that I cried for hours!

3 We loved the last film, but were bitterly **disappointed** by this one.

4 We waited too long! The ticket prices are now astronomically **high**.

5 The plot is shocking and the theme is **highly** controversial.

6 The government helped pay for the film. It was **heavily** subsidized.

62.5 ◀))

1 I was planning to buy tickets for the show, but now I can't.

2 The film had great special effects and a wonderful soundtrack.

3 He was chosen for the orchestra and played brilliantly.

4 This evening I'm going to have dinner and then watch a play.

5 They said that they would come to the launch party, but they haven't.

6 They should join in or not bother coming.

62.6 ◀))

1 The actors were good, but **seemed uncomfortable on screen.**

2 The performance starts at 8 and **ends just after midnight.**

3 You could buy a season ticket or **sign up for membership.**

4 The building is beautiful, but **doesn't have very good acoustics.**

5 The cast are all exhausted, but **very satisfied with the performance.**

6 The audience was very loud and **full of young children!**

62.8

1 **E** 2 **B** 3 **G** 4 **A** 5 **D** 6 **F** 7 **C**

63

63.2 ◀))

1 The book with the long title is the **one** I wanted.

2 The buildings in New York were taller than the **ones** in Paris.

3 If you still want a copy of that book, there are **some** over here.

4 If you need an umbrella, I can lend you **one**.

5 Have you seen her new sunglasses? The **ones** with the silver frames?

63.3 ◀))

1 They bought me a signed copy, **but I already had one.**

2 I think the most engrossing novels **are the ones about spies.**

3 If you want to join a book club, **make sure it's one with regular meetings.**

4 I know you want to buy a new car, **but the one we have is only a year old.**

5 If you need a plastic bag, **there are some in the box over there.**

63.4

Black Glasses is Martin Owens' fourth book in this series. Like the third book, this **one** is all about the brilliant detective Amanda Brook. Unlike the other **ones** in the series though, this time her personal life starts falling apart. Excellent plot as usual.

I have read some boring books in my time, but Sara Umborne's Pink Tree is the dullest **one** ever. Sadly, I can't tell you much about the book as I gave up after 20 pages.

Little Water Princess is a fabulous book for little children, or even older **ones**! There are few words, but the illustrations are beautiful. Lots of the pictures pop up, but **some** are 2D. A lovely gift idea.

There are endless books about cooking pasta, but How to Cook Pasta by Daniela Capril is the best **one** on the market today.

63.6 ◀))

1 I didn't like it, but my friend did.

2 Did you go to the show? We did, too.

3 You read a lot last month. I did, too.

4 Do I recycle? Yes, I do.

5 He works hard, but she doesn't.

63.7

1 False **2** True **3** False **4** True

5 False **6** False

63.10 ◀)) Model Answers

1 I hope not. / I hope so.

2 Jane Austen did.

3 I don't think so. / I think so.

64

64.2 ◀))

1 I tried to contact Max about the concert tickets, but wasn't able to.

2 My brother often forgets our dad's birthday, but this year he's promised not to.

3 Georgia was enjoying the performance. At least, she seemed to be.

4 Ian is going to the new nightclub, but I don't really want to.

5 The festival tickets cost a lot more than they used to.

6 I want to come with you, but I won't be able to.

64.4

1 True 2 True 3 True 4 False
5 False 6 False 7 True

64.7 🔊

1 I would like to read music, but it will be a long time until I'm **able** to.
2 Don't forget that it's supposed to rain tonight. Try to leave before it **starts**.
3 Some people aren't nervous about performing, but I'm too **afraid** to.
4 Some artists don't like to have family in the audience on the first night, but I **prefer** to.
5 It's such a shame. I would absolutely love to see him sing, but cannot **afford** to.
6 I've seen other artists who love talking to the audience, but I **hate** to.
7 You don't need to worry. I will come along to all of your recitals. I **promise**.

64.9 🔊

1 I asked him to come, but he didn't want to.
2 You can have one if you want.
3 You can stay, but I don't really want to.
4 If you're free to meet, I would still like to.
5 You can call me "Sam" if you want.

64.10 🔊

1 No, I decided not to.
2 Yes, I will try (to).
3 Yes, but I can't afford to.

65

65.2 🔊

1 These gardens are fabulous. Did you bring your camera, **by the way**?
2 Yes, but **as I was saying** before, I really think I could paint that myself.
3 No, I don't hate all modern art. I **actually** really like some street art.
4 **Anyway**, to get back to my question, would you pay two million dollars for that?
5 These paintings aren't the reason I come here. I **actually** prefer the architecture.

65.3 🔊

1 Aren't they? **By the way / Anyway**, where are we going for dinner?
2 Yes, but **as I was saying**, I'm getting really hungry.
3 We haven't, **actually**. There's another floor!
4 **Actually**, I'm really inspired. I love this landscape.
5 **Anyway**, we should head back to the car soon.

65.4

1 True 2 True 3 False 4 True
5 False 6 True

65.5 🔊

1 "Super-" as in "superhero" and "supernatural" **means "beyond."**
2 "Anti-" as in "antisocial" and "antibiotics" **means "against."**
3 "Pro-" as in "proactive" and "proceed" **means "for."**
4 "Neo-" as in "neoclassical" and "neoliberal" **means "new."**
5 "Post-" as in "postmodern" and "postwar" **means "after."**

65.6 🔊

1 Many children go to **pre**school before they are five years old.
2 My husband is 40 years old, but he still loves **super**hero comics and films.
3 A lot of the architecture here is **neo**classical and looks Roman.
4 I think that dropping litter in public is extremely **anti**social.
5 Before the ceremony began, we we told to wait in a small **ante**room.
6 Many 20th-century art movements have been called **post**modern.

66

66.4 🔊

1 Ahmed is getting his oven fixed.
2 Sally's having her nails painted.
3 Natasha got her photograph taken.
4 Gavin is cutting his hair.
5 Joe did the ironing at home.
6 Annie had some flowers delivered.
7 They're having their house painted.

66.5 🔊

1 I'm taking the car to **the garage to get it fixed.**
2 You should go to a salon **and have your hair cut.**
3 I don't want to cook. Should we **get a pizza delivered?**
4 They've just had their staff **trained to deal with malware.**
5 I'm going to have my computer **checked for malware. It's so slow.**
6 I took my daughter to the dentist **to get her teeth checked.**
7 They bought a dog and had **a deluxe kennel built for him.**

66.6 🔊

1 Remember, today we're **having** the bedroom carpets fitted.
2 Your coat is really filthy. **You should get it** dry-cleaned.
3 My eyes hurt when I read. I should **have** them tested soon.
4 My friend **had** his wallet stolen when he was in Barcelona.
5 I **have to get** my birth certificate translated into Spanish for my application.

66.7 🔊

1 No, **he gets / has it cleaned** by someone else.
2 The photographer's here. **She's getting / having her picture taken.**
3 Yes, but **I'm getting / having it fixed** on Monday.
4 The painter's coming. **We're getting / having the house painted.**
5 No, **I'm getting / having a pizza delivered.**
6 Yes, **I get / have my teeth checked** twice a year.
7 No, **we get / have it delivered** to the house.

67

67.2 🔊

1 The legal **department** in my office is the largest in the company.
2 Members of the **orchestra** are rehearsing in different rooms in the building.
3 The **government** is having an emergency meeting in New York.
4 The soccer **team** is arriving later this evening.
5 The entire **audience** was delighted by the guest performer last night.

67.5 🔊

1 I want to study economics.
2 Is athletics popular in your country?
3 *Cats* is a successful musical.
4 The Philippines is an island country.
5 Physics is my favorite subject.
6 *Hard Times* was written by Dickens.
7 The United States has nine time zones.

67.7 🔊

1 Neither her mother nor her father **was there to pick her up from school.**
2 Either a cat or a dog **is a great pet for a family.**
3 Either the diner or the coffee shop **is fine for our meeting.**

4 Neither the boss nor the workers **are happy with the announcement.**
5 We think that neither Tom nor Katya **has worked hard enough at school.**
6 Either the giraffes or the elephant **are the most popular animals in the park.**
7 Neither my car nor my motorbike **is safe to drive anymore.**

67.8
1 Not given
2 False
3 False
4 False
5 True
6 False
7 True

67.9 🔊
1 The school **is** getting new equipment for its technology department.
2 Computer studies **is** my favorite subject at college at the moment.
3 Neither the cable nor the batteries **are** included with the new digital radio.
4 The Bahamas **has** many beaches, including some with pink sand.
5 I don't know what's wrong with it! Either the engine or the fan **is** broken.

68

68.2 🔊
1 Even at the start of her career, she was **such** a well-respected scientist.
2 My brother fell off his bike this morning. The injury was **so** bad that we called a doctor.
3 Colds spread **so** fast between children, particularly in large groups.
4 I was hoping to get some positive news, but the test results were **such** a disappointment.
5 I'm pleased that he's **such** an experienced surgeon. It's very reassuring!

68.4 🔊
1 Dentistry is such a difficult job that **you have to train for many years.**
2 He recovered so rapidly that **he was soon able to walk again.**
3 She had such steady hands that **she could perform delicate operations.**
4 The medicine tasted so bad that **I nearly spat it all out!**
5 It is such a new treatment that **only a few patients have had it.**

68.7 🔊
1 Surgeons train hard, which is why they make **so** few mistakes.
2 I think these tablets work **so** much better than the others.
3 Doctors have to pass so **many** exams during their training.
4 Thank you, doctor. I feel **so much** better than I did last week.

68.8
Rats have a sense of smell that is **so** well developed that they can **detect** traces of TB in test **samples** given by humans. They signify when they smell TB by rubbing their legs together and are then given a treat through a syringe. There are a number of reasons why this is **such** an important breakthrough. First, the rats are able spot the **disease** in its early stages, which is so much better than testing later because then treatment can be started right away on any patients who have tested positive. TB is **treatable** if it is detected in its early stages. If left undetected, it can be **deadly**. Second, rats only take 30 minutes to test nearly 100 samples. This is so **much** more efficient than human laboratory **testing**, which can take up to four days to do the same number. Finally, using rats is so much cheaper than buying expensive devices and paying a lot of money per test. This is important because TB is still a global concern. The situation in Mozambique was so bad **that** TB was declared a national emergency in 2006. By 2014, 60,000 people were said, by the ministry of health, to be **infected**.

69

69.2 🔊
1 Apparently, **the** French horn is the most difficult instrument to play.
2 Alexander Graham Bell is often credited with inventing **the** telephone.
3 My sister has **a** saxophone that she plays in her school orchestra.
4 **The** blue whale is the largest animal that has ever lived on Earth.

69.4 🔊
1 I enjoy playing **the** piano, but I hated having lessons as a child.
2 Mountain **gorillas** are one of the most endangered species on Earth. / **The mountain gorilla is** one of the most endangered species on Earth.

3 In 2007 a Russian lawyer paid nearly $4 million for **a** violin.
4 **The sloth** is a slow animal, but the Galápagos tortoise is even slower.
5 Steve Wozniak designed and built **the** 1976 Apple I computer.
6 This concert is incredible. I love the sound of **the trumpet**. / This concert is incredible. I love the sound of **trumpets**.

69.6
The Space Race produced two truly iconic moments in **the** history of humankind. The first happened on April 12, 1961, when Yuri Gagarin became **the** first human in space. The entire Vostok 1 mission, including one orbit around Earth, lasted only 1 hour 29 minutes. Gagarin's voyage changed how people all over **the** world thought about **[-]** space.
Just over eight years later in July, 1969, **[-]** Neil Armstrong, "Buzz" Aldrin, and Michael Collins traveled to space in **the** Apollo 11 space craft. On July 20 1969, Armstrong stepped onto **the** Moon's dusty surface. What he actually said next is **an** interesting story in itself. For many years he argued that he said, "That's one small step for a man, one giant leap for mankind." After listening to repeated transmission recordings, however, he admitted that he accidentally dropped indefinite article "**a**." Either way, it was **a** huge step for mankind.

69.7
1 True **2** False **3** False **4** True
5 True **6** False **7** True

Index

All entries are listed by unit number.
Main entries are highlighted in **bold**.

A

"a" and "an" 54.2 68.1 68.3 69.5
abilities **5** 50.1
absolute adjectives 29.1
abstract nouns 55
academic life 17 *see also* education
acknowledgment 17.5
action verbs 2
actions 8 25.1 30.1, **34**
"actually" 65.1
adjectives **52** 64.3 68
   gradable and non-gradable **29**
   word order 4
adverbs 14.4 **29** 40.1 43.1 44
advice **9** 50.1 66.2
age 15
agreement, subjects and verbs 67
amounts 18 35
"an" and "a" 54.2 68.1 68.3 69.5
answering questions 23.7
apologies 30
art 61
articles 54 69 *see also* "a" and "an"; "the"
"as...as" comparisons **14** 18.6
asking questions 1.7 **23** 50
attention, gaining 17.5
auxiliary verbs 1.5 23.1 44.2 44.5 49.3
avoiding repetition 18.1 62.1 64

B

"be used to" 53.1
beliefs 3
body language 65.1
business skills 25 **26** 28 *see also* career

C

"can" and "can't" 38.1 49.1 50.1
career **21** 58 *see also* jobs
cause and effect 15.1
celebrity **41** 44
certainty and uncertainty 10.1 37.1 **38 43**
challenging (disagreement) 18.8
changing emphasis 19 34
changing meaning 28.3 28.4 34.4 34.6
   40 43
changing plans 60
classes (nouns) 52.4 69.3
classifying adjectives 29.1
clauses 40 45 47 48 63.8
closed questions 37.4
collective nouns 67.1

collocations 3 14 27.6
   lists of 6 11 16 21 26 36 41 46 51
   56 61
comparisons 12.1 12.4 **14 15** 68.5
complex verb patterns 24
conclusion markers 17.1 17.5
concrete nouns 55
conditionals 17 20 **32 39**
   first conditional 20.7
   mixed conditionals 39
   second conditional 20.7 32.1
   third conditional 32
   zero conditional 17.6
consequences 9.5 20.2 **34**
continuous forms 1 **2** 66.3
   future 58
   future perfect 59.6
   past 8.1 60.5
   past perfect 8.4
   present 1
   present perfect 1
contracted forms 9.6 32.3 32.7
contrasts 12 13 **14**
conversational skills 1 17.5 62.7 **65**
"could" and "couldn t" 9.1 32.2 37.1 38.1
   50.1 57.1
countable nouns 35 54.4 **55** 69.1 69.3
countries (nationalities) 52
courts and law **46** 47 48
culture and art 61
cultures and customs 51
CVs 22

D

deductions **38** 50.1
defining relative clauses 47
definite article 54.1 *see also* "the"
"definitely" 10.1
degrees of likelihood 10.1 *see also* predictions
dependent prepositions 34.1 34.4
direct objects 25
direct questions 23
disagreement 18.8
   discourse markers 12 17 65
distance, creating **42** 43.3
double comparatives 15.6
double object verbs 25
dropping clauses 64.3 *see also* ellipsis;
   shortened sentences
dynamic verbs 2

E

education **16** 17 20
effects 12.1 15.1
"either...or" 67.6
ellipsis 15.6 **62** *see also* shortened sentences
emphasis 12 14.2 27.4 35 **44** 68
   changing structure 5.4 **19** 45
   stress 7.6 12.1 19.7 **34**

entertainment 62 *see also* media
environment **31** 32
"-ever" (suffix) 40
exploration 69
extreme adjectives 29.1

F

facts 4 9.5 42
family **11** 12 13
"few", "fewer" and "fewer than" 18.2 **35**
   68.5
first conditional 20.7
focusing clauses 45
"for" 25.1 25.4 30.8
formal English 13.3 23.3 32.5 33.1 66.1
   discourse markers 12.4 17.1
   inversion 32.5 44.1
   "whom" 47.4 47.7
formal linking discourse markers 12.4
future continuous 58
future perfect 59
future perfect continuous 59.6
future tense (in general) 10 20 39.2 49 **56**
   57 60

GH

general discourse markers 17.5
general purpose (uses) 30.8
general statements **5** 54.4 55.4
generalizations 18 52.1 **69**
gerunds 22 24 28 30.8
"get used to" 53.1 53.2
"get something done" 66.1 66.3
gradable adjectives 29
groups 35.11 **52** 63.1 67 *see also* classes
   (nouns)
habits 13
"have something done" 66.1 66.3
"have to" 49.3
hedging language 43.1
hopes 57
"however" 40.1
hypothetical situations 20 39 50

I

"I wish" 32.12
idioms 8 10 11 26 36 41 46 51 56 61
"if" 17.6 20.7 23.3 32.2 37.4
"if only" 32.12
indefinite article 54.2 69
   see also "a" and "an"
indirect objects 25
indirect questions 23.1
indirect statements 43
infinitives 5 **28** 30.8 39.1 42.1 **64**
   modal verbs 50.1
   verb patterns 24.1
   with "used to" 13.1 53.5

informal discourse markers 65.1
informal English 30.2 30.4 35.3 45.7 66.1
    see also formal English
    conversation 1.5 62.7
    discourse markers 12.1 65
"-ing" endings 22.1 28 see also gerunds;
        present participle
interviews, job 23
intonation 1.7 see also stress
invention 69
inversion 44
"it is" and "it was" 5.1 45.6

JKL

jobs 21 22 23
law 46 47 49
"less" and "less than" 35.8 35.11
"likely" 10.1
likely events 20
linking information 12
"little" 35.2 35.3 68.5
living abroad 53
luck 36

M

main clauses 1.5 47
main verbs 1.5 28.4 30.5 45.6
"may" and "may not" 37.1 38.1 50.1
media 41 44
medical science 68
meetings 26 28
"might" and "might not" 9.1 10.1 32.2 32.7
        37.1 38.1
modal verbs 32.2 38 42.3 50
    in advice 9
    in future tense 49 57
    in question tags 1.5
movies 41
moving abroad 53
music 64
"must" 49.3 50.1 9.1 9.5
"must have" 38.1

N

narrative tenses 8.1
nationalities 52.1
negatives 29.7 33.2 49 50.1 63.8
        64.8
    adverbials 44.1
    consequences 9.5
    in question tags 1.5
"neither...nor" 67.6
neutral questions 58.7
non-defining relative clauses 47.6
non-gradable adjectives 29
"not as...as" comparisons 14
nouns 25.1 30.8 45.4 45.6 67.6 68
        see also pronouns

abstract and concrete 55
as adjectives 52
collective 67.1
in collocations 14
countable and uncountable 35 54.4
        63.1 67.3 69.3
phrasal verbs nouns based on 19.7
with relative clauses 47.6 48
numbers 18 35

O

objects 7.3 19.1 40.1 47 54.1
    with verbs 24.1 24.3 25
obligations 49 50.1
offers 50.1
omitting words 15.6 45.7 62 64.3 see also
        shortened sentences
"one / ones" 63.1
online learning 19
open questions 23 37.4
opinions 4 9 65
organizing information 17
"ought to" 9.1 9.5 50.1
"ought to have" and "ought not to have" 33.1
        33.2

P

particles 7 19.7
passive voice 19 42
past continuous 8.1 60.5
past participles 32.12 38.1 59.3 66.1 66.3
    in passive voice 19.3 42.3
    in third conditional 32.2 39.1
past perfect 8 32.3 39.1
past perfect continuous 8.4
past simple 8.1 20.7 37.4 39.1 63.5
past tense (in general) 13.1 32.12 33 37.1
        38 53.5
performance 64
permission 50.1
personalities 4 39
phrasal verbs 7 19.7 38
    lists of 6 11 16 21 26 36 41 46 51
        56 61
plans 28 59 60
plurals 19.7 54.4 67
    countable nouns 35 63.1 69.3
points (markers) 17.1
polite English 52
    questions 18.8 23 58
populations 15
positive clauses 1.5 63.8
possibilities 10 14.4 37
predictions 10 58 59
prefixes 65
prepositions 7.6 22 24.5 25.1 27.6 34
present continuous 1.1 58.1
present participle 8.5 58.3 59.3
present perfect 1.3

present simple 1.1 20.7 37.4
present tense (in general) 20.1 30.5 32.12
        58.11 63.5
presentations skills 26 see also interviews, job
pronouns 7.3 25.2 27 35.3 47
pronunciation 1.7 32.7 34.6 44 54.9 69.5
        see also stress
purpose expressing 30

Q

qualifiers 18.2 29
qualities 14 55.1
quantifiers 68.5
quantities 14 18 35
question words with "-ever" 40
questions 1 13.2 18.8 23 37.4 58.7
"quite" 29.9 35.6

R

reasons 12.4 30
recent past 1.3 see also present
        perfect
recommendations 9
reduced infinitives 64.1
reduced sentences 62 63 64 see also
        omitting words
reflexive collocations 27.6
reflexive pronouns 27
regrets 32 33 39.2
relationships 11 12
relative clauses 47 48
relative pronoun 47
repairs 66.1
repeated comparisons 15.6
repetition avoiding 18.1 62 63 64
reported speech 37.4
reporting verbs 42
requests 50.1 58.7
results 12.1 12.4 19.2 20.7 68.3
résumés 22

S

school 16 see also studying
second conditional 20.7 32.1 32.12 39.1
"self" and "selves" suffixes 27.1
separable phrasal verbs 7.3
sequencing markers 17.1
services 66.1
"shall" 50.1
shortened sentences 62 63 64 see also
        omitting words
"should" 9.1 9.5 50.1 66.2
"should have" and "shouldn't have" 33.1 33.2
silent letters pronunciation 54.9
singular 63.1 67 69.1

"so" 12.1 17.5 63.8 68
"some" 18.1 18.2 63.1
speculation 37 **38** 58.7
spoken English **7** 19.7 37.4 54.9
   conversational skills 1 17.5 62.7 **65**
   informal 12.1 30.2 32.7 **64**
   reported speech 37.4
stalling phrases 23.7
state verbs 2
statistics 18.4
storytelling 8
stress 7.6 12.1 19.7 **34** see also emphasis
studying **16** 17 19
subjects 15.6 27 40.1 45.4 50.1 65.1 **67**
   inversion and ellipsis 32.5 44 62.1
   in passive voice 19.1 19.3 42.1
   in questions 23.1 37.4
   in relative clauses **47**
substituting words 63
"such" 68
suffixes 27.1
suggestions 9.1 50.1
summing up 17.1
superstition 36
surprising numbers 18.6

T

taking notes 17
technology 56
television 41
tenses (in general) 8 32 37.4
   see also future continuous; future
   perfect; future perfect continuous;
   future tense (in general); past
   continuous; past perfect; past perfect
   continuous; past simple; past tense (in
   general); present continuous; present
   simple; present tense (in general)
"that" 5.1 42.1 45.6 45.7 47.3 68.3
"the" 15.6 52.4 **54.1 69.1** 69.5
third conditional **32** 39.1
three-word phrasal verbs 7.6

time adverbials 44.5
time markers 13.4 **33.6** 59.3 59.8
titles 54.1 67.3
"to" 25 **28** 30.8 64 see also infinitives
tourism 6 see also travel
tradition 36
travel 7 8
truths 5.1 17.6 43.3

U

uncertainty and certainty 10.1 37.1 **38 43**
uncountable nouns **35** 54.4 **55** 67.3
understatements 35.6
"unlikely" 10.1
unlikely events 20
unreal past situations 32
"used to" and "use to" 13 53.2 53.5
uses (purposes) 30.8

V

verbs 47.1 62.1 63.5 63.8 64.5 see also
     adverbs; infinitives
   action and state verbs 2
   agreement with subjects 67
   auxiliary verbs 1.5 23.1 44.2 44.5 49.3
   double object verbs 25
   gerunds 22 24 28 30.8
   hedging verbs 43.1
   main verbs 1.5 28.4 30.5 45.6
   modal verbs 32.2 **38** 42.3 **50**
     in advice 9
   in future tense 49 57
     in question tags 1.5
   patterns 24 27.6
   phrasal verbs 7 19.7 38
   reporting 42.1
vowels sounds 32.7

W

"want" 45.1 64.8
"was going to" 60.3
weather 40
"what if" 20.1 20.4
"whatever" 40.1
"when" 17.6 45.7 48.1
"whenever" 40.1
"where" and "whereby" 45.7 48.1
"wherever" 40.1
"whether" 23.3 37.4
"which" 47
"whichever" 40.1
"who" and "whom" 45.7 47
"whoever" 40.1
"whose" 48.5 48.6
"will" 10.1 49.1 50.1 **58** 60.1
"will have to" and "will not have to" 49.3
wishes 57
"won't" 10.1 49.1
work **21** 24 25 27 28 see also jobs
"would" and "wouldn't" 13.3 20.7 43.3
     50.1 57.1 60.1
"would have" and "would've" 32 39.1
written English 12.1 12.4 22 32.5 54.9

YZ

"yes" and "no" questions 23.3
"you had better" and "you'd better" 9.6
zero article 54.4 69.5
zero conditional 17.6

Acknowledgments

The publisher would like to thank:
Jo Kent, Trish Burrow, and Emma Watkins for additional text; Thomas Booth, Helen Fanthorpe, Helen Leech, Carrie Lewis, and Vicky Richards for editorial assistance; Stephen Bere, Sarah Hilder, Amy Child, and Fiona Macdonald for additional design work; Peter Chrisp for fact checking; Penny Hands, Amanda Learmonth, and Carrie Lewis for proofreading; Elizabeth Wise for indexing; Tatiana Boyko, Rory Farrell, Clare Joyce, and Viola Wang for additional illustrations; Liz Hammond for editing audio scripts and managing audio recordings; Hannah Bowen and Scarlett O'Hara for compiling audio scripts; Heather Hughes, Tommy Callan, Tom Morse, Gillian Reid, and Sonia Charbonnier for creative technical support; Vishal Bhatia, Sachin Gupta, Nehal Verma, Jaileen Kaur, Shipra Jain, Roohi Rais, Nisha Shaw, and Ankita Yadav for technical assistance.

DK would like to thank the following for their kind permission to use their photographs:
101 **Fotolia**: Maksym Dykha (top right). 111 **Alamy**: MBI (bottom right). 131 **Dorling Kindersley**: Malcolm Coulson (center right).

All other images are copyright DK.
For more information, please visit
www.dkimages.com.